RECKONING
with
RACISM

Landmark Cases in Canadian Law

Since Confederation, Canada's highest court – first the Judicial Committee of the Privy Council in England and then the Supreme Court of Canada – has issued a series of often contentious decisions that have fundamentally shaped the nation. Both cheered and jeered, these judgments have impacted every aspect of Canadian society, setting legal precedents and provoking social change. The issues in the judgments range from Aboriginal title, gender equality, and freedom of expression to Quebec secession and intellectual property. This series offers comprehensive, book-length examinations of high court cases that have had a major impact on Canadian law, politics, and society.

Other books in the series are:

Flawed Precedent: The St. Catherine's *Case and Aboriginal Title* by Kent McNeil

Privacy in Peril: Hunter v Southam *and the Drift from Reasonable Search Protections* by Richard Jochelson and David Ireland

The Tenth Justice: Judicial Appointments, Marc Nadon, and the Supreme Court Act *Reference* by Carissima Mathen and Michael Plaxton

From Wardship to Rights: The Guerin *Case and Aboriginal Law* by Jim Reynolds

Constitutional Pariah: Reference re Senate Reform and the Future of Parliament, by Emmett Macfarlane

No Legal Way Out: R v Ryan, *Domestic Abuse, and the Defence of Duress* by Nadia Verelli and Lori Chambers

Debt and Federalism: Landmark Cases in Canadian Bankruptcy and Insolvency Law, 1894–1937 by Thomas G.W. Telfer and Virginia Torrie

For a list of other titles
see www.ubcpress.ca/landmark-cases-in-canadian-law.

**LANDMARK CASES
IN CANADIAN LAW**

RECKONING
with
RACISM

Police, Judges, and the *RDS* Case

Constance Backhouse

UBCPress · Vancouver · Toronto

31 30 29 28 27 26 25 24 23 22   5 4 3 2 1

Printed in Canada on FSC-certified ancient-forest-free paper (100% post-consumer recycled) that is processed chlorine- and acid-free.

Library and Archives Canada Cataloguing in Publication

Title: Reckoning with racism : police, judges, and the RDS case / Constance Backhouse.
Names: Backhouse, Constance, author.
Series: Landmark cases in Canadian law.
Description: Series statement: Landmark cases in Canadian law | Includes bibliographical references and index.
Identifiers: Canadiana (print) 20220275491 | Canadiana (ebook) 20220283982 | ISBN 9780774868228 (hardcover) | ISBN 9780774868273 (softcover) | ISBN 9780774868280 (PDF) | ISBN 9780774868297 (EPUB)
Subjects: LCSH: Discrimination in justice administration – Canada.
Classification: LCC KE4395 .B33 2022 | LCC KF4483.C5 .B33 2022 kfmod | DDC 342.7108/73—dc23

Canadä

UBC Press gratefully acknowledges the financial support for our publishing program of the Government of Canada (through the Canada Book Fund), the Canada Council for the Arts, and the British Columbia Arts Council.

This book has been published with the help of a grant from the Canadian Federation for the Humanities and Social Sciences, through the Awards to Scholarly Publications Program, using funds provided by the Social Sciences and Humanities Research Council of Canada.

Printed and bound in Canada by Friesens
Set in Garamond by Artegraphica Design Co. Ltd.
Copy editor: Lesley Erickson
Proofreader: Helen Godolphin
Indexer: Judy Dunlop
Cover designer: Will Brown

UBC Press
The University of British Columbia
2029 West Mall
Vancouver, BC V6T 1Z2
www.ubcpress.ca

In memory of Joan Jones, who has inspired generations
with her antiracist ideas and activism

Contents

Acknowledgments

Researching *RDS* has been an extraordinary venture. When I began, I had little knowledge about anti-Black racism in Nova Scotia. As I began to uncover further information, I was staggered by the immensity of this history – its longevity, its range, its complexity. I have benefitted from the generosity of scholars, lawyers, judges, and community activists who shared their expertise with me. Their oral history interviews often left me bereft of words. It is impossible to apologize fully for my ignorance and for the racism I and other white Canadians have benefitted from.

I owe a debt of gratitude to the research assistants who have contributed enormously with their ideas, energy, and unstinting legwork: Vanessa Carment, Mirsa Duka, Desirée Hayward, Dayna MacDonald, Aleah McCormick, Hannan Mohamud, Josh Nelson, Julita Pacholczyk, Fregine Sheehy, Holland Stille, and Reakash Walters.

I am not able to thank everyone by name, the authors whose publications created a framework for this study, the people who spent precious time speaking with me, and the law students whose fresh perspectives added so significantly. I list here only a small group to whom I owe special thanks: Beth Atcheson, Olga Backhouse, Nancy Backhouse, Diana Backhouse, Jamie Benidickson, Stacey Birtch, Suzanne Bouclin, Kim Brooks, Rosemary Cairns Way, Natalie Carter, Rachel Cartwright, David Collenette, Penny Collenette, Hansel Cook, Sharon Cook, Elaine Craig, Maneesha Deckha, Adam Dodek, Barry Dorey, Mark Feldthusen, Colleen Flood, Chrystine Frank, Philip Girard, Lorraine Greaves, Shirley Greenberg, Michael Grossberg, Rebecca Johnson, Lynn Jones, Stephen Kimber, Craig Klafter, Andrew

Kuntze, Véronique Larose, Hester Lessard, Jamie Liew, Vanessa Mac-
Donnell, Diana Majury, Bruce Mann, Chloe Marion, Carissima
Mathen, John McLaren, Patricia McMahon, Cynthia Milton, Val
Napoleon, Peter Oliver, Maureen O'Neil, Jim Phillips, Cintia Quiroga,
Sylvia Rich, Leonardo Russomanno, Elizabeth Sheehy, Peter Showler,
Penelope Simons, Beth Symes, Walt Tanner, Laura Wheeler, Evelyn C.
White, Michelle Williams, and Ellen Zweibel.

I want to thank the two anonymous reviewers who read the manu-
script with such care and offered thoughtful suggestions and expert com-
mentary. I greatly appreciated the skilled professional assistance of the
UBC Press editorial staff and their trusted freelancers: Randy Schmidt,
Melissa Pitts, Ann Macklem, Lesley Erickson, Carmen Tiampo, Will
Brown, Irma Rodriguez, Helen Godolphin, and Judy Dunlop.

I am indebted to the University of Ottawa, the Social Sciences and
Humanities Research Council of Canada, the Molson Foundation,
and the Trudeau Foundation for research funding.

Joan Jones, one of the bedrock activists in Halifax's Black community,
left me with an admonition: "I'm always hesitant telling my story to
people. I never get it back. I always feel like, okay, off they go, and that
helps them, but it doesn't help me or my community. I feel very resentful
about that. We don't get it back."[1]

I know that a single study of the *RDS* case cannot live up to her
challenge, but I hope it represents a start toward reckoning with our
racist past, and a small step toward a better future.

RECKONING
with
RACISM

INTRODUCTION

I have been captivated by the *RDS* case since it began to weave its way through the courts.[1] What began as a simple criminal trial in 1994 in Nova Scotia Youth Court evolved into one of Canada's most significant race cases. When I taught *RDS* in my University of Ottawa criminal law class, the legal principle the students extracted was the importance of "objectivity." While their touching faith in objectivity is optimistic, even inspirational, the simplicity of the vision belies the challenges.

An African Nova Scotian teenager had been put in a choke hold, handcuffed, and charged for intervening in his young cousin's arrest. On appeal, the focus shifted from racist police practices to judicial racial bias. Never in its 122-year history had Canada's Supreme Court considered a similar complaint. Ostensibly, Canadians were content that their uniformly white judiciary exhibited no racism. In 1997, that complacency was shattered when the bench of nine white judges was asked to rule on *RDS*. The irony was that the impugned judge was Canada's first Black female judge. She was accused of racial bias against whites.

It struck me that delving deeply into *RDS* – the people, place, and time – might unearth useful tools to interrogate the role of racism in Canada's legal history. This narrative begins with the trial, broadens to examine the backgrounds of the individuals involved, and expands still further to elicit what we can learn about the history of African Nova Scotians more generally. It tracks the early history of slavery, the four larger waves of immigration, the discrimination that descended, and the experience of racialized policing. Then it moves back to the trial, analyzing how and why this case blew up, the fight over media access, successive appeals that culminated in the 1997 Supreme Court of Canada decision, the reactions of the individuals directly involved, and the views of whites and Blacks within the wider community.

A remarkable set of characters emerged: the white Halifax police officer who conducted the arrest; the Black teen charged with assault and obstruction; the notable cast of white and Black lawyers who argued the case; the white judges who deliberated on it; and the riveted community members who recognized the stakes involved. Probing the long history of the African diaspora community in Nova Scotia, the dynamics of policing in a predominantly Black neighbourhood, the environment that elicited criticism of the police, the shocked responses of the all-white legal authorities, and the backgrounds of the judges who grappled with the case helps to explore the meaning of *RDS*.

Today's cumulative videos of racialized police violence and the explosive resistance of the Black Lives Matter movement have lent increased urgency to the study of Canadian racism. Despite centuries of racial inequities, discussions of racism have rarely registered inside our white legal system. *RDS* upended the silence several decades before the George Floyd murder, forcing the police, lawyers, judges, academics, the media, and the wider society to consider racism. This case became a lightning rod, the centre of a painful, tumultuous, late twentieth-century legal debate about race.

Race is a socially constructed myth that purports to divide human beings into distinct categories. Fictional classifications have changed over time and place. Groups historically deemed "non-white" in Canada include Indigenous peoples, French Canadians, central Europeans, eastern Europeans, Asians, Indo-Canadians, Jews, and Muslims. Significantly, people already perceived as white decided who was white.[2] This is why many antiracists describe "race" in scare quotes. It is why we refer to *racialized* people, to signify that race is a fiction but racism is a reality. Because this study deals with specific geographic settings and times, for ease of reference I shall make use of simplified descriptors for individuals such as "white" and "Black" with occasional use of other terms of preference such as "African Nova Scotian" and "African Canadian."[3]

When naming the people described in this book, I have mostly adopted a preference for surnames, with some exceptions. Due to Rodney Small's youth during the arrest and legal proceedings, I have often referred to him as "Rodney," and have continued referring to him by his first name in later decades to avoid confusion. When describing the life backgrounds of other key figures, I have used their first names during their youthful years, switching to their surnames once they have commenced their careers. Although Judge Sparks's birth name was Corrine Sparks, she prefers to use "Connie" as her first name, and I have followed this preference except in formal references where her legal name appears.

Rocky Jones, the now-deceased African Nova Scotian defence lawyer in the *RDS* case, once expressed dismay that the author of the first book-length study of Black Canadian history, *The Blacks in Canada: A History*, was white.[4] He may have preferred that this book be written by an African Nova Scotian. I am a white woman, which presents particular challenges for this research. My racial experience is the product of a life contained almost entirely within a privileged white bubble. My academic research began with the legal history of sex discrimination.[5] I am indebted to the brilliant Black and Indigenous writers and activists who insisted that white feminists expand our essentialist focus on gender to encompass the complexities of race. Challenged by the courageous students of colour in my classrooms who demanded more inclusive learning, I have begun to shift my research to the legal history of racism.[6]

That so many people in this case are white means that while *RDS* is a study of Black resistance, it is also an inquiry into white racism. That may suggest specific responsibilities for white researchers. In the past, I have also faced allegations of bias on the basis of gender because of my femaleness and my feminism, an experiential background shared with at least two of the female judges who figure prominently in *RDS*. The richness of this case allows for substantial diversity of interpretation, and many voices register on the pages that follow. My hope is that readers will draw their own conclusions on the complex issues that emerged.

My understanding is that Judge Corrine Sparks, one of the principal
actors in this case, may write a memoir about her life after she retires
from the bench. She would undoubtedly narrate this story differently
than I have been able to do. I join with many others in hoping that
she does complete a memoir. It would make an invaluable contribution
to our deeper understandings.

The surviving legal records for *RDS* include the transcript of the trial,
the written factums containing the appellate submissions, the transcript and DVD recording of the arguments before the Supreme Court
of Canada, and the decisions from the Youth Court, the Nova Scotia
Supreme Court, the Nova Scotia Court of Appeal, and the Supreme
Court of Canada.[7] Biographical research on the witnesses, lawyers, and
judges was supplemented with oral history interviews of the teenager
charged, the arresting police officer, the lawyers for the prosecution,
defence, and interveners, and many of the judges.[8] The ninety-nine
oral history interviews that I conducted added observations from family
and friends of the individuals involved, journalists, community activists,
politicians, policing experts, critical race analysts, criminologists, psych-
ologists, social workers, law professors, historians, archivists, lawyers,
and judges.[9]

Written sources added context to the history of anti-Black racism
in Nova Scotia and its impact on policing, the criminal legal system,
and the political, economic, social, and legal environments that permeated this case. Gender and class formed key intersecting variables.
Canada's first Black female judge was forced to operate well outside
socially prescribed gender- and race-specific roles for women. The class
disparities between the accused Black teen, the middle-class white
police officer, and the elite white judges were impossible to miss.

All whose lives bump up against the criminal legal system are harmed.
The *RDS* case brings unavoidably to public view the pain inflicted on
the persons entangled in it. Making visible the depth of the harm carries
risk of further damage. While emphasizing the necessity of documenting
discrimination, Mohawk author Patricia Monture-Angus writes that
"no amount of social change discounts the pain those particular individuals carry who become the symbols of our struggle." She urges that

documentation be tempered with respect and compassion. The wisdom of her challenge is evident.[10]

There are several significant issues not covered here. The Indigenous communities on whose land the *RDS* events unfolded share with African Nova Scotians distinct but similar patterns of racist discrimination and resistance. The colonization of Mi'kmaw lands and cultures has evolved differently inside Black and white settler communities, yet, in 1989, the Royal Commission on the Donald Marshall, Jr., Prosecution found parallels for Blacks and Indigenous peoples in policing, criminal prosecution, and sentencing.[11] These and related matters of reconciliation and reparation deserve urgent attention, but the race focus here is specifically upon whites and Blacks.

Two related legal matters are not tracked in detail. The legal doctrine of judicial notice allows a court to accept certain evidence as fact without further proof, if the truth of it is so notorious or well known or so authoritatively attested that it cannot reasonably be doubted.[12] Rodney Small's defence lawyers chose not to argue that anti-Black police racism was sufficiently notorious to qualify for judicial notice. They were concerned about the voluminous, costly evidence potentially required to support judicial notice. They also feared that if the argument failed, it could be taken as a wider precedent denying the existence of racism. Since the argument was not made by the appellants, the Supreme Court chose not to consider it during the final appeal. Although future race cases will undoubtedly consider judicial notice as a key issue, in the late 1990s, the context was such that the omission was probably wise. There are two routes for allegations of judicial bias: an appeal or a complaint to a judicial council.[13] Judicial council complaints constitute a significant avenue for judicial oversight but will receive limited attention here because the prosecution chose the appeal route.[14]

We live in a time of unparalleled controversy over racism and racial dynamics within our police forces, the legal profession, and the judiciary. There has never been a more pressing time for a full-scale assessment of the *RDS* case, the arrest that precipitated it, the people who took it to court, the excitement that surrounded it, the dramatic impact it had on the individuals involved, and its significance for the Canadian legal system. This extraordinary case offers a unique focal point for a wider examination of Canadian anti-Black racism, judicial impartiality, police practices, and the race, class, and gender dimensions of the criminal legal system.

1

The Trial

On 2 December 1994, Rodney Darren Small appeared for trial before the Nova Scotia Youth Court at 3380 Devonshire Avenue in Halifax.[1] He was identified only by his initials (R.D.S.) because of his youth, but he has given permission to use the full name here.[2] A sixteen-year-old African Nova Scotian, slight in stature and younger-looking than his age, Small was charged with three *Criminal Code* offences: assaulting a police officer; assaulting a police officer with intent to prevent the lawful arrest of another person; and obstruction of a police officer.[3] It was his first time facing criminal charges. They all stemmed from one police altercation.

In the fall of 1993, fifteen-year-old Rodney Small was living with his mother in a two-storey rowhouse at 2438 Creighton Street in a predominantly Black neighbourhood in the inner city's North End. On a misty overcast afternoon, October 17, Rodney was riding home on a borrowed mountain bike after visiting his grandmother. Several blocks from home, he was startled to see a crowd watching a scuffle on Brunswick Street. One young boy shouted that Rodney's cousin was being arrested. Fifteen-year-old N.R., who lived down the street from Rodney, was struggling with a police officer while encircled by a crowd of more than half a dozen people. As Rodney would later explain, "When somebody is being arrested in the community, it brings attention."[4]

In 1993, at the time of his arrest on three charges, including
assaulting a police officer, fifteen-year-old Rodney Small
lived with his mother at 2438 Creighton Street, a rowhouse
in a predominantly Black neighbourhood in Halifax's North
End. This picture was taken in 2018.

Rodney was upset to see his cousin in handcuffs. Still on his bicycle,
he moved closer. The officer warned Rodney to stay away or he would
be next. Rodney ignored the officer and shouted to his cousin, "Do
you want me to go tell your mother?" The next thing he knew, he was
in a choke hold, arrested, and shoved into the police van alongside his
cousin. At the station, he was released on his own undertaking. Charges
were laid on 10 November 1994.[5]

Neither Rodney's mother nor grandmother had money to hire a
lawyer, but they sought help from the Black United Front, a Halifax-

Because he was under the age of eighteen, Small's case was heard in Devonshire Youth Court, a fast-paced court where Black youth were disproportionately represented.

based antiracism organization. There, they learned that there was a Black lawyer representing indigent clients through Dalhousie University's Legal Aid office. The lawyer was Burnley Allan Jones, whose nickname – "Rocky" Jones – was more frequently used.[6] Jones told them he believed the charges were "bogus," a clear example of the "shotgun approach" where the police laid multiple charges arising out of the same incident hoping some would stick. It was common for criminally charged individuals, especially poor ones, to accept a plea bargain, to plead guilty to one charge in return for dropping the others. Jones advised against this. He offered to take the case as part of a fight against police abuse of African Nova Scotians.[7]

Since Rodney was under eighteen, the case was heard in the Youth Court under the *Young Offenders Act.*[8] African Nova Scotians were disproportionately represented there as accused youths.[9] The pace of Youth Court was hectic, but many cases were diverted into community-service alternatives before trial. For reasons that were never made clear, Rodney's case was not on the diversion path.

The morning of the trial, Rodney arrived without family support.[10] His mother, who was angry with him, did not attend. His father was in jail. He had not asked his grandmother because he was worried about causing her more stress. The courtroom gathering was unprecedented: a Black accused (Rodney Small), a Black defence lawyer (Burnley "Rocky" Jones), a Black court reporter (Marva Welch), a Black deputy sheriff (Ray Lawrence), and a Black judge (Corrine E. Sparks). The only two white people in the room were the arresting officer (Constable Donald Stienburg) and the Crown prosecutor (Richard B. Miller).[11]

It was an unusual sight in a province that had long been criticized for having unjustifiably low numbers of Black lawyers, court workers, and judges. A 1989 Nova Scotia royal commission registered concern that there was only one Black judge in the province.[12] That was Judge Sparks herself. She was the first Black female judge in Canada. It was the first time Sparks had presided over a trial with a Black accused, Black defence counsel, Black court clerk, and Black deputy sheriff.[13] The trial would hear from just two witnesses, one white, one Black, both male.

CROWN WITNESS: A WHITE POLICE OFFICER

Prosecutor Miller opened by calling Constable Donald Stienburg to the witness box. A twenty-nine-year-old patrol officer, he had been with the Halifax police department for eight years. Stienburg stood over six feet tall, with a heavy-set athletic physique, a "big man" as Rodney described him. Some officers carried bad reputations within the African Nova Scotian community, but Rodney did not single out Stienburg as one of the worst. "He didn't have a rep like some of the cops that we know," Rodney explained years later.[14] Then he added, "But the reputation of the police in general is not good. There has always been a very bumpy relationship between the Halifax police and the Black community. It's ingrained in our history."[15]

Stienburg testified that he and his partner were in their patrol car on October 17 when a call came in that the police were chasing a stolen van. The van had been "dumped," and "five non-white males, young kids," jumped out and ran off. Stienburg said "two non-white males" ran across Brunswick Street in front of his car. His fellow officer ran after one fleeing boy, and Stienburg questioned the other, N.R., whom he arrested for theft and unlawful possession of a motor vehicle. He continued: "[T]here was a number of people milling around in the area. While I was holding [N.R.] a gentleman in a bicycle come ... He cut directly across the street on his bike, I believe it was a small mountain-bike type bike and drove right into my legs with the bike without stopping and started yelling at me."[16]

Stienburg identified the bike rider as Rodney Small, the teenager seated in court wearing a "white Miami shirt." Stienburg resumed: "He was straddling his bike at that time. He had put his feet on the ground. He was kind of on the ground straddling the bike and he was yelling at me at the time, pushing me with his shoulders and his arms away from the accused that I had arrested."[17]

Q. Can you tell us how you were being pushed?

A. He was using his upper body and his two hands to push me away from the person I had arrested.

Q. Can you tell me where on your body did R.D.S. touch?

A. In my upper body, in my arms.

Q. Can you tell me how many times you were touched by R.D.S.?

A. It was all at once. While he was – attempting to push me away from the person I had just arrested, it lasted for approximately a couple of seconds, not very long.

The prosecutor continued:

Q. Why did you arrest R.D.S.?

A. Because he was interfering with the arrest of the person I had arrested before.

Q. And did you advise him of that?

A. Yes, I did ...

Q. After you arrested R.D.S. what took place?

A. At that time I was calling for assistance from other police officers. Another police vehicle arrived and another couple of policemen assisted me.

Q. Okay. Was R.D.S. on his bike at this time or was he off his bike?

A. I believe he was straddling the bike while this was occurring. I can't recall exactly what happened afterwards but he was taken from my custody and placed in a police vehicle shortly after.

Q. Where were you and where was N.R. at this time after the arrest of R.D.S.?

A. N.R. was on my left and the accused was on my right after the arrest.[18]

Pressed for more detail, Stienburg replied, "I was holding both of the accused at the time trying to control both of them, because there was two people there and I was by myself. I believe I had them in a neck restraint, both of them at that time."[19]

When the trial turned to cross-examination, defence counsel Rocky Jones criticized the officer's reference to "non-white" males. He had objected for years to the police use of the term. In his speeches to African Nova Scotians, he often stressed, "You're not a 'non' anything. Don't accept this negative definition. It makes whites the norm."[20] Jones would always insist, "I am not 'non' anything. I am *Black*."[21] Jones noticed that Constable Stienburg became increasingly "tense and nervous" under this cross-examination.[22] The officer conceded that the description relayed over the radio could have covered "natives" and "East Indians." "There was nothing specific in this communication that would identify black kids?" queried Jones. "No," replied Stienburg. "Is 'non-white' a description that they [the police] usually use for people of African descent?" queried Jones. "It has been, yes," admitted the officer. The point had been made: the imprecise terminology led the police to search only for Blacks.

Jones homed in on the multiple charges. The officer had initially advised Rodney that he was being charged with obstruction. Two more charges were added before trial. Under continued cross-examination, Stienburg admitted that the check he ran on Rodney Small had uncovered no prior criminal record. It was "gross overcharging to say the least," claimed Jones.[23]

Jones turned to the physical interaction between the officer and Rodney:

> Q. And R.D.S. didn't get off his bike at any time?
> A. Not that I can recall, no.
> Q. And he didn't knock you over?
> A. No, he did not.
> Q. And you continued with your arrest of N.R?
> A. Yes, that is correct.
> Q. And the bike, if it did hit you, was not travelling at any high rate of speed?
> A. No, it was not.[24]

The first Jones had heard of the choke hold was at trial. Rodney Small had not thought to mention it during his pretrial interviews with his lawyer. Surprised that the officer had admitted this in his examination-in-chief, Jones felt he had been handed "a gift."[25] He highlighted the excess force: "You mentioned that you put both young people in the neck restraint, correct?" "Yes," replied Stienburg, "that's correct."[26] Jones hoped to emphasize the stark disparity between the towering, burly twenty-nine-year-old officer and the five-foot-eight-inch fifteen-year-old Rodney Small, weighing all of 104 pounds. Observers that day said Rodney's stature and weight made him look about twelve years old.[27]

DEFENCE WITNESS: A BLACK ACCUSED

Rocky Jones called Rodney Small as his only witness. "I was scared to death," Rodney recalled, "and it was my word against that of a white police officer. I thought it was going to be a slam dunk for the white cop."[28]

Q. Would you please tell the court what happened that day?

A. I was coming from my grandmother's going up to my mother's house and I saw like – I saw a police car and I saw a crowd ... Laurice came up on his bike. He said they got N.R. down. I said, "Where?" I said, "What did he do?" or something like ... So we were driving down, we drove Uniacke on the sidewalk, drove down on the Brunswick sidewalk and we was in the grass, because they was like in the grass like, and I was asking them when we got there, I said, "What's wrong with you N? What happened? What happened? I'll go tell your mother."

And he [the officer] said, "Shut up, shut up, or you'll be under arrest too." I said "What, what, do you want me to go tell your mother?" And then, boom, grabbed me – unexpectedly grabbed me in some choke-holds and said you're under arrest. Then he just put me in the choke-hold and I couldn't really breathe or nothing. And then a woman – some woman said, "Let that kid go, let that kid go." She was saying to me, "What's your phone number? What's your phone number?" And I couldn't talk. N.R. had to yell it out. Told the woman my phone number, phone my grandmother's house.[29]

The woman who called out was the aunt of one of the neighbour-hood children. The community relationships were on high relief that day: the aunt's intervention; Rodney attempting to get the details of his cousin's arrest so he could tell N.R.'s mother; N.R. calling on the aunt to call *Rodney's* grandmother. Both sides apparently approached the aunt to testify, but according to Rodney, the police intimidated her, and she "wasn't too adamant about stepping forward."[30]

Jones continued questioning:

Q. Now this crowd on the sidewalk, can you describe the crowd?

A. They were all little kids. None of them were older than 12, none of them.

Q. Now when you were coming down the sidewalk and you got to this crowd of kids, can you describe how fast you were going?

A. I was coasting. Like I was coasting down Uniacke. I was still coasting. I was coasting from coming down the hill so I was like coasting there.

Q. And when you were coasting down the sidewalk did you run into anybody?

A. No.

Q. Did you hit anybody?

A. No.

Q. Did you intend to hit anybody?

A. No.[31]

Jones turned to the officer's earlier testimony:

Q. Now you've heard the testimony of the police officer here. What differences would you say in what he said and what you've got to say?

A. I know I didn't hit him at all for sure.

Q. The police officer, you heard him say that you were – you had taken two hands and were pushing him on the chest. Did you do that?

A. No, my hands were still on my handlebars because I was like standing on my bike. I was still on my bike. When he grabbed me he grabbed me off my bike.[32]

Then it was prosecutor Miller's turn to cross-examine Rodney.

Q. [W]hen you heard what was going on and you heard N.R. was involved, you wanted to go right to the area, right?

A. I was like being nosey, I wanted to know what was going on, yeah.

Q. And obviously the place you're going to go to is the centre of the action, right?

A. Um ...

Q. At that time the police officer had a hold of N.R., did he?

A. No, I'm saying he already had handcuffs on him. He had the handcuffs on and the cop was just like [inaudible] and just holding his shoulder.

Q. So did you have any concern about N.R. at that point in time?

A. I was just – I wanted to go tell his mother what happened with him.

Q. Why didn't you?

A. Because I was under arrest. How could I go?

Q. You weren't under arrest at this time. You were sitting on your bike ... It's quite easy to take your bike and go to N.R.'s mother, isn't it?

A. No, it wasn't like that.

Q. Okay. Tell me how it was?

A. As soon as I came down I was asking him and then the cop like cut me off. "Shut up, or you'll be under arrest too." I said ... "Do you want me to go tell your mother what happened? What happened?" Then he said, "Shut up, or you'll be under arrest too." Then he grabbed me. I was still talking to N.R. and then he went and grabbed me, oh, "You're under arrest." Put me in a choke-hold so I just –

Q. How close were you to the officer at this time?

A. Talking distance. Right like – closer than what me and you are.[33]

Next, the prosecutor tried to discredit what he believed was an implausible story:

Q. So for just asking a question, this is your story, for just asking the question you were put in a choke-hold?

A. Yes.

Q. You did absolutely nothing to this police officer –

A. Nothing.

Q. – to deserve being put in the choke-hold?

A. Nothing.

Q. You didn't hit him with the bicycle?

A. Didn't touch him with my bike.

Q. You didn't touch him with your hands?

A. Didn't touch him with my hands.

Q. What happened after you were put in the choke-hold?

A. Some woman was yelling, "What's your phone number? What's your – get off that kid like that, what's your phone number?" And I couldn't talk and N.R. yelled my phone number out to her.

Q. And what was N.R. doing at this time?

A. He had N.R. in a choke-hold too. He had us both like that.

Q. And what were you doing?

A. I was – I couldn't do nothing. I couldn't breathe and my face was like – I was almost like knocked out. He had me right under the chin and it was –

Q. You weren't struggling, you weren't doing anything?

A. I couldn't move. I was almost – I was dizzy.

Q. And what about N.R., what did he do?

A. N.R. couldn't do nothing. He had handcuffs on.

Q. So you have no explanation as to why the police officer here today [is] testifying as to what he did?

A. No.[34]

THE LAWYERS' SUBMISSIONS AND THE DECISION

Defence counsel Rocky Jones stated that the court was faced with "two people giving two different stories." The officer claimed that Rodney Small ran into him and was trying to hit him with his hands. Rodney denied any intention to run into the officer and insisted that he had not touched him. Jones conceded that if Rodney was "close enough that the police officer can grab him in a choke-hold and take him off his bicycle," then "the bike may have touched the officer." But he insisted that the bike was coasting not speeding, that Rodney had never taken his hands off his bicycle, and that there was no criminal intent to assault. Jones asked the judge to find that "this young person is a credible young person who's come before the Court to state his case as clearly as he can." He emphasized that if there was "any doubt whatsoever it must be resolved in favour of the accused."[35]

Crown prosecutor Rick Miller agreed that it came down to whether "the police officer's version of events" was "to be believed over that of the defendant." He based his argument on his understanding of police operations:

If you look at the police officer, he's saying, well, he was assaulted, there was obstruction. Obviously, there was a wilful striking of the police officer by R.D.S. on the mountain bike. After that it was eventually the pushing, the shoving, therefore, in the police officer's mind he has to take action. That action is restraining R.D.S. and eventually placing him in a headlock. That is a very consistent, very normal explanation as to why people do, certainly police officers, why this police officer would do what he did.

Look at R.D.S's version of events. He's there, and even though he's concerned that his friend or his cousin is in some sort of trouble and he wants to contact his mother, for absolutely no reason he is placed in a choke-hold. I would submit, Your Honour, that does not make sense. If R.D.S. was there, as he alleges, making no contact with the police officer, simply having some concern for his friend, quite frankly he wouldn't be in the situation that he's facing today.

[I]t's simply a question of credibility here ... [T]here's absolutely no reason to attack the credibility of the officer. His explanation was straight forward. He was simply doing his lawful duty and carrying out the arrest of N.R. Again, it's just a question of, firstly, credibility and I would ask Your Honour to accept the evidence of Constable Stienburg over that over R.D.S. And secondly, based on the evidence of Constable Stienburg, would ask Your Honour to convict.[36]

Miller resisted the claim of overcharging, noting that it was "normal practice" to have charges in the alternative. He asked for a conviction on all three.

Judge Sparks delivered her decision that day, directly after the lawyers' submissions. In busy provincial courts, judges commonly issued oral decisions on the spot, unlike higher courts where judges often reserve, issuing written reasons later. Judge Sparks's oral decision summarized the contrasting testimony of the two witnesses. It was the handcuffs that gave her pause:

[T]his gives me some questions because first of all that was not noted by the Constable. At least I didn't hear the Constable note that N.R. was handcuffed. He gave the Court the distinct impression that he had a rather difficult job in trying to restrain N.R., but I really query in my own mind if this young boy was handcuffed what was the big ordeal about. It's a teenager, young person. I'm certainly not left with the impression based upon R.D.S.'s evidence that N.R. at that point was a threat to the officer. Again, nothing crucial turns on that point, but again I don't understand why it is that there is such a contrast in the evidence of R.D.S. and the Constable. And certainly, when R.D.S. indicated, I believe, two or three times, his distinct recollection that his friend, his cousin, N.R., was handcuffed when he approached the police vehicle this has a ring of truth, and it certainly provides some detail with respect to the actual incident.[37]

Then she considered the credibility of the two witnesses and delivered the verdict:

I must say that [R.D.S.] presented in a very positive way although his articulation was not as clear as it could be. He seemed to be a rather honest young boy. He said quite openly on cross-examination he was being nosey. He wanted to go down to the street corner to see what was going on. He seemed to have been struck by the hostility which greeted him by the police officer, and, of course, if I accept the evidence of R.D.S., this is a young person, N.R., his friend, was just approaching showing some concern. Why should a police officer be threatened by another young person who was merely trying to assist his friend in a non-threatening manner?

In my view, in accepting the evidence, and I don't say that I accept everything that R.D.S. has said in court today, but certainly he has raised a doubt in my mind, and therefore based upon the evidentiary burden which is squarely placed upon the Crown that they must prove all the elements of the offence beyond a reasonable doubt, I have queries in my mind with respect to what actually transpired on the afternoon of October the 17th.

The Crown says, well, why would the officer say that events occurred the way in which he has relayed them to the Court this morning. I'm not saying that the Constable has misled the Court, although police officers have been known to do that in the past. I am not saying that the officer overreacted, but certainly police officers do overreact, particularly when they are dealing with non-white groups. That to me, indicates a state of mind right there that is questionable.

I believe that probably the situation in this particular case is the case of a young police officer who overreacted. I do accept the evidence of R.D.S. that he was told to shut up or he would be under arrest. That seems to be in keeping with the prevalent attitude of the day.

At any rate, based upon my comments and based upon all the evidence before the court, I have no other choice but to acquit.[38]

Rick Miller and Donald Stienburg abruptly stood up and stalked out.[39] The accused teenager turned to his lawyer for confirmation. "He told me I was free," recalled Rodney. Choked with emotion, he felt "stunned."[40] And with that, forces were unleashed that would rile police, lawyers, judges, the media, and the public in protracted, bitter disputes for the next three years. It would ultimately be heralded as one of the most important, possibly the most important, legal decisions on race in Canadian history.

2

The People

DONALD STIENBURG

Donald Stienburg, the first witness at the trial, was born in 1965 in Ottawa but moved to Dartmouth, Nova Scotia, when he turned five. His father was an RCMP officer, his mother a dairy technician. Donnie, as everyone called him, grew up immersed in sports, a popular teenager who was elected valedictorian at Prince Andrew High School. Enrolled in engineering at Dalhousie University, he left before completion to follow his father into policing. Attracted by the physical fitness of the job, he emphasized, "I was a very physical person. I played hockey all my life." And his family history beckoned: "It was in my blood type-thing through my father." His younger brother, Dean, followed, joining the Halifax police force, where he was eventually elected head of the union.[1]

In 1986, when Stienburg began his police career, the life of a patrol officer demanded gruelling shift work: two twelve-hour days, followed by two twelve-hour nights, with four days on and four days off. Officers patrolled the streets and conducted their own investigations. Stienburg loved policing in Halifax: "It was a small enough police force that you got to know everybody, busy enough to keep you on your toes, but not so busy that you felt completely overwhelmed, or unable to make a difference," he explained.[2]

Donald Stienburg, in 2018. He left engineering school to follow his father into policing. An eight-year veteran of the Halifax police, he was the first witness at the trial. Rodney described him as "pretty big," "built nice," and "very athletic."

The day of Rodney Small's trial, Donald Stienburg showed up in court at 9:30 a.m. without sleep because he was just off the night shift. An eight-year veteran on the force, he was still inexperienced as a court witness. He had testified only two or three times a year before.[3] Recalling the officer's appearance that morning, Rodney Small described Stienburg as "pretty big," "built nice," and "very athletic," with brownish dark hair and a "kind of circle-y face."[4] For his part, Prosecutor Miller viewed his sole Crown witness as highly credible: "Donnie just sort of gives you the impression he'll tell you everything, tell you everything truthfully. You would never have the impression that you can't trust this guy. It's like if you had a favourite uncle, favourite cousin, whoever. When you sit down and talk to Donnie, [he is] very friendly, very honest."[5]

As for Stienburg himself, he remembered taking the stand and telling the story as recorded in the Crown brief. "I knew what happened. I was there. And I thought my testimony was fine," he recalled, "until the decision."[6]

RICHARD B. MILLER

Crown prosecutor Richard (Rick) Miller was born in Halifax in 1961 and grew up in the working-class North End like Rodney Small, except he was white. His father worked at the grain elevators, his mother was a homemaker; neither finished high school. "We weren't rich by any stretch of the imagination," explained Miller. He played baseball and hockey in high school, where he excelled academically, becoming one of two classmates to go to university. "Quite frankly," he explained, "a lot of people I grew up with went to jail." He left home at age nineteen and made his way through commerce and law at Dalhousie while working to support himself. Rick recalled "really liking law school," although he had little time to socialize with classmates while working thirty hours a week serving food and busing tables in the Victoria General Hospital cafeteria.[7]

Crown prosecutor Richard B. Miller, 2018. Miller grew up in the North End like Rodney Small and worked his way through law school. He represented legal-aid clients before switching to prosecution work.

Rick was called to the Nova Scotia bar in 1987. He began practice with a small criminal defence firm, took a stint as an in-house corporate counsel, and then opened up his own solo criminal defence firm. Representing legal-aid clients for a daily fee left him struggling to make ends meet, and he soon switched to prosecution work. At first, he could only get short-term contracts, but by the time of the *RDS* trial, Miller was working as a full-time Crown attorney at Devonshire Youth Court. He described prosecuting as "tough," even "pressured" at times, but thoroughly "enjoyable," even "fun." Of average height and build with sandy hair, Miller was perceived to be an open, talkative person with a friendly demeanour.[8]

When Rodney Small's trial began, Rick Miller had been in practice for seven years, yet people still thought of him as a novice. In his memoir, Rocky Jones described Miller as "pretty new to the game."[9] Constable Stienburg thought of Miller as "brand new."[10] Miller's earlier contractual criminal work had fallen under the radar. Years later, Miller expressed surprise that Jones was so dismissive. "Without meaning any disrespect," he emphasized, "Rocky was not somebody that I wanted to remove from the case. To say the least, *he* was very junior."[11] And Stienburg speculated about Miller's awareness that he was perceived as inexperienced, wondering whether Miller may have been "keen to do his job because he was brand-new."[12]

Stienburg spoke highly of Miller, describing him as a prosecutor with a "very practical approach," who was "thorough," "competent," "well-respected," and "personable."[13] Rocky Jones was less complimentary, tagging Miller as not one of the "heavy guns" and "a bit of a hawk."[14] As Miller watched *RDS* take on a life of its own, he reflected that "it was such a minor file. All I ever wanted to do as a prosecutor was just to present a fair case. This case had absolutely nothing to do with race. This turned into something it never was. It's the most bizarre thing I've probably ever been involved in."[15]

RODNEY DARREN SMALL

Rodney Small's family had deep roots in Nova Scotia. He traced his two-century heritage there to the arrival of Black Loyalists and Jamaican Maroons. By the year of Rodney's birth in 1978, his family resided in North End Halifax, a racially diverse, blue-collar enclave beyond the Citadel, dominated by the Halifax shipyard and the sprawling barracks of Canada's largest military base. The African Nova Scotian inhabitants had formed close community bonds and took pride in institutions such as the Cornwallis Street Baptist Church, the YMCA, local schools, and a recreation centre. But racial discrimination had impeded socioeconomic elevation, and the area was impoverished with high crime rates. The response, overpolicing, failed to stem the downward spiral.[16]

Rodney's family situation was a challenging one, as he would tell it years later. His mother, Denise Kelsie Small, was sixteen when she gave birth to Rodney.[17] In retrospect, he admitted that he had had little appreciation of "what it was like to have me at age sixteen," especially because his father, Rodney Cain, "was a lifer in prison."[18] He described his mother as an African Nova Scotian with "blue eyes," who "could pass for white" but would "get angry" if someone called her white. She was "self-educated" and "smart," he added, but without a "career orientation" and employed primarily in domestic work. Rodney described their relationship as troubled. She was "a bit short in bringing me up," he explained, a woman who was a strict disciplinarian and "didn't understand what I was going through."[19]

It was Rodney's grandmother, Maude Kelsie, who served as the primary parent, frequently the mediator between Rodney and his mother. Maude Kelsie had been raised in Gibson Woods, King's County, where she attended a racially segregated school. After moving to Agricola Street in Halifax, she cleaned hospital linens and raised fourteen children, "her own and some others, including me," Rodney emphasized. When her family had grown, she moved to the Brunswick Towers, where she still kept an eye on Rodney, who adored her in return. "My Grandma was the one who brought me up and was like my mom," he recalled. "I had a lot of hate in me as a young boy, but in my Grandma's eyes, I could do no wrong."[20]

Rodney attended Cunard Street Daycare and then St. Patrick's-Alexandra School. The autumn of his arrest, he was starting Grade 10 in high school. He described himself as a "fighter," protective of the "underdog," but also "a little bit of a bully," something he ascribed to the disruption and violence he witnessed at home. He played basketball, pool, and ping-pong at the YMCA, a "safe haven" space. He appreciated the North End's tight-knit "village-like" community where "you could go in anybody's house," but he deplored the police presence. "We were taught not to talk to the police, not to engage with the police, that it was dangerous," he explained. The memory of Constable Stienburg's choke hold was still searing years later: "I was dizzy. I thought I would asphyxiate. I had never had my breath cut off like that. I thought I might be brain-damaged. I thought this guy was trying to kill me. And then they will say it was a mistake."[21]

According to Rodney, it was not his decision to place himself in the middle of an unprecedented case. The wheels propelling the case to the nation's top court were set in motion by the officer who laid the charges. Then the raw urgency of the competing issues eclipsed everything else. Rodney's main recollection was of being "intimidated" and "scared to death." "I was a confused young kid," he added: "I wasn't fully confident with Rocky, my lawyer. And in no way, shape, or form did I feel like I had an advantage because there was a Black judge. I felt I was at a bit of disadvantage. I felt Judge Sparks would have to show why she was there, that she would convict."[22]

Surprised at the acquittal, he may have feared that Judge Sparks would lower the boom on him, yet another disciplinary parental figure like his strict mother. As some observers have noted, Black adults sometimes feel compelled to harshly discipline children to prepare them for societal racism.[23] Rodney also described himself as "a little upset" over Judge Sparks's verdict, wondering why she had speculated about the police.[24] Could her critique of police behaviour escalate the misconduct directed at him? An uncertain, emotionally troubled young man, he did his best to ignore what followed and to keep a low profile as the legal battle loomed over his future for three long years.

BURNLEY "ROCKY" JONES

Burnley "Rocky" Jones was born in Truro, Nova Scotia, in 1941, to a family descended from nineteenth-century Black Refugees. His parents, Willena Gabriel (a domestic worker and the first Black junior high school teacher in Truro) and Elmer Jones (a stationary engineer who tended industrial boilers) had ten children. They lived in Colchester County on "the Marsh," a predominantly Black neighbourhood composed of tarpaper shacks lacking furnaces and indoor toilets. The Zion Baptist Church was the cohesive centre of community life. The Jones men were all over six feet tall, known as "huge men" who were "extremely gentle," and Rocky grew up no exception.[25]

He excelled academically at Willow Street primary school but lost interest in school because of racial hostility from white teachers at the racially mixed Central Junior High School. It was then he noticed that his race defined what jobs he could hold, where he could sit in the movie theatre, which barbershop he could frequent, and which social activities he could join. By age seventeen, he dropped out of school and joined the military.[26]

Rocky's stint with the military was short-lived. His supervising officers complained that he "couldn't take orders," and they bristled when he spoke up about racism. Next, he drifted through Toronto, where, between pool hustling and poker, he attended meetings of the Universal Negro Improvement Association and the Toronto Negro Veterans' Association. He was introduced to Harry Gairey of the West Indian Federation and Stan Grizzle of the Brotherhood of Sleeping Car Porters in Canada. He also met and married Joan Bonner, a Black woman from Oakville. Joan was engaged in the race politics of the 1960s, and her infectious enthusiasm catapulted Rocky into a burgeoning wave of Black resistance.[27]

Before the Sixties were over, Rocky Jones had become one of the most visible faces of antiracist activism in Canada. He was a mesmerizing firebrand on the speaking circuit who could handle any challenge an audience could throw at him, an "eloquent" speaker with a deep, powerful voice. The coauthor of Jones's memoir, Jim Walker, described him as a "fast learner" who was "bright" and "good-looking." A physically imposing man, he had a larger-than-life presence – a devil-may-care agitator with a quick wit and a disarming smile.[28] African Nova Scotian cultural activist David Woods explained, "He had a facility to converse with anyone he met. He was a man everybody related to, everybody embraced. Even the ones he was fighting."[29]

Jones forged connections with antiracist organizations in the United States: Students for a Democratic Society, the Student Nonviolent Coordinating Committee, the Congress of Racial Equality, and the Black Panthers. He tried to explain to American activists the parallels he saw in Canada. They insisted that Canadian racism was less malevolent. To Jones, this was a distortion based on the erasure of Black Nova Scotian history. He believed Blacks were facing a "cultural genocide" in Nova Scotia, and he resolved to return home to turn this around.[30]

Burnley "Rocky" Jones, a descendant of Black Refugees and one of the most visible faces of antiracist activism in Canada, on a public-speaking tour.

A *Halifax Daily News* columnist described Rocky Jones as a "populist bohemian," someone "in the thick of every crisis, attending teach-ins, drop-ins, and sit-ins, spinning James Brown records and talking Marxism."[31] He confronted Halifax police over their intimidating tactics, accusing them of behaving like "an occupying force" in the Black community, and encouraged African Nova Scotians to resist. He emerged as a new form of leader, his revolutionary politics upsetting to some in both the white and Black communities who preferred change to come in more incremental ways.

Dissent within the African Nova Scotian community did not deter Rocky. His and Joan's home became the headquarters of the new civil rights movement in Nova Scotia, their kitchen table the centre of debate and strategic planning. They brought Stokely Carmichael and Rosie Douglas to Halifax and helped establish the Black United Front. In 1988, Jones made submissions to the Royal Commission on the Donald Marshall, Jr., Prosecution inquiring into the wrongful conviction of a Mi'kmaw youth. Jones's excoriation of the systemic racism against Blacks was one of the most powerful presentations the commission heard. He assisted the cultural "Black Renaissance" that showcased musicians, filmmakers, and poets. He coped with twenty-four-hour RCMP surveillance and survived regular death threats. Twice his house was burned down by arsonists; no charges were ever laid.[32]

In 1968, Rocky Jones went back to school. He enrolled part-time at Dalhousie as a mature student and graduated in 1974 with a BA in history. While there, he helped establish the Transition Year Program for Black and Indigenous school dropouts who wished to attend university.

◄ Joan Jones, Rocky's wife, addressing a 1999 news conference for Black History Month. Born Joan Bonner in Oakville, her efforts catapulted the couple into the front wave of Black resistance.

▼ Rocky and Joan brought the Black Panthers to Halifax and helped establish the Black United Front. Here, Rocky *(second from left)* poses with Miriam Makeba (South African musician), C.L.R. James (Trinidad activist and writer), and Stokely Carmichael (Black Panther) in 1968.

By 1987, he was running a North End employment agency for prison inmates and former prisoners. He was making a remarkable transition – from a symbol of Black radicalism to antiracist institutional builder – and moving closer to the rest of the African Canadian community as it turned increasingly to activism. As one observer noted, "In such a small community, the leadership of one person can be so critical, and so it was with Rocky."[33]

Rocky Jones graduated from Dalhousie, with Joan at his side, in 1974. While there, he helped establish a transition year for Black and Indigenous dropouts. In 1989, he helped create the Indigenous Blacks & Mi'kmaq Initiative to bring Nova Scotia Blacks and Mi'kmaq into the legal profession. In 1992, he became one of its first law graduates.

In 1989, he helped create the Indigenous Blacks & Mi'kmaq Initiative at Dalhousie law school to bring Nova Scotia Blacks and Mi'kmaq into the legal profession. In 1992, at the age of fifty-one, he became one of its first law graduates. Called to the bar in 1993, he took a job at Dalhousie's Legal Aid Clinic, the first and only Black lawyer on staff. That was where Rodney and his mother retained him. He had one year of practice behind him, but it was a fortuitous match. They could not have found a better lawyer for the case.[34]

CORRINE "CONNIE" ETTA SPARKS

Judge Sparks's Nova Scotian roots stretched back two centuries, with a heritage traced to Black Loyalists and Black Refugees. The family settled in Lake Loon, a segregated Black rural community in Preston township on the periphery of Halifax. Her father, Spencer Sparks, was employed as a custodian. Her mother, Helen Sparks, worked as a domestic, caterer, and teacher in a segregated school.[35] Judge Sparks described her parents as "honest, self-respecting, church-going people who worked long, hard hours at many jobs to support their family."[36]

Connie[37] Sparks was born in 1953, the eldest of nine children. With both parents working, household chores fell on her shoulders. "I was the oldest, so it was no surprise that I became the responsible one. I had to look after the younger ones," she explained. "My parents would always say, 'You have to be an example for the others.'"[38] Childhood friend Delvina Bernard recalled that Connie's mother "had high expectations" of her children in terms of "education, morality, and achievement" and that her home was "always spotless." Bernard added: "She always had time for young people. But don't mess with Mrs. Sparks, or she'll tell you right straight about yourself."[39]

Financial precarity was balanced with strong religious faith. Connie was baptized in Cherry Brook Baptist Church, which her family had helped found in 1902, and she carried her religion through a lifetime.[40]

Connie Sparks had Nova Scotia roots stretching back two centuries. She recalled being raised by honest, hard-working parents who balanced financial precarity with strong faith. She attended Cherry Brook United Baptist Church, which her family helped found in 1902.

She attended Lake Loon primary school, a segregated school with Black teachers, Black students, no library, and few resources. She sang in the church choir and attended Canadian Girls in Training (CGIT) and Explorers, church suppers, picnics, socials, and concerts. She sold wild blueberries in the summers and staffed the candy counter after school at the Mayfair Theatre in Dartmouth.[41]

Graham Creighton High School was her first experience of racial integration. "I would have to say, putting it mildly, there was a lot of racial tension there. Anti-Black racism was palpable," recalled Connie. "Certain teachers were very hostile," and Black students were "streamed away" from university-entrance programs. "If there was ever any infraction, it was always the Black kids who got punished, always more harshly than other students." Although Connie stuck to the university track, the talkative, outgoing personality of her younger years disappeared. She became quieter, more introverted, reserved.[42]

She found solace in the few racialized teachers who "took an interest" in her. Walter Borden, an African Canadian actor and playwright who taught her European history, introduced material on Black culture and politics. Some teachers helped her to overcome her lack of self-confidence. "They saw potential, something I did not recognize in myself," she mused years later.[43] High school principal Gerald K. Barry connected her with the local Rotary Club, which provided some funding for university, and the Sisters of Charity assisted with room and board. Connie enrolled at Mount Saint Vincent University, which had begun actively recruiting Black female students.[44] The first in her family to attend university, she obtained a BA in 1974, with a major in economics and a minor in psychology. During her part-time job at the university library, she read about the American civil rights movement, the Black Panthers, and Angela Davis, and she joined the Black Students' Association.[45]

After graduation, she worked briefly as an investigator at the Human Rights Commission, where she met Ken Crawford, a Black law student summering there. Connie said that his encouragement and her interest in human rights inspired her to apply to law school. Wait-listed for several months at Dalhousie, to her surprise she was admitted just before classes started.[46] Despite its ninety-five-year history, Dalhousie law school had graduated few Black Nova Scotians.[47] When Connie began in 1975, there were only two other Black students, Douglas Ruck from Dartmouth, and Mel White, an African Caribbean. Ruck described the threesome as "Black in a sea of white faces."[48]

Connie's reserved and deferential personality exacerbated her isolation, and she found law school "lonely, stressful, and intense." "Coming from a small segregated community, then a small liberal arts school, to a prestigious law school was challenging," she explained. "It was the first time in my life I had been exposed to the upper echelons of Canadian society." She hated being called on in class. Holding down two jobs to cover expenses added to the challenges, and many times she considered quitting.[49] Years later, her law professor Wayne MacKay recognized how difficult Connie's experience must have been: "The culture shock of being in this world, different from what your whole life experience has been, doesn't make it easy."[50] Another law professor, Leon Trakman, offered his impressions:

> My recollection of her is someone who was modest and warm by nature, astute in her judgement, and never ever oversold herself. She was also fair-minded in her reaction to others, some of whom were perhaps less worthy of the same comment in their treatment of her. But she was very perceptive. She was also conscious that others carried their own burdens, mine in being born a white South African; but she never sought to build on that guilt, very much to the contrary.[51]

Financial challenges required she take a year out for various paid jobs. Mel White dropped out permanently. Connie Sparks was the sole Black woman, and the sole Black person, to graduate in 1979.[52]

Sparks completed her articles with the Halifax City Solicitor's Department. City lawyer Donald Murphy had a reputation for hiring women and African Canadians who could not get placements elsewhere.[53] "I did traffic-violation prosecutions," Sparks recalled. After her 1980 call to the bar, she worked briefly as a trust officer for Canada Trust. Finding no jobs for Black female lawyers in Halifax, she uprooted

When Connie Sparks began Dalhousie law, she was one of three Black students "in a sea of white faces." When she graduated in 1979, she was the sole Black person.

herself to Calgary, a city perceived as a "financial mecca" where everybody who wanted a job could get one. There, she worked for another trust company and a small oil-and-gas company.[54]

Homesick, she soon returned to Dartmouth where she opened its first female law firm in 1981 with a white classmate, Helen Foote.[55] Under the shingle of "Sparks and Foote," from an office on Portland Street above a jewellery store, the two practised family, real estate, and personal injury law, along with "whatever came in the door." She and Foote secured appointments to the Residential Tenancies Board, resolving landlord-and-tenant disputes in the evenings, which helped pay the bills. It was, Sparks recalled, the "best years" of her practice career.[56]

When Helen departed for a larger firm later that year, Sparks joined her classmate Douglas Ruck, whose Dartmouth office was located on Prince Albert Road.[57] Over the next six years, she expanded her family and real estate practice.[58] Doug Ruck explained that both of them were "cognizant of what it meant to be Black in Nova Scotia" servicing primarily Black clients when "even they were not used to having Black lawyers." Ruck described how one white judge demeaned him in court. Surprised that a white client had retained a Black lawyer, the judge queried, "Why did she come to you?" When Ruck complained to the judge in his chambers afterward, he asked if the judge had ever before said such a thing to a lawyer in open court. "He couldn't name anyone."[59] Donald Oliver, another Black Dalhousie law graduate and the only one to land an unprecedented job with a large Halifax law firm, was advised it would probably take him longer than his white colleagues to make partner. Oliver summed it up: "You can't be a Black lawyer in Nova Scotia and not have experienced racism."[60]

In 1987, thirty-four-year-old Connie Sparks was appointed to the Nova Scotia Family Court. The first woman judge, Sandra Oxner, had been appointed to the Provincial Court in 1971. "I was the token woman," laughed Oxner, "and Connie Sparks was the token Black. No doubt about that."[61] The appointment made Sparks the first Black judge in Nova Scotia, and the first Black female judge in Canada.[62] With no application process, she had no idea she was being considered. She was taken aback when provincial Conservative cabinet minister Edmund Morris approached her to say he had put her name forward.[63]

Nova Scotia Conservative premier John Buchanan took great pride in Sparks's appointment. Years later, he called it "certainly historic, as far as we were concerned in 1987." He added, "I don't think anyone grasped the magnitude of what we were doing.

Sandra Oxner, the first woman judge in Nova Scotia, was appointed in 1971. She later commented: "I was the token woman, and Connie Sparks was the token black."

The newly appointed Judge Sparks with her parents,
1987. The appointment made her the first Black
judge in Nova Scotia and the first Black female
judge in Canada.

We knew there had never been a Black judge in Nova Scotia. Then
someone told me that the appointment would make Connie the first
African Canadian female judge in the country." It was, he remarked,
"long overdue."[64]

The African Nova Scotian community feted the newly sworn-in
Judge Sparks with a banquet, and she was inundated with congratula-
tions from across Canada.[65] Her visibility caused the Canadian Bar
Association to appoint her to the Task Force on Gender Equality. Its
Touchstones for Change report, released the year of Rodney Small's arrest,
would demand greater recognition of women in law and the judiciary.[66]
As the *RDS* case spun out of control, Sparks's prominence would only
grow – positively and negatively.

3

A Black History of Nova Scotia

Canada has long boasted of hosting the terminus of the Underground Railroad, a haven for Blacks fleeing American slavery.[1] Many are surprised to learn that slavery was practised here for over two hundred years.[2] Afua Cooper, Dalhousie University's Chair in Black Canadian Studies, emphasizes that slavery lies at the root of Nova Scotia Black history: "Nova Scotia was a premier North American site in which a unique Black identity was shaped and established. Black people came here to seek safety and a better life. Slavery and its shadow marked their movements."[3]

The first enslaved Black person arrived in what is now Canada in 1629, brought to Quebec by the Anglo-French adventurer David Kirke, who had just conquered the small settlement and held it briefly for England.[4] Colonists in French and English Canada enacted laws that assisted the sale of humans as property from 1689 to 1833.[5] The white settlers who flooded into the unceded traditional lands of the Mi'kmaq transported enslaved Africans with them.[6] Prominent Nova Scotians, including a governor and numerous clergymen, enslaved Black people.[7] Nova Scotia elites drew their fortunes from trade premised on the unpaid labour of slaves. Enslaved labour produced the rum, coffee, sugar, and molasses that travelled in triangular passage from the Caribbean through Nova Scotia to Britain. Black labour generated private capital for white settlers and taxes for the public treasury.[8]

This notice, about a "Negroe Girl named Thursday, about four and a half feet high, broad feet, with a Lump above her Right Eye" who ran away from her master, ran in the *N.S. Gazette and Weekly Chronicle* in September 1772. Canada prides itself on being the terminus of the Underground Railway, but slavery was practised within its borders for over two hundred years.

> RAN away from her Master JOHN ROCK, on Monday the 18th Day of August last; a Negroe Girl named *Thursday*, about four and an half feet high, broad feet, with a Lump above her Right Eye : Had on when she run away a red Cloth Petticoat, a red Baize Bed Gown, and a red Ribbon about her Head. Whosoever may harbour said Negroe Girl, or encourage her to stay away from her said Master, may depend on being prosecuted according as the Law shall direct. And whosoever may be so kind to take her up and send her home to her said Master, shall be paid all Costs and Charges, together with TWO DOLLARS Reward for their Trouble.
> JOHN ROCK.
> HALIFAX, Sept. 1st, 1772.

Slave auctions began in 1752, shortly after Halifax was founded. In 1769, white men sold "two hogsheads of rum, three of sugar, and two well-grown negro girls aged fourteen and twelve, to the highest bidder" on a Halifax beach.[9] In 1786, Halifax merchant Charles Hill advertised for auction a thirteen-year-old African boy.[10] The next large influx of enslaved people came with the New England Planters, who arrived in Nova Scotia in the 1760s to settle the Annapolis Valley lands confiscated from the recently deported Acadians.[11] Violence inevitably accompanied slavery. In Windsor, Nova Scotia, one enslaver killed a Black child with a hammer. In Annapolis, an enslaved man was whipped to death. In Truro, an enslaver cut a hole in the earlobe of a recaptured enslaved man, passed a knotted whiplash through the hole, and dragged him to his death. None of the white murderers was punished.[12]

FREE BLACK IMMIGRATION

Free Blacks were also among the first Nova Scotia arrivals. Mattieu da Costa came with Samuel de Champlain in 1608, and by the late eighteenth century, the province could count itself home to the largest free African population outside Africa.[13] There were four distinct migratory waves. Rodney Small's and Judge Sparks's forebears came with the first wave after the American Revolution. "Black Loyalists" had supported the British as soldiers, nurses, guides, domestics, and sea pilots. All told, these men and women represented about 10 percent of the Loyalists who settled in Nova Scotia.[14]

Promised freedom and land in return for their military service, Black Loyalists soon found themselves assigned land without formal grants, leaving them with insecure titles. Most received plots less than half the size of those allotted to white Loyalists, far from major settlements, on deep swamps or impenetrable woods, and on Nova Scotia's worst soil.[15] When the authorities did not honour pledges of rations and seed, mass starvation ensued. One Black man was hanged in Halifax in 1785 for stealing a bag of potatoes. Potatoes also figured in the case of Mary Postell and her daughters who, despite their manumission documents, were sold back into enslavement in 1791 for one hundred bushels of potatoes.[16] Others found their liberty contested when former white "owners" kidnapped and claimed them as slaves.[17]

Although they fought to hold British authorities accountable, many died of malnutrition, disease, and exposure. Some departed to set up a community of free Black people in Sierra Leone. Others persisted. Remarking on the Black Loyalists' notable success in founding Canada's first free Black community, African American journalist Evelyn C. White emphasizes that Nova Scotia "could have become the model for Black achievement in North America long before the Emancipation Proclamation."[18]

The Jamaican Maroons, to whom Rodney Small also traced his heritage, were Africans who had escaped enslavement to live in the mountainous Jamaican interior among the Indigenous Arawaks (Tainos). In a second migratory wave, over five hundred Maroons arrived after the British Jamaican governor, fearing the legendary warriors, offered them transport in 1796. Although Maroon skills proved essential in constructing the Halifax Citadel and Government House, starvation wages coupled with racist treatment dissuaded them from

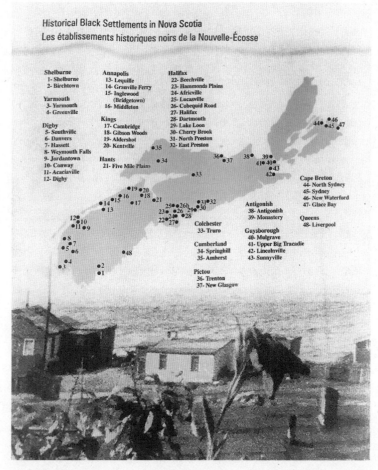

Historical Black Settlements in Nova Scotia
Les établissements historiques noirs de la Nouvelle-Écosse

Shelburne
1- Shelburne
2- Birchtown

Yarmouth
3- Yarmouth
4- Greenville

Digby
5- Southville
6- Danvers
7- Hassett
8- Weymouth Falls
9- Jordantown
10- Conway
11- Acaciaville
12- Digby

Annapolis
13- Lequille
14- Granville Ferry
15- Inglewood
(Bridgetown)
16- Middleton

Kings
17- Cambridge
18- Gibson Woods
19- Aldershot
20- Kentville

Hants
21- Five Mile Plains

Halifax
22- Beechville
23- Hammonds Plains
24- Africville
25- Lucasville
26- Cobequid Road
27- Halifax
28- Dartmouth
29- Lake Loon
30- Cherry Brook
31- North Preston
32- East Preston

Colchester
33- Truro

Cumberland
34- Springhill
35- Amherst

Pictou
36- Trenton
37- New Glasgow

Antigonish
38- Antigonish
39- Monastery

Guysborough
40- Mulgrave
41- Upper Big Tracadie
42- Lincolnville
43- Sunnyville

Cape Breton
44- North Sydney
45- Sydney
46- New Waterford
47- Glace Bay

Queens
48- Liverpool

Free Blacks were among the first settlers to arrive in Nova Scotia. In successive immigration waves over four centuries, they established forty-eight settlements. Rather than being called New Scotland, Nova Scotia could have been called New Africa.

permanent settlement. Many decamped to Sierra Leone, leaving only remnants of their community but a significant contribution to Nova Scotia bloodlines.[19]

Both Judge Sparks and Rocky Jones traced their heritage to the third wave, two thousand African Americans who supported the British in the War of 1812. Named the Black Refugees, they, too, were promised land but were assigned licences of occupation rather than title deeds and relegated to mainly barren lands.[20] Lord Dalhousie, governor of Nova Scotia and founder of Dalhousie University, stated that because the Black Refugees were "slaves by habit and education" and no longer working under "dread of the lash," their idea of freedom was "idleness" and they were "incapable of industry."[21] In 1838, the colonial secretary insisted that allowing Blacks to become landed proprietors rather than hired labourers was a "mistaken and mischievous notion."[22] Leading Halifax families funded the southern Confederacy during the American Civil War and pocketed large sums when Britain abolished slavery in 1833, choosing to compensate enslavers rather than Black people.[23]

Despite racially restrictive immigration rules, a fourth group from the Caribbean and Africa began to arrive in the 1800s. This group grew in number during the twentieth century, and continues to contribute to the swelling members of Nova Scotia's Black population today.[24]

With a four-hundred-year historical presence, African Nova Scotians have increasingly come to identify as a distinct people with a distinct culture, despite their erasure from the dominant cultural symbols.[25] Afua Cooper criticizes the artificiality of the designation of Nova Scotia heritage as "Scottish," with its symbols of the kilt, tartan, and bagpipes: "The province could easily have taken on a Loyalist identity, rather than a Scottish one. The African people came here before the Scots. It could have been called New Africa. Instead, it was reconceptualized as a settler identity, New Scotland. It's an erasure of heritage."[26]

THE PERVASIVENESS OF RACE DISCRIMINATION

It is difficult to know whether Nova Scotia was more racist than other provinces, but whites perpetrated race riots against Blacks from the earliest years. Disbanded white soldiers destroyed Black Loyalist dwellings in 1784 in Shelburne and Birchtown, in an effort to drive Blacks out.[27] Several years later, a mob of fifty white men attacked the Black settlement again, destroying property and livestock. Black Baptist minister David George was dragged from his church, beaten, and driven into the swamps. No arrests were made.[28] In 1880, rumours that a "coloured" man had "outraged" a white woman ignited another race riot in Bridgetown, which "put a white man in the grave and a black man on Death Row."[29]

When the First World War ended, race riots erupted in European camps for demobilized soldiers. After their return, bands of roving whites armed with clubs assuaged their fury on New Glasgow Blacks. Apologists attributed this violence to fear that Black soldiers, who had risked their lives on the battlefront might assert their rights at home, or that those who had experienced interracial socializing in Europe might dare to approach white Canadian women.[30] In the interwar years, racist attacks on Black Haligonians occurred almost yearly. White police and city officials did nothing to halt them.[31] In 1932, a five-foot Ku Klux Klan cross was burned on Halifax's Northwest Arm. Police admitted they knew who was involved but made no arrests.[32] In 1980, the KKK announced plans to set up a Nova Scotia chapter. In 1992, Halifax police advised that KKK material distributed on Halloween was not "hate literature" under the *Criminal Code.*[33]

Although Blacks paid taxes to support public schools, their children were often excluded. Nova Scotia legislation enacted in 1865 authorized racially segregated schools in Black neighbourhoods until the late 1960s.[34] White officials dismissed Black petitions and lawsuits calling for change.[35] Rodney Small's grandmother, Rocky Jones, and Connie Sparks all attended segregated primary schools. Even in integrated schools, Black students were often required to use separate doors and washrooms.[36]

By 1949, Black church leaders estimated that only twenty out of eight thousand children had reached high school, and Blacks could claim only nine university graduates in the province's history.[37] A 1962 survey found most dropped out between Grades 5 and 9 due to poverty and racist treatment.[38] White teachers perceived Black children as older, less innocent, and disruptive.[39] Halifax school records found them disproportionately suspended between 1987 and 1992, despite their parents' protests of race discrimination.[40]

Although Blacks paid taxes, their children were often excluded from public schools, and the province enacted legislation in 1865 to segregate classes. Rocky Jones, Connie Sparks, and Rodney Small's grandmother attended segregated classes such as this one at Guysborough Academy.

There was little incentive to obtain higher education when employers restricted Blacks to the worst occupations. The parents of Rodney Small, Rocky Jones, and Judge Sparks were relegated to low-wage domestic and custodial jobs. Black men toiled in the most arduous, dangerous, precarious jobs. Black women cleaned white women's homes. White employers paid skilled Blacks less than similarly skilled whites. Black unemployment rates were disproportionately high, and white unions denied them membership.[41] In 1978, the median income for Black Nova Scotians was 57 percent of provincial household earnings.[42] Racist landlords and creditors consigned Blacks to the least desirable residential districts.[43] The impoverished neighbourhoods where Rocky Jones and Connie Sparks grew up were well-known as Black wards. The paved roads, electricity, telephones, fire hydrants, garbage collection, plumbing, and sewage available to white settlements were rarely extended to Black communities.[44] When Clifford Oliver purchased a lot in the heart of Wolfville in the early 1900s, whites threatened to burn down any house he constructed there, and he was forced to build on the outskirts of town.[45] When an African Nova Scotian purchased a home in a white neighbourhood in Trenton in 1937, four hundred white rioters stoned him and destroyed the house and contents; he abandoned further efforts to occupy his property. The mob moved on to attack two other homes owned by Blacks, but the only person arrested was a New Glasgow Black man, who was convicted of assault.[46] Curfews excluded Nova Scotian Blacks from white "sundown towns" after dark.[47]

African Nova Scotians were often prevented from voting or holding public office.[48] They were excluded from jury service through geographic and property requirements.[49] During the First and Second World Wars, officers gave Black volunteers shovels instead of guns and told them it was a "white man's war."[50] Cemetery owners relegated the veterans of the No. 2 Construction Battalion to segregated burial plots.[51] Blacks worshipped in separate churches.[52] Nova Scotia courts upheld the rights of theatres, restaurants, recreational facilities, and lodging establishments to refuse Blacks.[53]

White child-welfare authorities used racially distorted definitions of "child neglect" to dismantle Black families.[54] In 1921, the Black community set up an orphanage for "coloured children" because other facilities refused them admission.[55] Banks refused loans and mortgages to Blacks. In the 1960s, nearly 80 percent of African Nova Scotians lived in "conditions of utter poverty." A 1973 Halifax housing survey revealed that 69 percent of Black homes still lacked indoor plumbing and 50 percent lacked central heating, while public transport was nearly nonexistent.[56] Although Black artists, writers, and entertainers had given flourishing expression to African Nova Scotian identity, the media, school texts, literary works, and theatrical revues disparaged or erased Black peoples.[57] Acclaimed Nova Scotia author Thomas Chandler Haliburton's writings "trafficked ruthlessly in images of comic or homicidal or shiftless blacks."[58]

BLACK RESISTANCE

The obliteration of Africville sparked some of the strongest opposition. A village of four hundred Blacks on the northern edge of Halifax overlooking Bedford Basin, Africville had been denied essential services for more than a century despite persistent petitions for schools, water, and roads. Facilities whites decried – a prison, sewage pits, garbage dumps, slaughterhouses, a fertilizer plant, and infectious disease hospitals – butted up next to Black homes. Yet generations of families took pride in the vital, close-knit community they fashioned there, in spite of it all.[59] Between 1964 and 1969, the City of Halifax bulldozed their homes and church in the name of municipal progress.[60] The defiance of the residents gained Halifax a reputation as the city with the most anti-Black urban planners, engineers, and architects in Canada.[61]

Between 1964 and 1969, in the name of municipal progress, the City of Halifax bulldozed the community of Africville, a village of four hundred Blacks. Protests by residents helped give Halifax a reputation as an anti-Black city.

George Elliott Clarke, an African Nova Scotian poet and literary critic, wrote that African Nova Scotians may have "started at the bottom in a society intent on keeping them at the bottom," but they "settled communities, campaigned for better schools, maintained a unique gospel and spiritual musical tradition [and] founded an independent church association" as well as issuing Black "newspapers and magazines despite the inhospitable market for their wares."[62] In 1932, the Halifax Colored Citizens Improvement League formed one of the first explicitly antiracist organizations. In 1945, the Nova Scotia Association for the

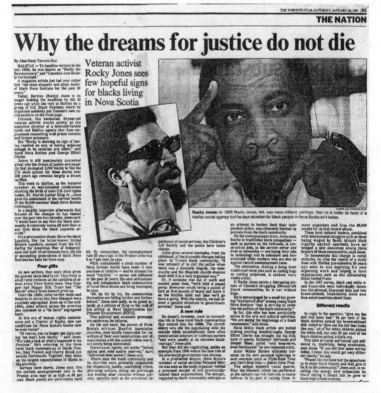

When Rodney Small and his mother needed a lawyer, they turned to the Black United Front, which Rocky and Joan Jones had helped found. It combined political advocacy with social services in the name of racial justice. This profile on Rocky Jones ran in the *Toronto Star* on 24 January 1987.

Advancement of Coloured People (NSAACP) protested the prosecution of businesswoman Viola Desmond for sitting in the whites-only section of a New Glasgow theatre.[63] Although the courts upheld her conviction, NSAACP activism inspired the first legislation prohibiting race discrimination.[64] Energized by the fallout from the razing of Africville, the civil rights movement in the United States, and the Halifax visit of Black Panther Stokely Carmichael, the community formed the Black United Front in 1969. It was the BUF that Rodney Small and his mother turned to when they needed a lawyer thirty-five years later. An umbrella group designed to make common cause for racial justice, it combined political advocacy with social services to Blacks. It was also the first Nova Scotia antiracist organization to take on systemic police discrimination.[65]

Michelle Williams, a Black Dalhousie law professor, describes the "common thread throughout African Nova Scotian history and contemporary experience" as a "denial of our basic human rights and freedoms on an individual and collective basis." Claiming reparations "for years of *de facto* and *de jure* segregation," she links the injustice directly to the "profoundly racist" environment of Nova Scotia. "We're stewed in it [and] steeped in it. It's how this place was built."[66]

Nova Scotia's distinctive Black history embodied centuries of racial violence and discrimination perpetrated against a substantial, firmly embedded, interconnected community of settled people from the African diaspora.[67] In all aspects of life – immigration, education, employment, housing, and economic, social, cultural, and political life – generations of resisters struggled to survive in a deeply racist society.[68] Their collective experience provides a striking background to the *RDS* case.

4

Race and Policing in Nova Scotia

As Rodney Small put it, "the bumpy relationship" between the Halifax police and the Black community was "ingrained in our history."[1] African Nova Scotians complained of discriminatory arrests, overcharging, and police violence, pointing to considerable concrete evidence of historical conflict between the police and themselves.[2]

In 1956, one of the *Halifax Chronicle-Herald's* first Black reporters described hearing "chilling stories about policing and overt racism in Black communities."[3] In 1967, the front page of *Maclean's* magazine profiled African Nova Scotian young people marching in protest against police discrimination.[4] Two years later, nineteen-year-old Thomas Ronald Drummond was walking home from work after midnight when the Halifax police stopped him at the corner of Gottingen and Gerrish Streets. Officers told the Grade 12 student to "get along." Words were exchanged. Then the teenager was charged with resisting arrest, handcuffed, and thrown into the patrol car, where a white officer repeatedly punched him in the head. When his uncle came to retrieve him from the police station, he found his nephew bruised and bleeding. A Halifax reporter located a witness in the cells who testified that the officer was still punching Drummond after the teen was locked up. The press coverage led to the resignation of one officer.[5]

BEATEN BY CITY POLICE, SAYS BLACK YOUTH

"I phoned the police station and they said there wasn't a mark on the boy," said Buddy Daye.

Daye, boxer turned youth worker, said he was seriously shaken when he arrived at the Halifax Police Station the next morning and found that 19 - year -old Ronnie Drummond had bruises on his head and that he had been bleeding from the mouth.

"It shakes my faith in something I've believed in," said Daye. "The kid had been beaten, he was scared and they wouldn't let him

RON DRUMMOND

make a phone call."

Drummond, a Grade 12 student at Queen Elizabeth High School until last month, had a confrontation with police on Creighton

POLICE - PAGE 10

POLICE - FROM 1

Street at about 1 a.m. and said he was told he was being arrested for loitering.

"When the police car came, they handcuffed me behind my back and threw me in the back seat," said Drummond. "One of them sat on my head, and after he got off he kept hitting me in the head with his right fist while I was handcuffed.

"It was the same policeman who kept hitting me and calling me names," said Drummond. "When we got to the police station they took off the handcuffs before they took me in, but this guy kept hitting me and other policemen told him to lay off."

A man being held in jail told The 4th ESTATE that he saw the policemen strike Drummond.

"I was bleeding in the police station and this guy still kept trying to hit me," said the youth.

When Drummond appeared in Police Court he was charged with resisting arrest.

"You're damn right I resisted," said Drummond. "I knew what they were going to do."

The youth is being represented by Halifax barrister Walter Goodfellow.

In 1969, Ronald Drummond's account of being beaten by police came to the public's attention through reports in the *4th Estate*. The nineteen-year-old had been walking home from work when police told him to "get along." An exchange of words escalated to a charge of resisting arrest.

Things exploded into public view again in 1989, after three days of racially charged violence at Dartmouth's Cole Harbour High School, which served students from the predominantly Black Preston township and a white working-class suburb of Halifax. When police intervened, Black students complained that officers had pepper-sprayed them, not the white students, and charged more Blacks than whites. Two Black students were convicted; all the white students were acquitted or had charges dropped.[6] David Nantes, a white provincial cabinet minister, rejected calls for a judicial inquiry, insisting that there was "no racism in Nova Scotia."[7] Frances Kent Potts, a white provincial court judge, dismissed complaints about disparate charging and prosecution. The police probe "may have been flawed" she ruled, but there was no proof of "racial bias."[8]

In 1993, white probation officer Cesar Lalo was charged with sexually abusing dozens of Nova Scotia boys under his supervision between 1973 and 1989. Most had been arrested for minor offences such as truancy or shoplifting. Some were sent for counselling simply because they were perceived to be at risk. Lalo was convicted, but the racism inherent in his crimes went largely ignored. Mark Knox, a white defence lawyer, was one of the few to emphasize that Lalo's "horrendous" predations involved "ninety percent African Nova Scotian kids from the poor part of town, often raised by single mothers and grandmothers" who entrusted their boys to Lalo's care because of his "interest" in their welfare.[9]

In the early 1990s, Nova Scotia police cracked down on prostitution. Black men from Preston complained they were "unfairly targeted and harassed," stereotyped due to the actions of a few.[10] One Black journalist wrote, "Breaking up a pimping ring is the job of the police; breaking down a community's reputation is the job of racists."[11] Although the RCMP admitted that all the men they charged were Black, they insisted that Blacks were not being "picked on."[12]

Jean Whalen became Nova Scotia's first Black female Crown prosecutor in 1989. In 1990, a white police officer spoke with her about a sexual assault charge against a Black teen. To Whalen's shock, he joked, "This guy's Black. He must be guilty," then added further racist comments.[13] Whalen pondered the risks of a novice Black female prosecutor bringing an unprecedented complaint of racism against a ten-year veteran on the force, but she did it.[14] The Nova Scotia Police Commission suspended the officer for seven days and recommended multicultural training, a penalty his lawyer insisted was "too harsh."[15]

In 1991, tensions built at a Halifax nightclub after young Black males claimed they were "refused admittance into the city's downtown bars." The *Halifax Daily News* agreed that race discrimination in the bar district had been "widely acknowledged" for years.[16] The province's threat to revoke liquor licences had little effect. On July 18, seven whites approached two Blacks in one of the only integrated bars. One of the whites threw the first punch, and a fight ensued. When the bouncers brutally beat the two Black males and banned them, but not the whites, from future admission, emotions reached a fever pitch. The next evening, a "rampage" involving hundreds of people and extensive property damage ignited "three nights of fury."[17]

Jean Whalen, Nova Scotia's first Black female Crown prosecutor, brought an early claim of racism against police in the province.

Confronting white police chief Vince MacDonald afterwards, Blacks queried "why police wore riot gear when confronting Blacks on Gottingen Street [but] didn't hit the white boys downtown."[18] Taxi passengers told the police chief that the police scanner had picked up references to "n*****s" and "Black bastards."[19] The national media covered the riot, and rumours flew that one officer had brazenly suggested that they should throw a "n***** off the bridge." On 1 August 1991, a mixed-race crowd over a thousand strong paraded through downtown. Some called it a "peace march" and others an "anti-racism rally."[20] Anthony Ross, a Black lawyer who practised in Halifax from 1973 to 1996, explained, "At that time, there was a line between police officers and Black people. Policing was at its worst."[21]

Police Chief MacDonald set up a review committee whose police members concluded that the altercation was "not precipitated by racial discrimination" but by Blacks "settling a score." The *Halifax Chronicle-Herald* reported that the officers were "tired of being criticized for doing their job." Tony Burbridge, a white constable who spoke for the police union, said that "morale is down" and warned that "allegations could

A mixed-race crowd of over a thousand strong paraded on 1 August 1991 for peace and against racism. The event was in protest of racially motivated policing and the outbreak of violence in Halifax's bar district.

leave a hesitant officer dead."[22] Stanford psychology professor Jennifer Eberhardt, a police trainer on racial bias, heard similar concerns from officers south of the border who viewed vilifications as yet "another burden added to the baggage they carry as they patrol the streets."[23] She added:

> They become bitter about putting their lives on the line for people who do not seem to respect them or appreciate their efforts. They become jaded as they bear witness to horrific acts of violence. They get worn down by living in a constant state of hypervigilance, not knowing where the next threat will emerge. And that leads to a vicious cycle that can sabotage communication and escalate even the slightest provocation.[24]

It was, she emphasized, the "fallout of racial disparities" that had taken centuries to accumulate.[25]

The Black members on Police Chief MacDonald's review committee underscored that the officers had allegedly "beat a Black man and shoved him through a window" and called another the "N-word" as they broke up a brawl. Their conclusion: the police had mishandled its internal investigation and failed to follow up on "complaints of excessive force and racial slurs."[26] Tempers flared within the wider Black community. African Nova Scotian sociologist Robert S. Wright observed that "Black consciousness was on the rise in a way it hadn't been since the 60s, early 70s."[27] Black journalist Charles Saunders complained of white erasures of racism: "From the black perspective, it is sometimes difficult to distinguish which is worse – acts of racism themselves, or the disavowals that invariably follow." He called the "repeated refusals" to consider "out-and-out racism" extremely frustrating.[28]

In 1991, Saunders chronicled how white police officers had watched, but made no effort to stop, three white men who attacked a South African Black man, Dennis Otto Mahlangu. With much of it caught on video, two whites held down Mahlangu while a third punched him in the face. The attackers were charged, but so was the innocent South African. Mahlangu complained to the chief of police that the officers also used racial slurs and physically abused him.[29] The police dismissed the complaint and charged him with mischief for filing it, a charge later thrown out by a judge who said it should never have been laid.[30]

In 1992, Dartmouth police took no action after discovering a burned cross and Nazi graffiti, despite admitting they knew about a local white supremacist camp. A police spokesman simply retorted, "[T]he Klan springs up wherever racial tension arises."[31] It was an unfortunate comment on the heels of six days of rioting in Los Angeles, following the acquittal of police who brutally beat Rodney King after he was hand-cuffed, face-down on the ground. Black activist Dolly Williams from East Preston clarified the connections in the *Halifax Daily News*: "People in Nova Scotia and Canada are saying that this can't happen here. We need to admit to ourselves that we too have problems."[32]

In 1993, Black activist Arthur Borden was convicted of threatening police officers after he rallied a North End crowd to complain that police unfairly targeted Black neighbourhoods for drugs. Under questioning by white prosecutor Adrian Reid, who would figure in the *RDS* appeal, officers testified that Borden threatened to beat them with their own nightsticks. Borden denied it. White chief justice Constance Glube, who would later also figure in the *RDS* appeal, rejected Borden's testimony, lecturing him to control his temper. "Most of us look to police for protection, not to harass them or prevent them from doing their job," she said.[33] Two months later, the *Halifax Chronicle-Herald* reported on a "smouldering dispute between Gottingen Street area teens and police who patrol the neighborhood," with teens insisting that "one officer makes a special effort to harass and embarrass them."[34] In 1994, three young Blacks filed complaints of assault against Halifax police officers for excessive force after they were ordered out of a taxi.[35]

In 1994, the Black United Front received fifty-four complaints from Black prisoners about racist prison guards at the Halifax Correctional Centre. The jail guard union mounted a picket to deny any racism, but their Black colleagues boycotted it, and Black prisoners inside disrupted the picket with shouts of "racists."[36] That year, the *Halifax Daily News* uncovered reports the RCMP had compiled earlier on Black Nova Scotian activists that referred to Black women as "prolific child bearers" and Black men as "layabouts, thieves, and drunks." Supporters of the Black Panthers were caricatured as "illiterate, semi-illiterate and hoodlums." The RCMP apologized. All the while, its officers were tapping Rocky Jones's phone, monitoring his house, and following his every move.[37]

Calvin Lawrence, raised in the same North End community as Rodney Small, was one of the first Blacks hired by the Halifax police in 1969. He recalled the reaction after Rocky Jones brought the Black Panthers to Halifax:

> [T]he Halifax police formed a riot squad specifically to deal with the imagined future of violent black unrest [and] purchased extra-large patrol wagons ... in preparation for the mass street riots they figured were inevitable. The cops were readying themselves for urban warfare; blacks were the enemy ... [I]n the late sixties and early seventies, conflict between the police and the black community was smouldering and could have burst into flames at any time.[38]

Lawrence overheard white officers uttering racial slurs and using the "N-word" and saw epithets like "Coon" scrawled over Black mugshots. He witnessed white officers "repeatedly" behaving "abusively" toward Blacks. Halifax officers would go "hunting" for arrests in the Black community just to prove their productivity – "to bolster their stats." Police practised "white supremacist behavior," he added, and they were not held accountable. Black officers who stood up against racial injustice were in a precarious position: "The minute you challenge somebody or label them a racist, then you have to watch out for them for the rest of your career – enemies for life." He wondered what his community expected of the few Black officers: "Did they think that a few black cops – us tokens – would be able to replace a deeply racist system with justice and equality?"[39]

EXPERT PERSPECTIVES

Donald Clairmont, a white Dalhousie criminologist, was one of the first to study race and policing in Nova Scotia. He developed a reputation for meticulous data analysis and time spent in squad cars doing rounds with police.

> I didn't see blatant racism, but there was a lack of trust, a sense that something could happen that you couldn't control. The relationship was one of underlying hostility. If the police had a call down to Gottingen Street or a disturbance outside a Black club, even with only a handful of people involved, they would send ten squad cars.
>
> If they had a call two hours later to Argyle Street, [with] big crowds of a thousand university students milling around, they would send one car. The expectation was that these are college kids, no sweat. They follow our instructions, no need to make a Hollywood production out of it.
>
> With a handful of Blacks, the police anticipated there could be fights and wanted a massive show of force. They knew there were many who didn't like them, who could mobilize crowds. They didn't know if they had the resources to deal with them. Clearly, a lot of animosity on both sides.[40]

Scot Wortley, a white University of Toronto criminologist, would later find significant overrepresentation of Blacks in Halifax police street checks.[41] While emphasizing that Nova Scotia was no worse than other parts of Canada, he called its situation distinct: "There is a policing culture involving systemic and cultural bias against people living in poor communities, with a particular focus on young men. Nova Scotia has had a large geographically segregated Black population for hundreds of years. Halifax almost feels like the American South. I have heard references to Nova Scotia as the Mississippi of the North."[42]

Craig Bennell, a white Carleton University psychologist and an expert in police training, agreed that there was "no question" that some races were overpoliced and that "sending a bunch of police cars to a scene" could "ratchet up" the likelihood of force. But Bennell stressed that most police-public interactions in Canada did not involve force. His study of "10.9 million police-public interactions" found physical force used in "only 0.1%."[43]

David Tanovich, a white Windsor University law professor, considered Donald Stienburg's choke hold of two fifteen-year-old boys – a serious use of force – as the heart of the *RDS* case. He explained that racialized stereotypes could lead police to "overreact" because they misperceived the danger:

> I was shocked that RDS was charged in the first place and then at the overcharging that followed. Officers are taught to use [the choke hold] as a last resort. It is an even more excessive use of force than a taser, and it has the potential for death. What could possibly explain a chokehold for such a minor incident? [T]here seems to be no other reasonable explanation than that the boys' race caused this officer to perceive himself to be in a more dangerous situation than he actually was.[44]

Even "well-meaning" individuals who were "not overtly biased" could stereotype, Tanovich added, and the more systemic the problem, the harder it was to prove.[45] In contrast, Bennell pointed out that what some might view as an overreaction could also be seen as an appropriate, proactive police response. "They are fearful. Police officers know the potential for danger [and] things can go wrong incredibly quickly."[46]

Wortley's perspective was somewhat different:

> The police are more likely to charge Blacks for lower-level criminal events. Young people will defy or question an officer, and the officers will say they were threatened and use force. We call it "contempt of cop" – *If you are going to be an a**hole, we can charge and arrest you.* Then [young Blacks] face discretionary charges such as obstruct justice, assault police. I've heard many stories similar to the one Rodney Small told.[47]

THE MARSHALL INQUIRY REPORT, 1989

In 1971, twenty-three years before Rodney Small's trial, Donald Marshall Jr., a Mi'kmaw youth, was convicted of the murder of Sandy Seale, an African Nova Scotian. Marshall served eleven years before a white man was uncovered as the murderer.[48] The Nova Scotia criminal legal system was castigated for failing Marshall "at virtually every turn," with indigeneity a contributing factor to the malfeasance of police, prosecutors, defence counsel, and the trial judge.[49] Yet during the 1983 rehearing, the white prosecutor urged the white appeal judges to conclude that the wrongful verdict was "not the fault of the criminal justice system or anyone in it, including the police, the lawyers, the members of the jury, or the court itself."[50] In 1985, retired white chief justice Ian MacKeigan claimed that Nova Scotia judges were "honorable men" and if any racist judges were sitting on the bench, he "doesn't know of any."[51] The appellate court's 1983 decision to belatedly acquit Marshall compounded the injustice by stating that he had contributed to his own conviction. In what many viewed as doubly shocking, the judges added that any miscarriage of justice was "more apparent than real."[52] This brought them before the Canadian Judicial Council (CJC) in a disciplinary review. The CJC found their words "inappropriate."[53]

It also served as the impetus for the province to appoint a Royal Commission on the Donald Marshall, Jr., Prosecution in 1986.[54] Although the central focus was anti-Indigenous racism, at the request of the Black community, anti-Black racism was added to the agenda. The inquiry documented a stunning degree of race discrimination against Indigenous peoples and what criminologist Donald Clairmont described as "a long legacy of negative Police-Black relationships in Nova Scotia."[55]

Various experts testified before the Marshall Inquiry in 1988. Edward Renner, a white Dalhousie psychologist whose research had revealed harsher treatment of racialized first offenders than white first offenders, testified that there was "racism within the criminal justice system from top to bottom."[56] Esmeralda Thornhill, an educator with the Quebec Human Rights Commission who would be appointed Dalhousie's inaugural Chair in Black Canadian Studies in 1996, offered an illustration with uncanny parallels to Rodney Small's subsequent *RDS* testimony. A Black male high school teacher witnessed a former pupil being manhandled by white constables. When he stopped to monitor it, officers threatened him "with clubs drawn" and ordered him to "move on." Thornhill charged that a "disproportionate number of Blacks experience[d] run-ins with the police" and were "labeled uppity" and "charged with mischief." She remarked that the common law contained no remedies for racism, because racial equality was "diametrically opposed to the national interest of colonialism." She recommended that the Criminal Code should contain a "distinct and separate infraction for racially motivated attacks on persons and properties."[57]

Rocky Jones appeared for the Black United Front. "There was a lot of apprehension about what I was going to say," he recalled. "The room was quite electric."[58] "I want to see if I can help the Commissioners understand what it's like to be Black in Nova Scotia," he began. "When we look at the police, the prosecutors, the judges, the juries, the coroners, the custodial staff, basically they're all white and basically they work to support the system which oppresses us. Given our history and oppression, it's no wonder that the police are able to treat us like they do. We haven't got a chance." He called for more Black police, lawyers, and judges.[59] His plea led to the creation of the Indigenous Blacks & Mi'kmaq Initiative at Dalhousie law school.[60] Jones was one of its first graduates, valedictorian of his class.

Marshall Inquiry surveys found Nova Scotians overwhelmingly agreed that "discrimination against blacks was an observable fact." Respondents "expressed concern with alleged police harassment" and reported that the police were "not very tolerant" when dealing with young Blacks, especially those who "question[ed] being stopped and asked for identification." The inquiry concluded that "the hostility of many Blacks to the police, and apparently of many police toward Blacks" was "well documented."[61]

In 1989, five years prior to Rodney Small's trial, the royal commission issued its final report. It found that "blatant and overt" as well as "unconscious racism and racial stereotyping" had contributed to Marshall's wrongful conviction. Citing a new Cole Harbour High School eruption, the commissioners emphasized that no one should assume racism occurred only in the past:

> We have heard disturbing accounts of racial stereotyping and overt discrimination against Blacks. A large portion of both Blacks and whites believe the police are the most likely officials in the criminal justice system to practice discrimination. Young Blacks are especially likely to hold this view ... Racism, we were told, is alive and well in Canada, and specifically in Nova Scotia ... The system does not work fairly or equally. Justice is not blind to color or status.[62]

WHITE DENIAL, ERASURE, AND FRAGILITY

The dismal historical record of interactions between the police and the African Nova Scotian community is clear. To some, it provided sufficient basis for Judge Sparks's statements. To others, the problem was linking the abysmal record to racism.

A cabinet minister claimed in 1989 that there was "no racism in Nova Scotia." Nova Scotia judges insisted in 1990 that there was no proof of "racial bias" and in 1993 that police did not "harass" citizens but "protected" them. In 1991, the conduct review committee characterized the police response to a racial brawl as "controlled and well-managed." RCMP officers claimed in 1993 that they did not "pick on" Nova Scotia Blacks. In 1995, the Halifax police chief rejected allegations of racism. Although a white officer was later disciplined for an improper strip search of three Black female teens, the chief stated: "[W]e stand on our record."[63] In 1996, with the *RDS* appeals well underway, Cole Harbour High School witnessed another interracial brawl. The police waded in with pepper spray, batons, and criminal charges. Despite claims that Black teens were disproportionately targeted, police spokesmen responded that "colour was not a factor."[64]

Carleton University psychologist Craig Bennell described the sensitivity involved in naming racism:

> I frequently talk to police. It's hard to deal with use of force without race issues coming up. The reaction from police, the moment race is mentioned, is, "Are you calling me a racist? I'm not." It stops the discussion. From an officer's perspective, they are annoyed. They see themselves as effective in de-escalating the majority of their interactions. I feel confident that most officers are not biased. The officers don't recognize that the broader literature suggests that most of us have these implicit biases. It comes back to, "Well, that's unfortunate, but that's not me."[65]

Afua Cooper, Dalhousie Chair in Black Canadian Studies, observed that white people often reject any linkage between racism and policing:

> White people's interaction with the police is different from African Canadians. In spite of all of the books and articles and exposés, they still don't believe it. They so want to believe that it's a fair and just society and everybody has equal opportunity. If you say otherwise, you're whining or ungrateful. There's not a lot of sympathy for Black people.[66]

At a press conference on Thursday, Halifax Police Chief Vince MacDonald defended one of his officers who allegedly strip-searched schoolgirls suspected of stealing $10 last month.

Police chief denies racism

■ continued from / A1

"I believe it's out of order."

The chief suggested that the lawyers used the news conference to air other beliefs as well.

"My view is ... (they're) taking advantage of a public forum to articulate certain points of view ... some relating to the case and obviously ... some that are maybe in a broader sense on ... a person's view of what they think the police department is all about."

Ms. Derrick, who represents one of the three girls, said Thursday that the news conference wasn't held to undermine the process but to outline the concerns of the girls' parents and guardian and to answer the public's questions.

"It was neither conducted as a trial of the complaint in public nor was it intended for that purpose," Ms. Derrick said.

"I don't see it as being particularly unusual."

Chief MacDonald said an officer has been appointed to investigate the girls' complaint and must report his findings within 60 days.

It's not known if that report will be made public, but results of such investigations usually are not.

Ms. Derrick, who'll also receive the investigator's report, said it will be her client's decision whether to release it.

Chief MacDonald said he hasn't yet spoken with Const. Campbell who has not been suspended, pending the investigation. It's believed she is out of town.

A second part of the complaint that questions the department's dealings with racially diverse communities will be dealt with by the city's police commission, the chief said.

As of Thursday, he hadn't received a report detailing the second allegation. But his department has been actively involved in many "progressive initiatives," such as race relations, he said.

The complaint and the furore surrounding it haven't compromised the department, the chief said.

"I don't see it as a step backwards. It likely points (to) a concern that Canadian society has ... in the area of race and particularly police-race relations."

In 1995, Halifax police chief Vince MacDonald rejected allegations of racism when one of his officers strip-searched Black schoolgirls suspected of stealing ten dollars.

Carolann Wright-Parks, an African Nova Scotian community organizer, added that responding to Black concerns is difficult for whites because they "don't want to admit [they] have reaped advantages from the way things are."[67] Canada's first African Nova Scotian female senator, Wanda Bernard, emphasized that when people name racism, whites who "take pride" in themselves as "impartial" and "unbiased" feel "personally attacked." Although "systemic racism" has been "ingrained in our systems and in our culture for hundreds of years," the issues get "personalized" and mired down in individual reactions. As for the police reactions to people calling it out "the way it is," she retorted: "It's called White Fragility."[68]

5

The Initial Fallout

The December 1994 trial heard two witnesses: Donald Stienburg and Rodney Small. The two agreed on some points, not on others. Rodney testified he rode up close to Stienburg, came to a halt straddling his bike, and called out to his handcuffed cousin, "What's wrong?" Stienburg testified Rodney drove the bike into his legs; Rodney denied his bike touched the officer. Rodney testified Stienburg warned him to "shut up" or he would be arrested next. Instead, he called out again to his cousin. Stienburg testified that, in an altercation lasting a few seconds, Rodney yelled at him and pushed him with his shoulders and hands. Rodney insisted his hands were still on the handlebars and denied hitting Stienburg. Both agreed the bike had not been travelling at great speed and that the officer was never knocked over. Both agreed that Rodney never got off his bike. Both agreed that Stienburg grabbed Rodney while he was straddling his bike and placed two boys in choke holds.[1]

Judge Sparks was left to decide whether the Crown had proved its case. Assessing credibility between contradictory witnesses is one of the most challenging aspects of judging. Sparks remarked that she did not accept "everything" Rodney said but that he seemed "a rather honest young boy" who admitted he was "being nosey." She observed that Stienburg failed to mention that the cousin was already handcuffed when Rodney arrived. She queried how one young boy could jeopardize an arrest under these circumstances. She remarked that she was not saying Stienburg had misled the court but believed he had "probably overreacted." She ruled that the Crown had not discharged its burden of proof beyond a reasonable doubt. Significantly, it was her comments about police officers overreacting with non-white groups and the "prevalent attitude of the day" that caused the uproar.

REPERCUSSIONS FOR VOICING RACISM

African American historian Ibram X. Kendi defines "racist" as the "support of a racist policy through actions or inactions, or the expression of a racist idea." He notes that it is a "descriptive term," better understood as a "peelable name tag" than a "permanent tattoo." He emphasizes that if we stop using the label, racism will not "miraculously go away." Instead, we will be frozen into inaction and unable to "identify racial inequity."[2]

Canadian courts rarely entertain discussions about racism. Defence counsel Rocky Jones broached the topic gently during Rodney Small's trial, cross-examining Donald Stienburg about the inaccuracy of the "nonwhite" term the police used for suspects. Judge Sparks used the term "nonwhite" in her decision, rather than "African Canadian" (or *Black,* which Jones preferred). No one noted for the record that Stienburg was white. No one mentioned the word "racism." Yet the backlash that erupted was considerable.

Four months later, Rocky Jones's efforts to raise racism openly would cause calamity. Working with white Halifax lawyer Anne Derrick on a file involving a strip search of three African Nova Scotian schoolgirls, Jones asserted that a white female police officer took unnecessary measures because of the girls' race. The officer then sued the two lawyers personally for defamation because she perceived they had called her "racist." Her successful lawsuit culminated in the largest sum ever awarded in a Nova Scotia defamation trial. The verdict was overturned on appeal, but the message was clear. Do not complain of racism.[3]

Fourteen years later, Constable Stienburg could recite from memory almost the exact words Judge Sparks had said: "*I'm not saying Constable*

*Stienburg misled the courts, although police officers have misled the courts
in dealing with non-white youths. I'm not saying Constable Stienburg
overreacted, but certainly police officers have overreacted in dealing with
non-white youth.* Then [Judge Sparks] said, '*This was a young police
officer who overreacted.*'" Stienburg continued:

> It seemed to me that she didn't want to say these things to me, trying
> to candy coat it, and yet that's what she felt. The comments were in-
> consistent. It was upsetting. [It was] disappointing and offensive.
>
> She relied on something that had no relevance to the trial. I have
> no problem with "not guilty" verdicts, but when you start pointing
> fingers and saying things – basically calling me a *racist* and that I over-
> reacted – it was upsetting. As a police officer you look at the courts as
> being fair. You look up to judges. I honestly felt that her comments
> were very unfair. In my opinion they were *biased*.[4]

It was Stienburg who first used the language of "racism." Back at
the station, it was he who spread the word among his colleagues. As
Stienburg emphasized, these were challenging times, and the officers
were "under a lot of scrutiny," dealing with "volatile situations" involving
Blacks outside the downtown clubs. "We were constantly being accused
of being racist," he recalled, and we were "very careful not to overstep
our boundaries as a result. That was another thing that was discouraging
with this decision." Stienburg added, "I find judges don't often hammer
somebody personally. I felt it became personal when she started making
comments about racism and overreacting." Although one Black officer
counselled caution, "Donnie, you may be right, but I don't think you
want to go down that road," Stienburg lodged a complaint with his
police union and his staff sergeant. In retrospect, he admitted: "I
probably wouldn't have pushed this at all if I had known what I would
be in for over the next five years. I probably would have let it roll off
my back and moved on."[5]

Police Chief Vince MacDonald was known for his efforts to increase
community policing and hire racialized officers, but that day he backed
Constable Stienburg.[6] Speaking on behalf of "all the officers in Halifax,"

Family Court chief judge Robert France Ferguson received a complaint against Judge Sparks launched by police chief Vince MacDonald in the name of "all the officers in Halifax."

he launched a complaint against Judge Sparks with white Family Court chief judge Robert Ferguson.[7] Dalhousie criminologist Donald Clairmont explained: "They see it as a critique of their style of policing. Obviously, they know that the trust between themselves and the Black community is not strong. [They] agree there could be better communications, more trust. But, personally, they think, 'I'm not doing any of this stuff.' When you say 'racism,' they hear it as grounds for punishment or dismissal."[8]

Crown prosecutor Rick Miller was equally perturbed. He began to second-guess his case. There had been a passenger in Stienburg's patrol car that day, a schoolteacher who was part of a "ride-along" program for the public to observe police work. Miller hoped to call her as a witness, but she took ill. Under workload pressure to try Youth Court cases quickly, Miller chose to proceed with Stienburg alone. Whether the teacher's back-seat position in the car would have permitted a clear sightline to the fracas was never tested in court, but Miller wondered whether her testimony might have helped. He also queried whether any of the officers who loaded the two youths into the paddy wagon might have seen what happened. He had not interviewed them earlier, reluctant to overuse police resources in a simple case.[9]

Years later, Miller ruminated over his closing address: "Obviously, as in any trial, you argue that one person's not telling the truth and the other is. I can't tell the judge, 'Donnie's a really nice guy.' But I indicated Donnie doesn't have any reason to lie. Whereas the accused is protecting his cousin, protecting himself." Miller continued:

When this whole thing started to blow up ... and there were so many articles in the paper, television ... I mean I sat there, and I marvelled how a bland, little, routine trial turned into this. Essentially, because it was my comment that Donnie had no reason to lie. Perhaps with a different judge, different prosecutor, the comment might never have been made. I think it obviously snowballed after that.

My view of the justice system is pretty clean. The paranoid people out there who think that they can't get a fair trial, I don't think they've had the right exposure to the justice system. I don't argue that police officers don't lie. But my experience with police is they've told the truth to me. I have never thought an officer lied on the stand. There were many cases where I wish they wouldn't have said something they said, but I never thought they were deceitful.[10]

Miller explained that relations between prosecutors and judges can sometimes be excellent, sometimes less so. The connection between Miller and Sparks, while always professional, was uncomfortable. Although counsel rarely interrupt judges in court, Miller did so five times during Rodney's trial.[11] His last intervention halted Sparks in the middle of her decision, to remind her of an earlier statement he had made.[12] The uneasy relationship may also help explain Miller's strong reaction to her ruling, which he characterized later as an interruption itself: "Judge Sparks interrupted and said – 'Woah' – essentially 'police officers lie, white officers lie.' She turned it into a racial thing. I'm thinking, Wow, where did this come from? It had nothing to do with anything in the trial."[13]

He reiterated how devoid of race he felt the case to be:

This is a case that had absolutely nothing to do with race. If you knew the players involved – Donnie, and I think myself – this is not a case that had any aspect of race in the facts. How people view it, I can't control. [B]ut this was such a routine case, that had no aspects of race involved whatsoever, other than that the accused was Black and Donnie was white, but so what, you know?

I've heard stories [that] this particular officer did this or that. Very few stories, but you hear them. Things happen down in the US. You see it on TV, and it is more prevalent than what happens here in Canada. Whereas here, I know certain people seem to have the wrong impression ... She was making these comments, and I was thinking, I know Donnie's a great guy, he's certainly not lying, he has no reason to lie.

Miller added, "[Judge Sparks's] statements were quite ... I don't know if shocking is the proper word to use ... I mean it was something. You can't have police officers walk into a courtroom and all of a sudden have judges say, 'I can't trust you, can't believe you.'"[14]

THE STRUGGLE FOR MEDIA ACCESS

Adding fuel to the fire, someone tipped off the press. Headlines of "Top Cop Considers Action against Judge" and "Cop Complains about Judge's Remarks" appeared.[15] When Halifax reporter Barry Dorey learned that Judge Sparks had criticized police conduct toward "non-white groups," he cast the story as a "judge's race comment." Years later, he wondered why the newspaper had not viewed it as an issue of racialized policing. "Was it that the tip came from a cop?" he queried. Reflecting that the *Halifax Chronicle-Herald* was an all-white workplace, he added, "Maybe my whiteness and youth meant I had no proper perspective or life experience on the matter. Why would a white cop hassle someone? That was the thinking."[16]

Dorey appeared before Judge Sparks on December 7 to request a copy of the trial record. Because Youth Court records were protected from public disclosure, nonparties had to convince the trial judge to grant access.[17] Judge Sparks balanced the right to privacy against the public right to know and ruled that RDS would be revictimized by publicity and that reporters had no valid interest in the transcript of a teen acquitted of non-serious charges.[18]

The press appealed the denial of access before Associate Chief Justice Ian Harold Morton Palmeter. A prominent member of Halifax's white legal elite, Palmeter had long-standing ties to Conservative politics and membership in several prestigious all-white Halifax clubs.[19] He sat on a panel that absolved a white Provincial Court judge of

METRO

Cop complains about judge's remarks

Comments about how minority teens treated spark review

By BARRY DOREY
Crime Reporter

A family court judge's comments about how cops treat minority teens are under review by the Halifax Police Department after a constable complained the remarks were disparaging.

Police union spokesman Sgt. Tony Burbridge said a constable contacted him last Friday about closing remarks by Judge Corrine Sparks. After hearing the officer's concerns, he advised him to write a report to Chief Vince MacDonald.

Sgt. Burbridge revealed Thursday that another officer had voiced concerns about comments the judge made in October. That officer was advised to submit a report to management, although it wasn't known

■ Corrine Sparks

Thursday if that had been done.

Meanwhile, this newspaper resumed its quest Thursday to hear a tape of the judge's comments and the trial, in which a black Halifax teenager was acquitted of charges of assaulting a white police officer and resisting arrest.

Lawyer Virve Sandstrom, representing The Chronicle-Herald and The Mail-Star, appeared Wednesday afternoon before Judge Sparks to argue the media has the right to listen to the tape.

Judge Sparks reserved decision

while she considers the submissions of counsel. A decision is expected shortly.

Senior police officials received taped copies of the proceedings Wednesday, but haven't decided to take any action.

Police investigate one or two complaints of comments from the bench each year, Chief MacDonald said. The comments typically concern the quality of a police investigation.

Past cases have been resolved by sending an officer to discuss the judge's concerns or lodging a complaint with the chief family court judge, the chief said.

The Chronicle-Herald tried to listen to the tape Monday morning, but was denied because the court was short-staffed. Reporters were told they could hear it later in the day, if

court officials became free, but that changed when court officials consulted with Judge Sparks.

On Tuesday, officials cited a section of the Young Offenders Act that says only police, lawyers and family have unrestricted access to family court records.

Under this section, others, including media, must apply to the presiding judge and prove that disclosure is in the interest of the proper administration of justice.

John MacKinnon, director of family courts, said officials were ensuring proper procedures are followed, not throwing obstacles in front of the media.

Court officials say it's the first third-party request they have ever received and they are proceeding cautiously.

When Halifax reporter Barry Dorey heard about the case, he cast the story as a "judge's race comment" rather than as an issue of racialized policing. His articles ran with headlines such as "Top Cop Considers Action against Judge" and "Cop Complains about Judge's Remarks."

making anti-Black racist comments in 1985. That one-sentence decision found "insufficient evidence" to warrant discipline.[20] In 1992, he dismissed the Charter claim of a Black single mother who was asserting equality rights to public housing for Blacks, women, and social assistance recipients.[21] It was a life résumé with little connection to Judge Sparks or the African Nova Scotian community.

Overturning Sparks's ruling, Palmeter granted press access on condition that there would be no identification of Rodney Small. He found that Judge Sparks had failed to balance freedom of expression with the right to privacy. He disapproved of her decision and quoted from her oral ruling in part. Judge Sparks had said, "Also, I should add in the circumstances of this case where there was evidence of the accused being manhandled by the investigating officer, this fortifies my conclusion that there is heightened reason to be guarded and protective of the court record as there could indeed be repercussions for the accused in his community." Palmeter described this as "extraneous comment" and an "error in law: "I find the term 'manhandled' somewhat unusual, but even if it were true, how could the release of the record cause

When Judge Sparks ruled against releasing the trial record to Barry Dorey and the press, the press appealed denial of access before Justice Ian Harold Morton Palmeter, a prominent member of Halifax's white legal elite.

repercussions for the accused and his community unless the identity of the young person was revealed, which it could not [sic]."[22]

The dismissal of Sparks's non-access decision reflected traditional hierarchies between upper-level Supreme Court judges and lower-level Family Court judges. Condescension from upper-court judges would establish a larger pattern in this case, but this seemed more pointed than most reversals. Palmeter's refusal to equate a choke hold and handcuffs with "manhandling" seems surprising, but his comments also reveal insensitivity to the tensions between Halifax police and young Black men, where almost anything could spark an explosion. It was a noteworthy contrast, a Black judge expressing concern about repercussions for African Nova Scotians, and the white associate chief justice dismissing any such notion.

Although a police tip apparently set this in motion, it was Donald Stienburg who expressed alarm about the fallout from publicity:

My name was basically dragged through the mud. I didn't realize that this would attract that kind of attention from the media. I think they were fair ... yet I didn't understand why my name would have to be put in there. I grew up in Dartmouth. I know a lot of people, it's a small area, and it was embarrassing for me. People would come up and say, "Donnie, what happened there?" They are reading and not understanding ... "This isn't the Donnie I know ... who I played hockey with." It was embarrassing each time I had to explain.[23]

THE IMPLICATIONS FOR JUDGE SPARKS

Judge Sparks was never formally advised of Police Chief MacDonald's complaint to Family Court chief judge Ferguson, and it appears that nothing further came of this.[24] But in parallel with Constable Stienburg, the press subjected Judge Sparks to increasing scrutiny, exacerbated because she was the only Black female judge in Canada. Some questioned how the Black woman who had generated such controversy had ever come to be appointed.

The impetus for the 1987 appointment came first from the African Nova Scotian community. Three months prior, the Black United Front and the Congress of Black Women had complained of a two-justice system in Nova Scotia, one for Blacks and one for whites. They called for Black prosecutors and Black judges.[25] The new white Nova Scotia chief justice, Lorne Otis Clarke, appeared receptive to diversity, advocating for younger and more female judges.[26]

Edmund Morris, the white Conservative minister of social services, sealed the deal at the cabinet table.[27] Morris's interest in naming a Black judge marked him out as an innovator.[28] Described by colleagues as "short," "feisty," and "talented," the former Halifax mayor was sometimes criticized by Black advocacy groups.[29] But he was also known for his support of the first Black deputy mayor, Graham Leo Downey, as the latter pushed for more public housing, the revitalization of the North End, and the elimination of race discrimination.[30]

Morris's preferred candidate was Connie Sparks, the only Black female lawyer in Nova Scotia, someone he knew well from her family law practice. She had a human-rights background and was active in her community, volunteering with the Canadian Mental Health Association and the Nova Scotia Home for Colored Children. She had recently represented two Black youths expelled from school, a high-profile case that heightened her visibility.[31] Morris conducted credit and security checks and called her into his office to announce his wish to see her become the first Black judge in Family Court.

Family Court, with its limited jurisdiction for matters related to dependent parents and children, was a "very difficult court," less sought

▸ Edmund Morris, Conservative minister of social services and former mayor of Halifax, pushed for the appointment of a Black judge and favoured Sparks as a candidate.

▾ Mayor Edmund Morris with Elizabeth Iona Hampden, crowned Miss Halifax in 1976.

after by lawyers who generally preferred appointments to the Provincial Court or the Supreme Court Trial or Appellate Divisions.[32] Sandra Oxner, the first white woman appointed to the Nova Scotia Provincial Court, explained: "It was harder to get people to go to the Family Court because of the stress of it – so much anguish. Most of the physical violence that occurs in court occurs in Family Court."[33] Perhaps some thought there would be less pushback if the first step in the racial diversification of the judiciary began with the Family Court.

Morris was aware that Sparks might face charges of tokenism. He told her she was not selected because she was Black but because she was qualified. Sparks asked for time to reflect: "My life flashed in front of me. I knew I was giving up my privacy, and that it would be a field of predominantly white men. I knew that there would be enormous isolation. Thirty-three is very young to be a judge, but if I hadn't accepted the position, I probably would never have got another chance to be on the bench."[34] She spoke with Anthony Ross, a Black lawyer who had been practising in Halifax since 1973. Ross recalled attempting to allay her apprehensions. "You are the most senior lady lawyer," he stressed. "I'm the only one!" she retorted. "That's what I told you," Ross replied. "You're the most senior."[35] Sparks agreed to let her name stand.

The next hurdle was Sparks's lack of political affiliation. Although the Sparks family was known as "hard-working" and "very religious," its members were not active politically. And as a former cabinet minister emphasized about Nova Scotia judicial appointments years later, "*All of it* used to be political."[36] It meant Morris had to rally more support based on Sparks's merit alone. Terry Donahoe, Nova Scotia's white attorney general, knew Sparks well and agreed to support her.[37] Tom McInnis, the education minister whose riding encompassed Sparks's Cherry Brook–Lake Loon neighbourhood, had assisted the Black community before. Calling her "bright" and "articulate," he strongly backed the nomination, but added: "You would imagine it would have been controversial. I absolutely guarantee [there would have been] questions from the Bar Society [although] I didn't witness it personally. I'm sure we had discussion about it in cabinet, but it went through pretty quick. Edmund Morris was pushing it."[38]

White Nova Scotia premier John Buchanan, who claimed to know "just about every lawyer in Nova Scotia," added:

> When Connie ... we always called her Connie ... came along, she was the very first Black female, as I recall, to become a member of the bar. Connie had an excellent reputation as a lawyer, and she was supremely qualified. We had very few lady lawyers in Nova Scotia. When she practised law, particularly family law, she was extremely able and well liked. She was an exceptional lawyer. She was a community kind of gal.[39]

Premier John Buchanan supported
Sparks's appointment to the bench
and recalled no opposition at the
time of her appointment.

It was "an extra bonus" – two for one – that the appointee was both
Black and female.[40] Decades later, Buchanan characterized Judge Sparks
as an excellent choice:

> I guess, as with a lot of people in Nova Scotia at the time, there was
> some racism for many of the Black community, and she experienced
> some of that herself, as she said at the time. But back in the 1970s and
> '80s, I don't recall anybody who said a bad thing. Edmund Morris
> thought at the time, as I recall, that he and I would face opposition
> when we appointed her, but I can't recall any opposition in our cabinet,
> in the Legislature, or in the press at the time of her appointment.[41]

Then he qualified his last statement, adding that "there might have
been some underground kind of comments."[42]

Indeed, resistance rumbled around the edges. Doug Ruck, Sparks's
African Nova Scotian law partner, described some of the negativity as
"downright vicious," even from some he "hadn't expected to hear it
from."[43] Helen Foote, Sparks's former white law partner, recalled "shock"
in the legal community. "I heard the chatter [that] basically she wasn't
qualified. That she wasn't at the bar long enough, didn't have the
grounding, didn't have enough experience."[44] Family Court appointees

required a minimum of five years' practice; Sparks had seven.[45] As Foote emphasized, "I'm sure that people didn't want to be seen to say anything about race, so they gave other reasons for grumbling."[46] Marva Welch, the Black court reporter at the *RDS* trial, was upset over criticism of a woman she described as the "epitome of class," someone her community strove to emulate.[47] African American journalist Evelyn C. White speculated that the quibbling was rooted in "entitlement." "Who was the white man who should have had that slot instead of Sparks?"[48]

Australian law professor Margaret Thornton describes "merit" as an abstract term with "no meaning" without reference to social context. Frequently acclaimed without articulated criteria, the "meritorious best person" is assumed to be "instantly discernible to all, as if by magic." White males, who have been the benchmark for centuries, carry an assumption of competence and tend to favour those who "look most like themselves as a testament to their own worth." As she notes, it made skepticism toward female and racialized judges inevitable.[49]

Douglas Ruck, Sparks's African Nova Scotian law partner, described the reaction to Sparks's appointment as "downright vicious."

Helen Foote, Sparks's former white law partner, recalled that the white legal community was shocked by Sparks's appointment, alleging she lacked experience.

Negative commentary about Judge Sparks fit within patterns of disrespect toward other "outsider" judges.[50]

The success of the nomination ultimately reflected the reputation of Connie Sparks herself. One supporter described how she was viewed within the African Nova Scotian community: "She is very proper, reserved, and measured, with a mild temperament. At the same time, she has an air about her that comes across as very thorough and competent and serious."[51] That Connie Sparks's reputation as quiet, gentle, and respectable had permeated the highest reaches of Nova Scotia political elites was a plus. "You wouldn't think she'd ruffle any feathers," said one observer.[52] Unlike someone of Rocky Jones's reputation, Sparks must have seemed inoffensive and safe. Until she wasn't.

SUPPLEMENTARY REASONS

The turmoil her oral decision created induced Judge Sparks to release "supplementary reasons" on 13 January 1995. These were subsequently ruled inapplicable on appeal because she had not "reserved" her earlier decision and was without further jurisdiction.[53] Yet her additional analysis offers insight into her thinking. Judge Sparks questioned the necessity of "choke-holding a young person of such a slight and slender build," adding that the forcible arrest was "not routine," but a "harsh physical restraint" rarely disclosed in Youth Court. She rejected prosecutor Miller's assertion that her task was to "choose which version" of the divergent testimonies to accept. The burden of proof beyond a reasonable doubt lay with the Crown. She rejected his claim that there was "no reason to attack the credibility of the officer," who was "simply doing his lawful duty." She emphasized that "a police officer, like any other witness, must establish his credibility." She cited the Marshall Inquiry and provided additional observations about the courtroom dynamics:

> On cross-examination ... the police officer admitted that his police department routinely refers to African-Canadian persons ... as "non-white." At this point in his *viva voce* evidence, the officer became ruffled;

and in my view became tense. The line of questioning by defence counsel was that this labelling of "non-white" was a pejorative categorization of African-Canadians. Generally, the court observed that this witness appeared nervous when he commenced giving evidence. It was not unnoticed by the Court that this may have been due to the racial configuration in the court which consisted of the accused, the defence counsel, the court reporter and the judge all being of African-Canadian ancestry.

She reaffirmed the acquittal "on all three counts."[54]

It sparked still more controversy. The initial ruling had made no overt reference to "racism," and the phrase "nonwhite groups" appeared once. The supplementary reasons were more direct, with two references to "nonwhite" persons, two to "African Canadian" persons, and one reference to "persons of colour." The race of the officer remained unidentified, and there was no reference to "racism." But Sparks ventured that the officer's obvious nervous tension may have been due to the "racial configuration" of the courtroom.

This was no backing off, but a clearer articulation of how race was implicated in the case. It was an attempt to describe what it might have felt like for a (white) police officer to experience anxiety, possibly even suspicion and fear, when facing a "Black" courtroom. Sparks refrained from mentioning that African Canadians might feel similarly when confronted with a "white" courtroom. But she drew on Constable Stienburg's visible discomfort in the witness stand to address why his testimony did not meet the

The turmoil her oral decision created induced Judge Sparks to release supplementary reasons in January 1995.

Crown's burden of proof. By implication, it linked the officer's unease in a Black courtroom with what he may have felt when faced with the intervention of a Black teenager at the corner of Brunswick and Uniacke.

Reactions to the supplementary reasons were deeply divided. Some celebrated them as brave statements from a courageous African Canadian judge giving long-overdue expression to the realities of racially infused policing. Others saw them as more evidence of unfairness, a contestable leap linking an officer's nervousness in the witness stand to the racial composition of the courtroom and then, potentially, to an earlier incident on the street. The reference to the Marshall report, which had not been cited during the trial, some saw as more overreaching. As many would conjecture, it was difficult to know whether the supplementary reasons strengthened or undermined Judge Sparks's decision.[55] The Supreme Court of Canada would later dismiss the document in its entirety.

6

The Appeals Begin in Nova Scotia's
Supreme Court

Although prosecutors rarely appealed Youth Court acquittals, Rick Miller believed Judge Sparks's decision should be overturned, and he forwarded the case to the appeal litigators at the Public Prosecution Service.[1] Policy required that appeals be based on the "public interest," the "seriousness of the error of law," protecting the administration of justice from "disrepute," and the "potential impact of the decision as a precedent."[2] The deciding factor appears to have been the perceived allegations of police racism. Jean Whalen, who had been appointed as the province's first African Nova Scotian prosecutor in 1989, recalled that "people were just livid" that race had been raised.[3] Yet it was not police racism that served as the fulcrum but the allegation of judicial "bias." Constable Donald Stienburg had been the first to voice the word, shifting the focus from white racism to the impartiality of Canada's first Black female judge. That set the framework for the notice of appeal filed against Rodney Small's acquittal in December 1994.[4]

THE SUPREME COURT OF NOVA SCOTIA

White prosecutor Adrian Charles Reid stood in the Supreme Court of Nova Scotia on 18 April 1995 to argue that Judge Sparks had based her decision on her "own preconceptions regarding the attitude of the

Prosecutor Adrian Charles Reid *(second row from bottom, five from left)*, a Dalhousie grad and the Crown's best trial lawyer, argued that Judge Sparks based her decision on her own preconceptions about police rather than the evidence.

police towards minorities" rather than on the evidence. Adopting Stienburg's language of "bias," Reid complained that Judge Sparks's ruling flowed from her "racially based bias against police."[5] As Officer Stienburg recalled, Reid "went after it like a bulldog."[6]

Adrian Reid was a Dalhousie law grad called to the bar nineteen years earlier. A man with short, reddish-blonde hair, he had the reputation of an authoritative, uncompromising personality. Described by his colleagues as "very bright," a "dogged cross-examiner," and their "best trial lawyer," he handled a "lot of tough cases."[7] Reid prosecuted the infamous Gerald Regan case, a former Nova Scotia premier charged in 1995 with sex-related crimes against multiple women. Reid would lose that in 1998, prompting *Maclean's* to describe him as a "brooding Crown prosecutor" and the verdict as a "huge setback" for an office "already under fire for its controversial handling of recent high-profile cases."[8]

Lawyers are generally loath to accuse judges of bias since the assumption that judges are impartial lies at the heart of their authority. Judges are equally uneasy about labelling a colleague "biased" because of the disrespectful implications for the bench as a whole. The allegation, rarely made, is usually couched in diplomatic language, a claim that the judge may have created a "reasonable apprehension of bias." It is a step back from tarring a judge directly with the epithet of bias, arguing only that a reasonable outside observer would perceive bias. Reid went much further. He claimed that Judge Sparks's decision not only created an "appearance of unfairness" but exhibited "real bias."[9]

Rocky Jones questioned whether the "same objections would have been raised if a white judge had made similar comments," which roused Reid to "object strenuously."[10] Jones also insisted that the prosecutor was unfairly quarrelling with Judge Sparks's factual findings. Trial judges were the ones who heard the witnesses. Their factual conclusions were not usually disturbed by appeal judges, whose bailiwick was correcting errors of law and whose courtrooms were restricted to lawyers' legal arguments. But Constance Glube, the white chief justice of the Nova Scotia Supreme Court, made short shrift of Jones's argument. While agreeing that an appeal court would not normally "substitute its own view of the facts for the trial judge," she stated that it could set aside a verdict that was "unreasonable or not supported by the evidence." "If there is to be found an apprehension of bias," she added, "then the verdict would not be supported by the evidence."[11]

Chief Justice Glube seemed surprised that Reid had accused Sparks of "real bias" and not just the "appearance of unfairness."[12] She was not prepared to go so far herself: "The test of apprehension of bias is an objective one, that is, whether a reasonable right-minded person with knowledge of all the facts would conclude that the judge's impartiality might reasonably be questioned." It was an accurate statement of law, and more respectful of Judge Sparks than Reid had been. But Glube found Constable Stienburg's plight compelling. She quoted from Reid's argument that Stienburg "could not hope for a fair hearing" because Judge Sparks had exhibited an "apparent preconception [against] the police generally."[13]

Glube reviewed Jones's argument that Sparks had made "findings of fact based on the credibility of the witnesses" and that her comments "dealt with the police in general and not the specific actions of Constable Stienburg." Then she stressed that "fundamental justice requires impartial decision makers" and ruled that Judge Sparks should not have spoken about police overreacting and the "prevalent attitude of the day" because there was no evidence before the court on either point. Unforthcoming on the racial identity of those involved, she offered a racially neutral decision that a "reasonable apprehension of bias" existed and ordered the charges remitted to Youth Court for retrial "in front of a different trial judge."[14] The *Halifax Daily Mail* described it as "an extraordinary rebuke," a rare example of one judge ruling another judge "biased or even apparently biased."[15] It was a stinging indictment of Judge Sparks. It also meant that the new trial would be held before a white judge, since she was the only non-white judge on the Family Court.

Constance Rachelle Glube was not the judge that observers might have predicted would issue such a strongly worded reversal. She, too, was an outsider to Nova Scotia's legal elites. Judge Sparks may have been the first Black woman on the Family Court, but Glube was the first woman appointed to the Nova Scotia Supreme Court, in 1977, and its first female chief justice, in 1982. Judge Sparks's appointment made her the first Black female judge in Canada. Glube's chief justiceship made her the first woman to achieve such recognition in Canada.[16]

CONSTANCE "CONNIE" GLUBE: FIRST FEMALE CHIEF JUSTICE

Born in 1931 into an Ottawa Jewish family, Glube, like Corrine Sparks, preferred to be called "Connie." The year she started law school, she married Richard Glube, an MBA graduate from the University of Chicago, whose family owned an upscale furniture store in Halifax.[17] One of two women to graduate from Dalhousie law in 1955, she found herself never fully accepted:

I came first in my second year, and I was pregnant. Dean Horace Read said, "Two heads were better than one." He was an interesting character. Women were not his thing. I was kind of offended, because the person who [ranked first in second year] had always been offered a scholarship to Harvard. But I was not offered. He offered me a scholarship to take my master's in legislation at Dal, and he offered it to me in the hall. I was so annoyed, I said no. Stupid and childish, I know. I could have used it![18]

When she graduated in second place, Dean Read joked that maternal responsibilities kept her from the gold medal, irritating her still further.[19]

There were then no married women, and no Jewish women, practising law in Halifax, and without family connections, Connie Glube would never have obtained an articling position. The city's large law firms hired no Jewish associates.[20] By 1950, Jewish lawyers made up 6 percent of the Halifax bar, more than their 1 percent of the city's population, but most practised on their own or with one partner.[21] Jewish lawyer Leonard Arthur Kitz, known as a "human-rights trailblazer," finally took her on, but his Kitz Matheson law firm did not ask her back after her 1956 call to the bar.[22]

Glube was devastated, fearing that her legal career was over before it started. "They said they didn't think I was serious about practising," she explained. She spent the next five years juggling part-time retail jobs with four children at home until she found herself going "stir-crazy," desperate to rejoin the legal world. "They looked at me as if I were out of my mind," she remembered. "Everybody turned me down. Finally, the people I had articled for let me come back." Clients were scarce. "If I could get clients, I could keep them, but I didn't attract them because I was a woman."[23] Unwelcome sexual propositions and harassment were incessant. Several years later, she opened the firm of Fitzgerald Glube, doing criminal and divorce cases. In 1969, she joined the City of Halifax legal department and, in 1974, became its first female city manager.[24]

Glube served for years as president of the Shaar Shalom Synagogue Women's League and as a member of Hadassah WIZO.[25] Her Jewish religion increased her isolation in a profession with a long history of anti-Semitic discrimination, although she was usually reticent to discuss it.[26] The smallness of the Jewish community in Halifax was often cited as a factor mitigating the harshness of anti-Semitism, but religious intolerance remained significant.[27] The first Jewish judge on the Nova Scotia Supreme Court, Justice Louis Dubinsky, was not appointed until 1967. When Glube joined him in 1977, she became the second.[28]

Discrimination did not wane after her judicial appointment. "Walking into the judges' common room that first day was not easy," she recalled. "It was not easy being one of the early ones."[29] Her chief justice, Gordon Cowan, was "highly skeptical" of Glube, and she remained the only female on her court for twelve years.[30] By the time she heard *RDS,* there was one other woman (and no visible minorities) on the Nova Scotia Supreme Court.[31] It was an era when the typical federally appointed Nova Scotia judge was male; born in Halifax to middle-class, white, Protestant parents; practised at a large law firm; became active within the Barristers' Society; and worked as a fundraiser or campaign organizer for the governing political party.[32] Justice Glube was an outsider on these criteria. As Dalhousie law professor Wayne MacKay quipped, "Glube was the first in so many ways. Race was almost the only 'first' she didn't have."[33]

Glube's appointment to the bench occurred in the wake of Prime Minister Pierre Elliott Trudeau's "just society" campaign. Trudeau and his justice ministers hoped to improve judicial appointments through wider consultations, diversifying the pool beyond the political cronies frequently recommended by regional ministers.[34] "They obviously wanted to appoint a woman to the bench," explained Glube. "I was the most senior, so they picked me."[35] Her promotion to chief justice came the year of another Trudeau initiative, the adoption of the *Canadian Charter of Rights and Freedoms.* The new policy role it bestowed on the courts fanned a growing sense of urgency for a more inclusive judiciary. Glube recalled her telephone conversation with Trudeau in 1982. When she asked him why he chose her, "He paused and said, 'I

Constance Glube's court in 1993. The court was all white and included only two women: Chief Justice Glube *(middle front row)* and Justice Margaret Stewart *(far right back row)*.

Chief Justice Constance Glube in her judicial robes, 2003. Glube was the first woman appointed to the Nova Scotia Supreme Court, in 1977, and its first chief justice, in 1982.

appointed Bertha Wilson to the Supreme Court of Canada last week, I'm appointing you chief justice this week, and I'm appointing [another woman] to the immigration court, and she isn't even a lawyer.'" Glube's reaction: "At least he was honest."[36] Her retorts minimized what it had taken to succeed that far.

Given her background, some were surprised that Chief Justice Glube so abruptly quashed Judge Sparks's decision.[37] Had she gone from "outsider" to "insider-outsider," absorbing consciously or unconsciously many of the legal attitudes of the white male colleagues she had worked with for so many years? Her decision certainly reflected an assimilationist worldview, of a piece with the predominant judicial mindset. Alternatively, did she seek distance from Sparks's *RDS* decision because she experienced her own position as fragile? She described her judicial philosophy as cautious, expressing reluctance to be "too dominant" because she was "the only woman among all the male judges."[38] The journey from "outsider" to "insider" could take a toll. Philip Girard's biography of Bora Laskin, who was appointed the first Jewish chief justice of the Supreme Court of Canada in 1973, suggests that Laskin felt he had to "choose his battles very carefully," wary of squandering his "reputation for impartiality" and "the respectability he had built up so carefully."[39] Glube may have felt the need to stress her own firm attachment to the judicial ideal of "complete impartiality."[40]

As sensitive as she seemed toward allegations of racism against white officers, she may also have been less sensitive to racism allegations against a Black judge. She had been remarkably gentle to John R. Nichols, a white Provincial Court judge accused of racism against Blacks in 1985. An all-white jury acquittal of a white man who killed a Black man had raised consternation among the Black community. Nichols, the trial judge, spoke jocularly to a reporter: "You know what happens when those Black guys start drinking." The reporter published the comment. The attorney general chose not to appeal for racial bias, but there was a misconduct complaint to the Nova Scotia Judicial Council. Both Chief Justice Glube and Justice Ian Palmeter sat on the council's review panel, which exonerated Nichols. Their one-sentence decision found "insufficient compelling evidence" of judicial misconduct.[41]

POLICE REACTION TO THE GLUBE DECISION

The official response from the Halifax police department was silence, understandable reticence with tensions so high. Police culture dictated that officers should endorse the actions of fellow officers or refrain from speaking. "Defend or don't talk" was the watchword. Most officers believed they responded to street crime as well as they could. Many worried that unsubstantiated allegations of race bias raised the prospect of unfair discipline or job termination. Some were concerned that anxiety over racism claims would stop them from carrying out the important responsibility of properly policing minority communities.[42]

The only public comment came from police union spokesperson Corporal Tony Burbridge. An eighteen-year-veteran of the force known for his "forthrightness," Burbridge was a founding member of the police union who sat on its executive for ten years, six as president.[43] Although the union had taken the lead in assisting Constable Stienburg with his original complaint, Burbridge announced that it did not intend to get "involved further." Attempting to smooth the waters, he told the *Halifax Daily News* that he "didn't want to speculate on what Sparks was thinking when she gave her ruling." Burbridge added that "many other officers have testified in her court and haven't had any problems."[44] Two weeks later, taking a more assertive tone, Burbridge complained that arrests would continue "despite the pressures of a minority community that wants to turn every arrest of a minority into a possible racial issue."[45]

THE REACTION OF THE BLACK COMMUNITY

The reaction was different in the Black community, where Judge Sparks was held in high esteem. Pearleen Oliver, one of Nova Scotia's most respected antiracist advocates, had described Sparks's judicial appointment as the "first down payment with interest" on the "debt of justice" to the African Nova Scotian community.[46] Wanda Thomas Bernard, who would be appointed to the Canadian Senate in 2016, emphasized that the first Black judge "represented the hope of our ancestors for a

Judge said too much, higher court rules

By MARLA CRANSTON
The Daily News

A Halifax family court judge who made critical remarks about police conduct was indirectly reprimanded by a higher court this week.

Judge Corrine Sparks is reported to have made disparaging remarks about how Halifax police treat minority youths as she acquitted a black teenager Dec. 2 on charges of assaulting an officer and resisting arrest.

It's hard to know what she said exactly, since no reporters were present and Sparks has denied public access to the transcript and court tape.

At the Crown's appeal of the verdict Tuesday, Chief Justice Constance Glube continued Sparks's publication ban on the remarks but said the judge went "two paragraphs" too far.

Sparks thoroughly reviewed the facts of the case and based her decision on the credibility of the accused, Glube said in Nova Scotia Supreme Court.

"Had it ended there, there would have been no basis for this appeal .... Unfortunately the decision did not. The learned trial judge went on for two more paragraphs," Glube said.

Ruling Sparks might have been biased against police, Glube ordered a new trial for the youth with a different judge.

At the appeal, Crown attorney Adrian Reid said Sparks's verdict seemed based as much on her "preconceptions" about police attitudes toward minorities as it was on the evidence.

Defence lawyer Burnley (Rocky) Jones said his client got a fair trial and Sparks's comments dealt with policing in general and not any specific action of the arresting officer, Const. Don Steinburg.

Glube also criticized Sparks

for sending supplementary reasons for her verdict to the appeal court, which is "not a practice that a judge should follow."

Section 682 of the Criminal Code states a judge can submit further reasons behind a ruling only when a higher court requests them.

Sparks rejected a request from the Halifax Herald Ltd. to hear the trial tape. The newspaper and the CBC are appealing that ruling next week in Nova Scotia Supreme Court.

Steinburg filed a complaint about Sparks's comments. The police union directed him to the proper channels, but isn't getting involved further, said spokesman Cpl. Tony Burbridge.

Burbridge said he didn't want to speculate on what Sparks was thinking when she gave her ruling. Many other officers have testified in her court and haven't had any problems, he said.

Corporal Tony Burbridge, speaking for the Halifax police, told the *Halifax Daily News* that he didn't want to speculate on what Sparks was thinking.

better future for African Nova Scotians. There was an excitement and an energy around her appointment, and a lot of positive enthusiasm."[47] It was also important to the community that both before and after her judicial appointment Sparks kept contact with her family, participated in community events, attended church regularly, sat on their charitable boards, and mentored African Nova Scotian youth.[48]

The high regard did not mean that anyone anticipated special treatment. Like Rodney Small, who admitted that he initially felt "at a bit of disadvantage" with a Black judge, many predicted that the first on the bench would feel pressure to rule as harshly, if not more so, than her white counterparts.[49] And Judge Sparks was reputed to "cut them no slack."[50] Social worker Robert Wright, who appeared before Judge Sparks, observed that she was not "a lenient judge" and could be a "stern, parental figure." He added:

She would not have had the ability to behave like many of the people she would see before her – young offenders and parents in child welfare cases. I think she took her own experience as a Black woman very seriously. [She] understood the scrutiny they were under and how you survive as a Black person. People who thought they might get a break were sorely mistaken.[51]

Judge Sparks was also regarded within her community as "conservative," someone who had never been "really vocal" on race issues.[52] It made the *RDS* decision all the more surprising. George Elliott Clarke had a vivid memory of the day the decision was released, when "everybody was talking about it."[53] Carolann Wright-Parks, a community organizer from Beechville, was elated with the explicit reference to police unfairness:

We thought, Wow, this was amazing. We never expected it. For her to say that the police have a tendency to do that ... She understood the analysis and our lived experience. The *RDS* case gave us a sense of relief. Somewhere in the justice system, it's recognized that this happens to us. We aren't asking for a leg up. We just don't want to be mistreated anymore.[54]

Social worker Sherry Bernard, who worked from the same courthouse as Judge Sparks, explained that Sparks was "aware of how the police acted. When she expressed that, they said, 'I'm offended by what you said.' Well, we said, 'I'm offended by *what you did.*'"[55] Lynn Jones, a trade union activist, added: "We were used to being dismissed and used to people not believing us, compared to authorities or the state. With *RDS,* everyone totally believed the kid, and that the cops were doing a cover-up. There wasn't even a question in the Black community. I'm sure with the white community it was more of a question."[56] Sylvia Parris-Drummond, an antiracist educator from Guysborough County, emphasized "how courageous [Judge Sparks] had to be to make that statement."[57]

Delvina Bernard, a director of nonprofit organizations who had grown up in Judge Sparks's neighbourhood, expressed outrage over the appeal:

> When Rocky Jones won the case, everybody was, like, "Yes!" This is the first time you have a Black client, Black lawyer, Black judge, and it's about time people be told. Then it ricocheted. We know darn true the police are biased. And she said it in the most polite language ... How dare they appeal this? When they won the appeal, everybody was just aghast. People could not find words to describe how upset they were.[58]

Senator Wanda Thomas Bernard added that "racism was being played out right before our eyes, leaving African Canadians across the country questioning our place, our right to have equitable access to justice."[59] Michelle Williams, director of Dalhousie's Indigenous Blacks & Mi'kmaq Initiative, declared: "Just the slightest scintilla of truth brings the whole system crashing down on this Black female judge. The Black community was enraged by what happened to her."[60] Afua Cooper, Dalhousie's Chair in Black Canadian Studies, explained why she thought the authorities had been so affronted by Sparks's decision:

> White people have a very hard time seeing Black people in authority. It could have been the stereotype of Black incompetence. "She's a judge but clearly doesn't know the law." People knew the *RDS* case was hugely significant. [They] saw Rodney as almost a hero, [and] Connie Sparks and Rocky Jones in the same way. People also had this sense of outrage. Here, again, we were wronged. And they didn't expect us to do anything. They expected us to just roll over once again.[61]

Jalana Lewis, who graduated from Dalhousie law school more than a decade after *RDS,* had much to say about Canada's first Black female judge:

> I didn't understand until I went to law school what it means to be a judge, how isolating it is socially, professionally. To be a Black female

Jalana Lewis, who graduated from Dalhousie law more than a decade after the decision, commented that Sparks, as a Black female judge, must have been isolated socially and professionally, forced to witness members of her community being mistreated over and over again.

judge in criminal court in Nova Scotia, you would see a lot of your community being mistreated over and over again. That would be very challenging, I'd imagine. And there's also who she is in her family, in her community ... What kind of pressure was there on her when she graduated, was called to the bar, went into private practice? There was all this extra baggage she never asked for, that was undeserved. If only Judge Sparks could have just been a judge and done her job, but there's all this extra stuff that others don't have to deal with. Not to be dramatic, but her treatment on the bench sounds like a horror movie.[62]

The groundswell of Black concern spread well beyond Nova Scotia. Juanita Westmoreland-Traoré, a lawyer then serving as the Ontario employment equity commissioner, who would be appointed the first Black judge in Quebec in 1999, praised Sparks's recognition of "the impact of racial disparities." "For this, she was pilloried. It sent a message to all minority communities, but to African Canadians in particular, that their gem, their shining star, Connie Sparks, could be treated this way, because she is a strong leader, a woman of integrity and principle. When you see that this can happen, it's a very grave blow."[63] Micheline Rawlins, Canada's second Black female judge, appointed to the Ontario provincial court in Windsor in 1992, agreed with Sparks's decision. "The problem was she hit a nerve, like a sensitive tooth. She identified covert racism, not the sort that hits you over the head but the kind that is always coming sideways and zinging."[64] Jamaican-born Hugh Fraser, one of the few Black male judges in Ontario, called Sparks to offer support. "Is it realistic to expect a judge to divorce herself from the experience she has lived all her life? I really felt a lot of empathy for her."[65] Lincoln Alexander, appointed Canada's first Black lieutenant-governor in Ontario, in 1985, was also publicly supportive.[66]

Denise Dwyer, a lawyer then starting her career as an Ontario Crown attorney, described the impact on young Black prosecutors: "For me, it sent a clear message that there was a hierarchy of Crowns. Your life experience lens was illegitimate. How do I practise with the same value as my white colleagues, if by virtue of the colour of my skin, I might not be seen as impartial?"[67] Arleen Huggins, an employment lawyer in Toronto, recalled that Ontario lawyers saw the *RDS* case as "one of the most important ever." She counted Sparks as a role model for Black lawyers, especially Black females, and saw the backlash directed at her as "disheartening and hurtful."[68] Ghanaian-born law professor Elizabeth Adjin-Tettey, who taught *RDS* to her University of Victoria students, had similar concerns. "Judge Sparks got into trouble for saying something that we all know. At least in the United States, they can name it. But it is un-Canadian to do that. We don't talk about the burden of people like Sparks, carrying this weight on their shoulders. I found it painful to think and talk about."[69] Word even spread among Black American judges, one of whom happened to express concern to Judge Sparks that there was a Black judge up in Nova Scotia who was unfairly under attack, unaware that she was talking to the individual concerned.[70]

Joan Jones published a scathing column in the *Chronicle-Herald*, pointing out that it was "no surprise to African Canadians" that Judge Sparks had come under fire and lauding her for "courageously" expressing her reasons for "finding a young black man not guilty."[71] Jones, partnered to Rocky Jones, was an antiracist activist credited for initiating the civil rights movement in Canada in the 1960s, for nurturing its participants in her Halifax home, and for hosting vibrant political discussions around her kitchen table while raising five children and caring for countless activist houseguests.[72] "Until very recently, our criminal justice system, no matter how racist or biased, was virtually unchallenged," she asserted. She applauded Blacks for becoming "more outspoken" and lamented that they were "criticized for doing so." She complained that minority judges were "expected to reject their background and adopt a Euro-centric point of view."[73] Years later, she continued to express outrage over Chief Justice Glube's decision:

> That just hurt me to the heart. I felt so bad for [Judge Sparks.] She was
> so right, and so ahead of her time when she said that. I also felt, which

▲ Joan Jones published a scathing column in the *Halifax Chronicle-Herald* that lauded Sparks for courageously expressing her reasons for finding a young Black man not guilty.

◄ Joan Jones in her Halifax kitchen, 2018.

I'm sure she would not be at liberty to say, but I felt she got punished. Shame on them for punishing Connie Sparks. And it hurt all of us. We all felt for her. White folks should have done something about it.[74]

It was Rocky Jones who picked up the baton next. He vowed to try again. On 18 May 1995, he filed a notice of appeal to review Chief Justice Glube's decision before the Nova Scotia Court of Appeal.[75]

7

Nova Scotia Court of Appeal

Judge Corrine Sparks now carried another "first" of distinction. The history of racism in Canada suggests that race issues may have infected many trials, but the Dalhousie law team that helped prepare the *RDS* appeal could locate no Canadian precedents of judges found guilty of race bias.[1] It meant that *RDS*, singling out Canada's first Black female judge, generated extraordinary interest.

On 13 October 1995, a panel of three white male judges from the Nova Scotia Court of Appeal sat to review the case.[2] Rocky Jones submitted that Chief Justice Constance Glube had erred in finding "reasonable apprehension of bias." He argued that Sparks's comments did not constitute "bias" against the police but "merely reflect[ed] an unfortunate social reality."[3] He claimed that the comments "stemmed from her experience as a Black woman in Nova Scotia" and the "common-sense knowledge" she brought to the bench. Jones stressed that all judges brought "their own experiences to the bench" and that they should not be overturned when they spoke about it, "especially when it's racism."[4] The *Halifax Daily News* interviewed Jones directly after his submissions:

> [I]n a society where racism didn't exist, judges should completely ignore the issue of race. But where racism is a reality of our society, racism will be unwittingly perpetuated if, as Glube's analysis demands, judges studiously

ignore race. [Judge Sparks's comments] display a sensitivity to the real-life context ... exposed by the Marshall Inquiry to be infected by racism.[5]

Prosecutor Robert E. Lutes appeared as opposing counsel. The white, Moncton-born specialist in appellate litigation had two law degrees, from the University of New Brunswick and King's College, London, United Kingdom, with two decades of practice behind him. Defence lawyers described him as a man with a "huge heart," and his Crown colleagues sometimes referred to him jocularly as "the social worker." He had a positive relationship with Rocky Jones. It may have helped that both had a reputation for a great sense of humour. "I thought well of him," explained Lutes, "and I believe he thought well of me."[6]

Lutes reminded the judges of Sparks's comment: *"I'm not saying that the constable misled the court, but police officers have been known to do that in the past."* Lutes felt those words sealed his case. "Why did [those remarks] come up?" he queried. "They just don't fit." He argued it was wrong to take "general information on racism" and relate it to specific cases "if no evidence pointing to it" arose at the trial.[7] It was an argument that resonated with the editors of the *Halifax Daily News,* who characterized Judge Sparks's comments as "personal feelings":

> For justice to be blind, in the proper sense of disinterest, it ought also to be color blind. A judge has to let the defence and prosecution hammer out matters such as prejudiced witnesses, and then hand down a verdict dispassionately. Judge Sparks is as aware of tensions between police and blacks as any intelligent citizen should be. But a judge has to set aside personal feelings and work only with the evidence. Race is a volatile element in courtrooms, as trials in the U.S. have shown. Our courts ought to be free of racial bias.[8]

When all three judges agree, they issue a unanimous decision. If they disagree, the "majority" decision carries the force of law. The judge who disagrees can issue a "dissenting opinion," which has no binding impact but might become persuasive to future jurists. *RDS* split the court two to one.

THE MAJORITY JUDGMENT:
FINDING A REASONABLE APPREHENSION OF BIAS

Two appeal justices, Edward (Ted) John Flinn and Ronald Newton Pugsley, ruled against Judge Sparks. Flinn wrote the judgment; Pugsley signed on. One decade after the *RDS* decision, Charles E. Haliburton profiled every judge who had been appointed to the Nova Scotia high courts over two-and-a-half centuries.[9] Justices Flinn and Pugsley looked like cookie-cutter versions of the norm.

Halifax-born Flinn held degrees from Saint Mary's University and Dalhousie, was called to the bar in 1960, and practised as a law partner for three decades in Halifax. He was a Fellow of the American College of Trial Lawyers and had served as president of the Barristers' Society and of the Federation of Law Societies. He sat on the Halifax school board, Saint Mary's board of governors, and the Nova Scotia Law Foundation. He was a member of the Halifax Club and served as its president. He described his hobbies as "sailing, photography, music and golf." He was a fundraiser for the Liberal Party when Prime Minister Jean Chrétien appointed him to Nova Scotia's highest court. The 1995 appointment meant he was a rank newcomer to the bench when he sat on *RDS* the same year.[10]

Toronto-born Pugsley, with a two-year head start over Flinn, was appointed in 1993 to the Court of Appeal by Brian Mulroney. A graduate of Upper Canada College with multiple Dalhousie degrees, he had practised as a senior partner at Atlantic Canada's largest regional law firm. Like Flinn, he

Edward (Ted) John Flinn, one of the two Nova Scotia appeal justices who ruled against Judge Sparks. Appointed in 1995, he was a newcomer to the court.

Ronald Newton Pugsley, the other appeal justice who ruled against Judge Sparks, was appointed in 1993 and another newcomer to the court. He had previously defended white police and judges accused of racial bias.

was a president of the Barristers' Society and a Fellow of the American College of Trial Lawyers. He described his hobbies as "choir, tennis, golf, and grandchildren."[11] He had appeared at the Marshall Inquiry, defending a white detective accused of shoddy investigation. The inquiry found his client had drawn a premature conclusion about Marshall's guilt based on racist assumptions. Another of his former clients was Judge John Nichols, whom he successfully defended before the Nova Scotia Judicial Council on a complaint of racist remarks.[12] Lawyers are not to be confused with their clients, but these cases would not have greatly expanded his racial expertise.

Both Flinn and Pugsley were appointed in the aftermath of the *Marshall Reference*, which had thrown the Court of Appeal into disrepute for its treatment of a Mi'kmaw man wrongly convicted of murder.[13] The 1989 royal commission uncovered "a legal system rife with racism, incompetence, and overt political favouritism."[14] The new chief justice, Lorne Clarke, took as his mission the rehabilitation of the sagging court. On record as supporting diversity, his first inclination was to seek heavy-weight litigation lawyers.[15] Flinn and Pugsley brought strong credentials to the bench, but like Justice Palmeter, who had little comprehension of the strain between police and Black teenagers, their life experience had little in common with young Rodney Small, and little in common with an African Nova Scotian female judge raised in the segregated community of Lake Loon. How would these two elite white men assess Judge Sparks's statements?

Although Chief Justice Glube's decision made no reference to racial identities, Flinn's judgment identified the race of the two trial witnesses on the first page. It was a step forward from the earlier erasure. Although he said nothing about Sparks's race, Justice Flinn described Rodney Small as "African Canadian" and Donald Stienburg as "caucasian." This was a word typically capitalized although not by Flinn. African American historian Nell Irvin Painter, who researched the adoption of the term "Caucasian," has noted it had fallen into disuse years earlier.[16]

Justice Flinn did thorough research on the legal test for judicial bias. Quoting from previous cases, he offered a list of legal principles:

> [T]he apprehension of bias must be a reasonable one, held by reasonable and right minded persons, applying themselves to the question and obtaining thereon the required information. [T]hat test is "what would an informed person, viewing the matter realistically and practically – and having thought the matter through [–] conclude."[17]

> [T]he court does not look at the mind of the justice himself ... The court looks at the impression which would be given to other people. Even if he was as impartial as could be, nevertheless, if rightminded persons would think that, in the circumstances, there was a real likelihood of bias on his part, then he should not sit. And if he does sit, his decision cannot stand ... Nevertheless, there must appear to be a real likelihood of bias. Surmise or conjecture is not enough ... The court will not enquire whether he did, in fact, favour one side unfairly. Suffice it that reasonable people might think he did.[18]

> The keystone in this structure is the neutrality of the judge. Should even the appearance of it be lost the usefulness of the court is at an end and the structure collapses. In a celebrated, if overworked, phrase, "Justice should not only be done, but should manifestly and undoubtedly be seen to be done."[19]

Justice Flinn's description of bias as the inability to act "in an impartial manner" captured the essence of the issue. That complaints must contain something more than "conjecture" seemed equally important, although, as he noted, it was not necessary to prove "actual bias."[20] To put the test as high as "actual bias" would set a standard almost impossible to meet. Adrian Reid's hubris aside, most prosecutors would not have been pleased with a test that needed proof of actual bias.

To require an evaluation through the medium of a "reasonable person" was a device with a long history in common law. It was designed to caution a judge to stand back and gauge what another person standing apart from the particular dispute might think. Some commentators wondered whether the mechanism really worked to separate the judge's own view from the fictitious "reasonable person." The test had also been critiqued on the issue of gender. In its early versions, reference was always to a "reasonable man," provoking complaints that the male perspective was entrenched in the concept. Even when the terminology was neutered, doubts lingered. Questions about whether that fictitious "reasonable person" also embodied a white racial identity were less frequently asked.[21]

Next, Justice Flinn addressed the Sparks decision:

> Counsel for the appellant argues that these comments do not indicate that the Youth Court Judge is biased against the police. He says they merely reflect an unfortunate social reality. That may very well be so; however, it does not address the real issue here. The issue is whether or not the Youth Court Judge considered matters not in evidence in arriving at her critical findings of credibility, and, hence, acquittal. From the general proposition that "police officers overreact when they are dealing with non-white groups," the Youth Court Judge concluded that Constable Stienburg overreacted ...
>
> There was no evidence before the Youth Court Judge as to what was the "prevalent attitude of the day"; nor, indeed, was there any evidence as to why Constable Stienburg overreacted. If there were concerns in this regard, they were not canvassed in the cross-examination of Constable Stienburg; and, as a result, Constable Stienburg had no opportunity to address any such concerns in his testimony.[22]

Summing up, Justice Flinn wrote: "The unfortunate use of these generalizations by the Youth Court Judge, would, in my opinion, lead a reasonable person, fully informed of the facts, to reasonably conclude that the Youth Court Judge would consider the important issue of credibility in this case, at least in part, on the basis of matters not in evidence; and, hence, unfairly."[23] He dismissed the appeal and upheld Chief Justice Glube's decision to overturn the acquittal.

THE DISSENTING JUDGMENT:
QUESTIONS WITH RACIAL OVERTONES

Gerald Borden Freeman, who wrote the dissenting judgment, had fewer markings of elite status than his two colleagues. He was not from Toronto or Halifax but born and raised in Liverpool on Nova Scotia's South Shore.[24] He took his early schooling in racially integrated public schools, a far cry from Pugsley's private Upper Canada College. Most of the Blacks in the Liverpool area lived outside the town, but they attended Liverpool schools. Although racial equality was far from evident, Freeman had had African Nova Scotian classmates as friends.[25]

His path to law and the judiciary was also distinct. After graduating from Acadia University, he worked in Halifax and St. John's, Newfoundland, as a journalist with the *Halifax Herald* and Canadian Press before heading to law school at McGill and Dalhousie. Then he returned to Liverpool to do "small town law," handling "a little bit of everything," as he described it. His firm boasted one of the only female lawyers then in practice. He served as president of the Red Cross and the Kiwanis Club and was active in the Conservative Party.[26]

Unlike Justices Flinn and Pugsley, his career as a judge did not commence with a direct appointment to the Court of Appeal. In 1988, Brian Mulroney's Conservative government appointed Freeman to the county court, where he assessed the credibility of conflicting trial witnesses as part of his daily docket.[27] It was unusual for county court judges to be elevated to the appellate courts, but within two years, Mulroney promoted Freeman to the Appeal Division of the Nova Scotia Supreme Court, where he replaced a retiring judge who had participated in the notorious wrongful conviction of Donald Marshall Jr.[28] A man

Justice Gerald Borden Freeman wrote the dissenting judgment. Appointed to the court in 1990, he attended racially integrated public schools in Nova Scotia's South Shore and was something of an outsider on the court.

with a voracious love of poetry, English literature, and nature books, when Freeman was asked for a list of his hobbies, his reply was "writing, reading, and country living." The first person from the South Shore on the Court of Appeal, he was something of an outsider at the province's top court.[29]

Justice Freeman's dissenting decision identified the race of everyone involved. In his first paragraph, he described Rodney Small as a "fifteen-year-old black youth" and Donald Stienburg as a "white police officer." Midway through, he referred to the "African Canadian ancestry" of the accused, the defence counsel, the court reporter, and the judge. The first time he used the phrase "non-white youths," he put scare quotes around the language the police used in their radio transmission that day.[30] Perhaps he felt similarly to Rocky Jones on that.

Justice Freeman concurred with his colleague's summary of the judicial bias rules. It was the application that he disagreed with. "In my view, it was perfectly proper for the trial judge, in weighing the evidence before her, to consider the racial perspective. I am not satisfied that in doing so she gave the appearance of being biased herself."[31] He noted that the prosecutor had urged Sparks to accept Constable Stienburg's evidence over Rodney Small's and suggested that her comments may have been intended to explain why she rejected his submission. "The officer and the accused entered Judge Sparks's courtroom on an equal footing," he explained. "Her duty was to determine credibility when their testimony was in conflict. This is a notoriously difficult and inexact exercise in adjudication in which the judge's whole background experience plays a role in the assessment of demeanour and other intangibles."[32]

Justice Freeman observed that Sparks's remark about the "prevalent attitude of the day" could have referred to the "attitudes exhibited" on the day of trial. There had been four African Canadians present in court that day. Rocky Jones had mentioned it in his appeal argument, and Judge Sparks had described the "racial configuration of the court" in her supplementary reasons. Freeman accepted this as evidence grounding Sparks's comment, although he was quick to add that the supplementary reasons played no part in the appeal.[33]

The "overreaction" comment was more difficult. He thought Judge Sparks might have introduced the concept to explain the conflict in testimony. Freeman stressed that if police officers were known to mislead or overreact, that was "a far cry from stating that Constable Stienburg did either." Judge Sparks had made it "clear, initially, that she was not saying he did" and that she did not attribute any "questionable" state of mind to Constable Stienburg. "Rather," noted Freeman, "she seemed to be directing herself to a need to take certain possibilities into account." And then, he emphasized, she "immediately tied it to evidence." She was concerned that the charges might have arisen "more as a result of RDS's noisy verbal interference" than because of the "physical acts, assaults, and obstruction with which he was charged." The officer failed to mention the handcuffs. He laid three charges as the result of an incident that was "minor" by "any standard." Freeman resolved that Judge Sparks's finding of "overreaction" was "within the purview of the trial judge."[34]

In contrast to the majority, Freeman was direct about the race implications of assessing credibility:

> The case was racially charged, a classic confrontation between a white police officer representing the power of the state and a black youth charged with an offence. Judge Sparks was under a duty to be sensitive to

the nuances and implications, and to rely on her own common sense which is necessarily informed by her own experience and understanding.

It is unfortunately true and within the scope of general knowledge of any individual that police officers have been known to mislead the court and overreact in dealing with non-white groups.

Assessing credibility is an art as much as a science and it draws upon all of the judge's wisdom and experience. Questions with racial overtones make the difficulties more intense, yet these questions must be addressed freely and frankly and to the best of the judge's ability. Because of their explosive nature they are more likely than any others to subject the judge to controversy and allegations of bias, but they cannot be ignored if justice is to be done ... I consider Judge Sparks's remarks to be more consistent with a fair inquiry into delicate subject matter than suggestive of bias.[35]

Justice Freeman was more explicit here about racism than Judge Sparks had been. Yet no one complained that his judgment was biased. No one apparently even considered doing so. Of course, his view was only a dissent. Yet white male privilege also shielded him from the opprobrium directed at Judge Sparks.

Reflecting upon his dissent later, Justice Freeman admitted he was "sorry" he had to "write an opinion that contradicted" Chief Justice Glube's. "I liked Connie," he explained. "I respected her." He was less sorry about differing with Ted Flinn. Flinn "didn't see eye to eye with me on *RDS*," recalled Freeman. In fact, his colleague tried to talk Freeman out of the dissent, expressing concern that it suggested "racial prejudice existed in Nova Scotia." Freeman believed Flinn was wrong to object. Racial prejudice *did* exist. And although he "liked and respected Ted Flinn," and his colleague's disapproval "slowed me down," in the end, added Freeman, "he didn't change my mind."[36] Years later, retired Tax Court judge Valerie Miller, an African Nova Scotian, commented: "The only one who had his head on was Freeman. The others were in the same place as the judges who decided *Marshall*. If they say something, it's not considered racist, but if Connie Sparks did, it was."[37]

INTENSIFIED FOCUS ON JUDGE SPARKS

The media frenzy over Sparks's reversal made repeated reference to her "controversial remarks about police." The *Halifax Chronicle-Herald* depicted her as having "waded into controversial waters" and reminded readers that she had been overturned earlier when she "caused a media flap" by forbidding press access. Reporters emphasized that she had been "admonished" for "violating the freedom of the press."[38] No one mentioned that she chaired the judicial education committees of the Nova Scotia Provincial Court Judges' Association and the Canadian Association of Provincial Court Judges, Atlantic Region.[39]

With the *RDS* case under the microscope, Judge Sparks's marginalization intensified both within and outside the judiciary. Rumours critical of her work began to spread. Her former law partner Helen Foote wondered if the unjustified gossip could be traced to disrespect: "It could be pure and simply they don't respect her as a judge, so they have to find something wrong with how she is doing the judging."[40] Criticisms were sometimes raised about other judges, but when attached to Nova Scotia's first Black judge, they took on added resonance. The criticism fit a pattern of holding early minority judges to a higher standard than other judges, with disparagements often based on racist stereotypes rooted in slavery.[41] Thurgood Marshall and Clarence Thomas, the first two Blacks on the US Supreme Court, faced similar critiques.[42] The racist context sullied perceptions, making it impossible to evaluate individuals fairly.

Connie Sparks had known from day one that her new status as a judge would pose challenges. Her biggest concern was separation from her own community. She had to resign from community groups that were seen as having an advocacy function. "I knew that my role would be different from that of a lawyer," she said. "I knew that perceptions about me would change and that I'd experience isolation."[43] Although the African Nova Scotian community celebrated her appointment, elevation carried a price. Antiracist educator Sylvia Parris-Drummond described the distancing that could result: "When the community

Sherry Bernard, an African Nova Scotian social worker who appeared before Judge Sparks in Family Court, described her as "very conscientious" and "fair."

speaks about people who [are] achievers ... they are guarded. You hear rumblings ... *'Are they really a community person now?'*[44]

Yet there was no question that her community backed Judge Sparks in the wake of *RDS*. Anthony Ross, an African Caribbean lawyer practising in Halifax, underscored the support. He rejected the gossip circulating about her capacities as a judge. She had a "good reputation," he emphasized. "When she started at first, the most junior judge, she was a little uncertain, but by the time she did [*RDS*], she had enough confidence. She learned on the job. She is not the only judge who learned on the job." Ross thought the problem lay with the Nova Scotia legal profession: "There is an in-group and an out-group. When it came to Black people, they were judging them against perfection. There were a lot of people who would have preferred not to see her on the bench – a lot of lawyers, a lot of judges."[45]

Sherry Bernard, an African Nova Scotian social worker who appeared before Judge Sparks in Family Court, described her as "very conscientious" and "fair." She added, "Being the first and only Black judge for so many years, she had a lot to deal with. She had to be aware that she was being watched and what she said could be misconstrued. We were very disturbed by how the judicial system treated her."[46] Robert S. Wright, an African Nova Scotian social worker and sociologist who appeared as a child welfare worker in Judge Sparks's court, regarded her as "thoughtful," "respectful," "compassionate," and "open to innovation."[47] Heather McNeill, an Indigenous member of the Milbrook

First Nation and a Dalhousie Legal Aid lawyer, characterized her as a "very competent" judge, respectful of counsel and their clients, who reviewed the evidence and made her decision supported by the evidence."[48] Shawna Paris-Hoyte, an African Nova Scotian lawyer who frequently appeared in Family Court, added: "She was an exceptional judge. Her decisions were well articulated, direct, clear, and fair. We're always held to a different standard, always questioned. Look at what happened to her. The lesson was clear.[49]

Delvina Bernard, founder of the Africentric Learning Institute of Nova Scotia, grew up in Sparks's neighbourhood and recalled the outrage the Black community felt and their certainty that Judge Sparks had been "done wrong."

Delvina Bernard, who grew up in Sparks's neighbourhood, described the consternation within the African Nova Scotian community:

> People who didn't even understand it were outraged. They didn't understand court appointments, criminal justice workings, the relationship of the *RDS* case to the backlash against Connie ... but people in the lay world knew her. The Connie they knew, they had that much faith in her professionalism and her competence that they absolutely knew that she'd been done wrong even if they didn't know the details.[50]

Bernard reflected on the relayed pain this must have caused Judge Sparks's mother:

> This is your first child, the golden child of the community. She followed all the rules: go to school, get a degree, get another one, live well,

establish a career, don't get in trouble. And after you do everything right, someone decides they are going to do a takedown of you. At least if she did something wrong, there's causality. Like if she had really screwed it up. But she didn't.[51]

Dianne Carter, an African Canadian lawyer working in Toronto pondered whether Judge Sparks must have wondered, in every subsequent case she presided over, "Is this person going to ask me to recuse myself?"[52] African American journalist Evelyn C. White added, "You're on the bench every day and you're accused of being biased. How do you go to work every day? How did she survive the impact on her mother?"[53]

Judge Sparks chose not to seek support from her wider community during the appeal process.[54] Sylvia Parris-Drummond knew that some would have reached out but observed that Sparks was "careful how much she said even to a close friend." She thought Judge Sparks felt that she needed to "carry this herself," to be strong because of "the impact [on] the Black community."[55] Delvina Bernard added, "She kept it totally to herself. It was a very lonely time for her."[56]

As for Rodney Small, the young man at the centre of the case, who had maintained a conspicuous absence from all the appeal proceedings, he was back to square one. Awaiting retrial.

8

Gender Matters

RDS was understood to be about race. But it was also gendered. As critical race researchers emphasize, racism and sexism intertwine.[1] Judge Sparks's Black female identity and the racialized masculinity of others added a heavy imprint.

THE ARREST, THE ACTORS, THE TRIAL

Gender was on display from the first moments of the arrest involving Rodney Small, his male cousin, and a male police officer. The youths escaping from the stolen van were males, the focus of most policing. When police use physical force, as Constable Stienburg did, Canadian research shows 91 percent of the tackled suspects are male.[2] When Rodney Small and Donald Stienburg squared off surrounded by a circle of wide-eyed children, the white officer was instilling a lesson not to challenge police. Sociologists describe these as "deference rituals," where officers who see themselves as symbols of law expect deference, especially from lower-status groups.[3] Rodney's interventions challenged police authority in front of a crowd of Black youths. When officers perceive "bad attitude," it can trigger discretionary decisions that vary by gender, race, and class. Where the suspect is young, this reduces the sense of confrontation, but in a racist society, even young Black males are seen as menacing.[4] Rodney Small wanted to prove he did not suffer overpolicing passively. Both males were exhibiting what criminologists call the "swagger factor," performing racialized masculinity before a crowd.[5]

Would a less masculinized culture reduce the potential for harm? Would the situation have played out differently if either had been female? Campaigns to recruit policewomen emphasize the new approach they might bring to the job, assuming that "conciliatory" females generate less confrontation.[6] Here, women were at the periphery. As caregiving mothers, grandmothers, and aunts passing by, they were the rescuers the boys looked to for help.

The gendered male dynamics continued in the courtroom. The accused, defence counsel, deputy sheriff, police officer, and prosecutor were men. That was no accident. People charged with crimes are predominantly male. Police, prosecutors, criminal defence lawyers, and deputy sheriffs are predominantly male. The exception was Judge Sparks, a woman vastly outnumbered in a cohort of male judges. The physically most diminutive adult in the room, her femaleness was palpable.

Gendered socialization had impacted the lives of each individual in the case. Rodney Small played basketball and pool in all-male company, he portrayed himself as a street fighter, and he masked his fears about testifying: "I would not admit I was afraid – that's my facade."[7] Donald Stienburg studied engineering, a predominantly male discipline. Then he and his brother followed their father into the force. A tall, physically imposing man who "played hockey all his life," he chose policing for its "physical" aspects. He worked with the Emergency Response team, sometimes referred to as the "SWAT team," the most daring of units.[8] Rick Miller, a devotee of hockey and baseball, bore an aggressive reputation as "a bit of a hawk."[9]

Broad-shouldered and tall, Rocky Jones had served in the military and survived within the informal male economy as a card-playing pool hustler. He was devoted to manly outdoor activities, hunting and fishing. He played basketball and hockey "well after you'd expect given his age and physical condition." His deep booming voice commanded silence when he addressed a crowd. His prominence as Canada's foremost antiracist activist was attributable not only to skill and courage but also to gender. His equally talented wife, Joan, found her activism too often sidelined with womanly tasks of caretaking. Rocky Jones's teach-in at St. Francis Xavier University in 1968 was titled "The Black Man in Nova Scotia."[10]

GENDER AND THE JUDGE

Connie Sparks came from a family with strict gender roles. Her mother, who took on domestic and teaching positions while raising nine children, delivered exacting lessons about women's responsibility for Christian humility.[11] Connie attended all-girls Canadian Girls in Training meetings. Her first paid jobs, as candy-counter cashier and library assistant, were female ones. At university, she lived in the Sisters of Charity convent.

The masculine world of law posed a stark contrast. Her Dalhousie law class was 69 percent male.[12] In 1979, she became the second Black woman to graduate. Irene Ayodele Healey, the first, graduated in 1976 and then departed the province.[13] Nova Scotia premier John Buchanan hailed Sparks as the "first Black female" called to the Nova Scotia bar.[14] In fact, Healey was called three years earlier but never practised.[15] In 1980, Sparks became the first Black woman to practise in Nova Scotia.[16]

The first white female lawyer in Canada, Clara Brett Martin, was called to the Ontario bar in 1897.[17] The first white female lawyer in Nova Scotia, Frances Lilian Fish, was called in 1918.[18] Racialized female lawyers followed decades later. Canada's first Black female lawyer, Calgary-born Violet King Henry, was called to the Alberta bar in 1954.[19] Myrtle Blackwood Smith, Ontario's first Black female lawyer, was called in 1960.[20] Nova Scotia was noticeably behind. For a province that boasted English Canada's first law school and one of the oldest continuously settled African Canadian communities, Sparks's call to the bar was long overdue.

Gender exacerbated race discrimination when Sparks tried to find her footing in practice. She articled for the Halifax City solicitor, who was reputed to hire women who could not find articles. She worked as in-house counsel, a lower-tier predominantly female practice, and

Connie Sparks was only the second Black woman to graduate from Dalhousie Law, in 1979. Irene Ayodele Healey *(fourth row down, fifth from right)* was the first. She graduated in 1976. Antigua-born Castor Williams, the first Black male appointed to the Provincial Court, in 1996, was in her class *(fifth row down, fourth from right)*.

Frances Lilian Fish, Nova Scotia's first female Lawyer, 1918.

▲ Violet King Henry, Canada's first Black female lawyer, 1954, with articling principal, E.J. McCormick.

◄ Sparks in her Dartmouth office, 1984. After articling for the Halifax City solicitor, Sparks worked as an in-house counsel and then opened an all-female law firm in Dartmouth.

then opened an all-female law firm in Dartmouth. At age thirty-four, Sparks was young for the bench. Her working-class upbringing and storefront practice were worlds away from the elite Halifax law firms that were the source of many of the province's judges. Gender, race, age, and class intersected to make her a striking anomaly.

Although Sparks's appointment led politicians to claim that her sex was an "extra bonus" – two for one – the first women judges met fierce resistance.[21] Pressure had been building to appoint women judges since the 1970s, spurred by a burgeoning feminist movement, but Sandra Oxner recalled an uproar over her own appointment as the first (white) woman on the Nova Scotia Provincial Court in 1971. "Many lawyers didn't like it," she explained. "I was told that some said they would never appear before me. There was such rigidity against the women."[22] Oxner was still the lone woman when Sparks arrived at the Family Court in 1987.[23]

As a Provincial Court judge, Oxner was entitled to preside over the separate Family Court too, but she did not, because she preferred criminal cases over family or youth matters.[24] Sparks became the third female out of twenty-three judges in the history of Nova Scotia's Family Court. The two white women who preceded her were Elizabeth Ann Roscoe, appointed in 1984, and Margaret Jane Stewart, in 1985. Both moved up to the Nova Scotia Supreme Court within a few years.[25]

It is impossible to separate sexism from racism, yet some of the rancour directed at Judge Sparks fit with patterns of criticism meted out to other women judges. Bertha Wilson and Claire L'Heureux-Dubé, the first two on the Supreme Court of Canada, faced malicious slurs about their competence. Lawyers and judges griped that they had not "merited" their appointments. Stereotypes cast women judges as weak, emotional, illogical, manipulative, incapable of exercising authority, and lacking in objectivity.[26] Male colleagues excluded them from information-sharing circles and mentoring. Lunchroom banter about sports and golf scores, laced with sexist jokes, isolated them further. Women judges who answered a Canadian Bar Association (CBA) survey described "amused tolerance" as the gentlest reception on offer.[27]

Judges' conferences included "a lot of drinking in hospitality suites," off-putting to Judge Sparks, a woman raised in a "strict Christian home" with little drinking.[28] The sexualized culture of the gatherings upset many women judges, who reported "scandalous" incidents of sexual harassment, particularly at the provincial court level.[29] Judge Sparks suffered sexual harassment intersected with racism, a twisting of the knife that intensified the harm.[30] Although white female judges understood the dangers of sexual harassment, few understood racist overtones, wrongly suggesting to Sparks that she was overreacting. "Nobody has to expose themselves to that kind of hostile environment," Sparks explained. "You have to extricate yourself."[31] Her absences, while fully understandable, did nothing to further connect her with colleagues.

However, it made her stand out when the CBA was seeking a "woman of colour" to join its Task Force on Gender Equality in the Legal Profession, chaired by Bertha Wilson.[32] It was transformative for Judge Sparks, who found the consultations "opened her eyes" to how much her own experiences resembled those of other racialized women lawyers and judges.[33] Lawyer Melina Buckley, the task force director, described her pivotal contribution. "Judge Sparks would pick her battles," recalled Buckley, but her "quiet courage" contributed to a hard-hitting report.[34] The task force confirmed that racialized judges experienced "sexism and racism on the bench" and lauded them for displaying "remarkable courage and determination in extremely trying circumstances."[35] When the report was greeted with fiery backlash, it further isolated the authors.[36]

That would have been challenging in most workplaces, but judicial life places a rift between people on the bench and others. The ease with which non-judges speak their minds and behave in public is no longer feasible. Socializing with other judges is one of the only options left.[37] Judge Sparks was already distanced from her African Nova Scotian community, something she had worried about when considering the appointment. Then she was segregated within her judicial circle. She took refuge in travel. She attended meetings of the Delos Davis Law Guild of Ontario, the newly formed Black lawyers' association.[38] She became active in its larger American counterpart, the National Bar Association (NBA), founded in 1925 to represent Black lawyers denied entry to the American Bar Association. By the time Sparks joined, the NBA numbered thousands of African American lawyers, judges, educators, and students.[39] Neither organization was gender-balanced at the time, but both offered Sparks significant external support.

Back in Nova Scotia, Judge Sparks's conference travel created a backlash.[40] Unjustified criticism circulated over her absences. When *RDS* blew up, there was no support from her colleagues. She stood alone, with no one to throw her a life preserver.

A GENDERED DECISION
AND GENDERED BACKLASH

"Quiet courage" might also describe the tone of Sparks's *RDS* decision, delivered in what some described as a "female voice."[41] She used mitigating phrases: "I have queries in my mind with respect to what actually transpired," and "this gives me some questions." She emphasized that she did not "accept everything that RDS has said," and was "not saying that the Constable has misled the Court" or "overreacted." Her verdict was styled as one of probability: "I believe that probably the situation" was of a "young police officer who overreacted."[42] Some judges leave no doubt about their hierarchical authority. Judge Sparks was not one of them. Her decision was tempered, designed to take the edge off her findings of credibility.[43] Whether this reflected a lifetime of socialization to speak as a female or her own perception of her fragile status, it may have worsened the situation. While some observers supported diverse adjudication styles, others read the decision as internally inconsistent.

Gendered dynamics were on display as the uproar escalated. The male prosecutor requested his superiors review the file. The male officer complained to his male staff sergeant, who complained to his male police chief, who complained to the male chief justice of the Family Court. Rocky Jones accused the press of leading a "witch hunt" against Sparks, the province's "only Black judge."[44] He did not emphasize that she was the province's only Black *female* judge. The first public statement in defence of Judge Sparks said nothing about gender. Later, before the Nova Scotia Court of Appeal, Jones finally mentioned gender, noting that Sparks's comments "stemmed from her experience as a black woman in Nova Scotia." Then he pivoted to focus on race.[45] Malcolm X once described Black women as the "most disrespected" demographic in America.[46] Did Rocky Jones ask himself whether, had she been male, the same witch hunt would have erupted?

"Do I think a Black male would have been subject to the same treatment?" queried Michelle Williams years later. The director of Dalhousie's Indigenous Blacks & Mi'kmaq (IB&M) Initiative answered her own question: "Probably not. There's a certain vulnerability [attached to] Judge Sparks's femaleness. I don't think they would have gone after [a Black male judge] the way they went after her."[47] African Nova Scotian senator Wanda Thomas Bernard added, "I don't think we should even be questioning did gender play a part. Of course, it did. Not just in the way she was perceived and how people reacted to her decision, but also the fallout afterwards, and the lengths they went to prove she had done something wrong."[48] Arleen Huggins, a prominent Ontario Black lawyer, pointed out that critics attack female judges "personally." They complain that male judges made a "bad decision," but they call females "bad judges."[49]

Maryka Omatsu, the country's first Asian Canadian female judge, emphasized that racialized women judges were "more under the microscope" and "much more vulnerable."[50] Philip Graham, an African Canadian lawyer whose Toronto practice encompassed workplace discrimination cases, saw gender as central. "Do I think the firestorm around Sparks was because she was female? For sure."[51] Barrington Walker, Canada's leading Black male historian, concurred: "Honestly, I don't think they would

Michelle Y. Williams, director of Dalhousie's Indigenous Blacks & Mi'kmaq Initiative, said Judge Sparks's femaleness made her vulnerable.

have treated a Black male judge the same way. It's not a walk in the park for a Black man in these institutions, but the kind of overt, outward displays of disrespect shown to Black women is distinct."[52]

Jean Whalen believed that a Black male judge would have received the same treatment. When she was appointed to both the Nova Scotia Provincial and Family Courts in 2009, she followed Castor Williams, the first Black male appointed to the Provincial Court, in 1996. It made her the second African Nova Scotian female judge. "When I listened to Connie's stories, Castor's stories, and mine," she observed, "there was a pattern."[53] Evangeline Cain-Grant, North Preston's first Black lawyer, and the first Black woman in Canada to open a solo law practice, added: "If Judge Sparks had been a Black male judge, there would have been the same uproar. Our Blackness is seen first, before anyone sees our femaleness."[54] Delvina Bernard, founder of the Afri-centric Learning Institute of Nova Scotia, agreed:

> [T]rying to disaggregate [race and gender] presents a challenge. Gender is always operative, and it's a highly male-biased system, an old boys' network. You don't belong to the closed inner circles. Decisions are made in bathrooms over urinals. That's not where the women of the legal system find themselves and certainly not the Black women. [But] I think the same thing would have happened to a Black male.[55]

Judge Castor Williams, the first Black male appointed to the Provincial Court, in 1996.

Anthony Morgan, an African Canadian lawyer and antiracist advocate, characterized the *RDS* courtroom as saturated with sexism. "Who dominates these rooms? Masculinity plays into that," he stressed. Tall physically powerful Rocky Jones sparred with the tall physically powerful Officer Stienburg, yet it was "white masculinity," Morgan observed, that was dominant. Intersectional race and gender elevated the authority of Stienburg and Miller while diminishing the power of Jones and Sparks.

Speculating further, Morgan added:

The white male prosecutor and the white male officer were steamrolling the Black female judge. "Even though you are a judge, it is still our courtroom. If you are going to sit on our bench, we have to show you your place and the place of others. We and our people created the rules, and you are all just visitors to the court system." It was part of the disciplining of her. In her body as a Black woman, she couldn't represent authority. Consciously or unconsciously, they would have been considering, "Who's going to protect her? I can say what I want about her credibility, her judgment."[56]

"I would be very surprised," concluded Morgan, "if that wasn't operating in the culture and space and energy of that room. Because of the ways we are socialized to devalue women, and especially Black women, it made her an easier target."[57]

THE PUZZLE OF CONNIE GLUBE

Chief Justice Connie Glube was the first female judge to rule against Judge Sparks. It would be naive to assume that one female judge would offer unwavering support to another, although there was much to suggest Glube's familiarity with prejudice. She faced sex discrimination in law school, during articling, in her law practice, and from fellow judges. She was the first woman and the first Jewish woman appointed to Nova Scotia's Supreme Court and the first female chief justice in Canada. She was the only woman on her court for twelve years. In

1995, the year she decided *RDS,* 88 percent of federally appointed judges were male, and 97 percent were Gentile.[58]

Did Sparks's arrival on the Family Court elate or disappoint Glube? Did her presence inside the judiciary improve or detrimentally complicate Glube's life? Some clues suggest that Glube nurtured her other female colleagues. Described as an "unfailing source of support, encouragement, and mentorship for women in law," she was hailed as a "feminist hero." Praised for her commitment to "equal opportunity in her chosen profession," she was said to be dedicated to "overcoming the gender, ethnic, and religious barriers of her era."[59] Apparently, she phoned Judge Sparks directly after she filed her *RDS* decision, hoping to soften the blow by breaking the news to her personally, but there was little warmth in the exchange between the two.[60]

Did Glube's decades of marginalization help explain her ruling? Those who shatter glass ceilings suffer stigmatization and heightened scrutiny. Glube would have known that even minor errors could be fatal, implicating not just an individual but an entire group. She had a reputation as "all business," known to be harsh when things did not meet her standards.[61] If she believed that the first Black female judge had blundered, she may have felt the need to issue a strong rebuke. Dalhousie law professor Richard Devlin suggested that it was "not totally surprising" that Glube took the position she did: "She was a woman. She was Jewish. You don't want people to accuse you of being partial, so you have to step up in a certain way."[62]

Class issues may also have complicated this. Glube, the lawyer's daughter and wife of a prominent businessman, had little in common with Sparks, raised in a segregated rural township by parents employed as a domestic and a custodian. As chief justice, Glube moved in elite legal and social circles far removed from Sparks. Superior court judges could be condescending in their dealings with lower court judges. Judge Sparks's Family Court was one of the lowest tribunals in the judicial hierarchy.

Ultimately, the most plausible explanation remains race. Black women had long complained that white women betrayed Black women whenever they saw a chance to better their own position.[63] It would have been surprising if Glube had exorcized herself of the rampant racism that suffused her society. Overt or unconscious racism may help to explain why a white feminist intimately aware of sexism missed the gender discrimination against Judge Sparks. Sparks's gender, intertwined with race, may simply have disappeared from Glube's view.

THE CENTRALITY OF GENDER

Missing the gender dynamics struck some observers as a signal weakness in the discussions of *RDS*. Antiracist activist and poet El Jones believed that gender was at the heart of Sparks's decision to speak about racist overpolicing. Black women have "always been the leaders," she emphasized, but "sexism and misogyny inside the community" meant that discrimination was characterized as racism. "That's always bothered me about this case. There was no recognition of intersectionality."[64] She cited Paula Giddings, an African American historian who chronicled the essential contributions and abuse of Black women in the abolitionist movement, the southern antilynching campaign, and civil rights activism.[65] "*RDS* is a racial profiling case," El Jones stressed, "but it's also about what happens to a Black woman judge who steps out of line. The case is not read through that lens – a Black woman judge being challenged as a Black woman."[66]

Her perspective was buttressed by Anthony Morgan:

In the conversation and literature about Black activism, it is Black women who put their bodies on the line. Judge Sparks took her lived experience and made a general comment consistent with the realities. Would a Black male judge have done that? Honestly, I'm a bit sad to say I think a Black male judge would not have. Something provoked Sparks, something that runs deeper, something that compelled her to speak the truth.[67]

Appeal to the Supreme Court of Canada

ASSEMBLING IN THE OTTAWA COURTROOM

Monday, 10 March 1997, was a bitterly cold, blustery day in Ottawa. The previous night's temperature had dipped to fifteen below zero Celsius and the windchill was numbing. It did not deter the crowd that lined up two hours before the court's start. Rodney Small was not among them. He had plans to leave Nova Scotia. "I told Rocky I was never coming back – guilty or not. [Tell] them to come and arrest me!"[1] Denise Kelsie Small was there to represent the family. "I'm his mother," she recalled, "and I wanted to see what happened."[2] She was near the front of the line, accompanied by Sharon Jones (Rocky Jones's second wife) and Folami Jones (Sharon and Rocky's daughter).[3]

Rocky Jones's younger sister Lynn, a trade union activist nicknamed "the network queen" for her ability to rally the community, led a large delegation of African Nova Scotians.[4] They were joined in line by African Canadians from Quebec, Ontario, Alberta, and British Columbia representing antiracist and feminist organizations.[5] As the line swelled, several chartered buses arrived, packed with white law students who had reserved seats. Fearing there would be no seats left, Lynn Jones intervened. "What's going on here?" she exclaimed, not knowing of the advance reservation. She insisted that there were "enough people of colour to fill the room."[6]

The students graciously stood back, the African Canadians took seats, and the rest found places in two overflow anterooms with closed-circuit TV. The crammed room surprised Rodney's mother. "When I looked around," she said, "I was just amazed how many people were there. It was a packed house!"[7] Others marvelled at the assemblage of so many African Canadians: representatives of community organizations, activists, scholars, lawyers, and even a Supreme Court law clerk.[8] One lawyer described it as a "celebratory atmosphere – they came to bear witness."[9]

Lynn Jones examining her archival collection of photographs, 2018. On the day of the appeal, Jones, Rocky Jones's sister and a trade union activist, led a large delegation of African Nova Scotians and their Black and feminist allies to the court.

Rocky Jones entered in black barrister's robes and white tabs, bleary-eyed from final preparations that had stretched into the small hours of the morning.[10] He felt "nervous as hell" with "the weight of all these Black people square on my shoulders." His sister Lynn had reminded him the night before that he should "just say it the way he would talk if he was at home."[11] Armed with the knowledge that he "probably knew more about racism than all those judges put together," he approached the counsel table.[12] Robert Lutes came over to greet him. Sensing Jones's anxiety, Lutes motioned to the assembled throng to reassure his adversary that the audience was on his side.[13] Jones was not seated when the red-and-white-robed judges filed in to take their elevated chairs. "Three judges come in, and I go to move to my spot, and then another judge comes in, and another. I had no idea there

Yola Grant *(left)* and
Carol Allen, two Black
lawyers from Toronto
who represented
intervener groups,
entering at security.

were nine judges," Jones lamented.[14] Rodney's mother murmured, "Oh
my. You have to convince every judge up there? Courts scare me."[15]
Jones was still struggling to assist his white co-counsel, Dianne Pothier,
legally blind since birth, and intervener counsel April Burey, a Toronto
lawyer of African Caribbean heritage who was in a wheelchair.[16] The
Dalhousie team was supplemented with lawyers representing intervener
groups. In addition to Burey, there were two Black lawyers from
Toronto, Yola Grant and Carol Allen. Grant and Allen, who had mistaken the 9:30 a.m. start time as 10:00 a.m., had panicked when they
were held up at security. "Thank heaven they didn't start without us,"
said Grant, who remembered the room as "hot." "It's rare that you walk
into a courtroom and the room feels warm. You had this sense of a lot
of bodies breathing in a confined space – every seat taken – a sea of
faces of Black people."[17]

Six Black lawyers and articling students – four female and two male
– sat at the counsel tables.[18] On the bench directly behind them, African
Nova Scotian Carol Aylward was caught up with the symbolism: "For
the first time in the history of this country, the Black community had
rights-based organizations who not only intervened in the case, but

had Black lawyers to argue their positions."[19] The presence of so many Black lawyers, students, and community observers had turned the courtroom into another version of the Halifax Youth Court that fateful morning. Except now an unprecedented number of Blacks were facing an all-white bench of judges.

ORAL SUBMISSIONS FROM APPELLANTS

Rodney Small's legal team was well prepared. Debates over rules concerning witness credibility, the test for bias, judicial notice, social context, the Charter, the Marshall report, policing studies, and tactical strategies had consumed untold hours.[20] Dalhousie law professors and their clinic students provided *pro bono* assistance, funds were obtained from the Court Challenges Program, and a written "factum" containing the legal arguments had been sent to the court in advance.[21]

Rocky Jones opened strongly. He cited two cases prior to *RDS* in which white male judges had acknowledged racism. In 1992, Nova Scotia Family Court judge Paul Niedermayer conceded that racism existed in Nova Scotia. Referring to the Marshall report, Niedermayer added that "a person would have to be stupid, complacent or ignorant not to acknowledge its presence, not only individually but systemically and institutionally."[22] In 1993, Ontario Court of Appeal justice David Doherty had written:

> Racism, and in particular anti-Black racism, is a part of our community psyche. A significant segment of our community holds overtly racist views. A much larger segment subconsciously operates on the basis of negative racial stereotypes. Furthermore, our institutions, including the criminal justice system, reflect and perpetuate these negative statements.[23]

Neither white judge was challenged for bias. "The allegation of bias arose in this particular case," Jones emphasized, "because Judge Sparks, a Black woman, was adjudicating the trial of a Black accused and she explicitly recognized that the case had racial overtones." "For centuries," he asserted, "people of colour have made claims about bias in the courts," but the court had been "deaf to those claims." As soon as "one Black judge even raises the issue of race," claims of judicial bias "seemed to be well grounded."[24]

It was a demonstrable double standard – two unimpeached white male judges and one Black female judge accused of racism. Lynn Jones recalled spontaneous cries of "amen," "right on," and "yeah, brother." "They stopped the case at one point," she added, "and warned us. I almost got kicked out of the place!"[25] For Carolann Wright-Parks, a seventh-generation community organizer sitting in the courtroom, the exhilaration was memorable: "Oh my God, this is just amazing. Law and justice could go hand in hand. For a brief moment, it made me want to go to law school."[26]

Dianne Pothier took the podium next. She urged the court to measure bias against the right to racial equality in section 15 of the Charter.[27] Although this was her first appearance as counsel at the Supreme Court, she was ready. The Halifax-born law professor of Acadian heritage had stood first at Dalhousie law school, carrying off almost every prize. She had articled with the Dalhousie Legal Aid Service, clerked for Chief Justice Brian Dickson at the Supreme Court, and taught at Dalhousie since 1986.[28] Pothier identified herself as legally blind, due to an inherited genetic condition of albinism. Her expertise on Charter equality law and her lived experience of disability discrimination made her an ideal choice as co-counsel.[29]

She explained that erasing Judge Sparks's identity as a Black judge – as all the previous judges except Gerald Freeman had done – was "a stark example of what happens when we officially pretend that race is not an issue in the justice system." The racial majority might be comfortable "not talking about race," but that was not a "neutral" position. She reminded the judges that before the Marshall Inquiry, the Nova Scotia judiciary was "all white." She emphasized the importance of counteracting the long "history of racism, both intentional and non-intentional." Judge Sparks's comments, she argued, reflected sensitivity to the "real-life context in which the justice system impacts upon 'non-white' groups."[30]

Supreme Court judges often interrupted counsel with questions, and Chief Justice Antonio Lamer interceded then. A man of mixed French Canadian and Irish heritage, who had grown up in the 1930s in East End Montreal, where French Canadians, English-Canadians, and Italians lived on separate blocks, Lamer had little exposure to Blacks. As he explained in a 1994 interview, "[W]e didn't have a black problem, there weren't that many and the few we did have were working in the train station as porters or as shoe-shines in washrooms. They weren't visibly taking jobs ... there was no black problem, because there were no blacks, not because we were tolerant."[31]

His questions veered from anti-Black racism to speculation about French Canadians. "To some people I'm a honky, to others I am a frog ... Am I to say that ... an English policeman arresting a French Canadian, that we take into account that there are social tensions right now and factor them into every case? ... I'm wondering how far we're going?"[32] Nervous laughter was the initial audience response. His next interruptions drew startled murmurs.[33] To growing discomfort in the courtroom, he referred to Chinese clients from his earlier law practice as "tremendous gamblers." Citing the problem of the Montreal casino "constantly occupied by people of the Chinese community," he added that "Chinese people have a propensity for gambling." He queried "how far down the slope we're going to go once we do this?"[34]

Pothier replied that negative generalizations about persons accused of crime would "further marginalize" rather than "decrease marginalization" of vulnerable groups.[35] She diplomatically did not suggest that Lamer had just supported a derogatory stereotype about a racialized minority.[36] Lamer continued, referring to the Roma, whom he called "gypsies," with the hypothesis that 95 percent of them might be "pickpockets." He added, "What if there is empirical data to the effect that a certain ethnic group doesn't have great respect for the oath?"[37] Again Pothier replied that these illustrations compounded the section 15 problem.[38] Watching from the next table over, Yola Grant observed, "She was using very simple language, really good analogies, and staying the course. She was passionate and she delivered clearly."[39]

The Dalhousie legal team at the Supreme Court. *Left to right:* Lianne Lagroix, Dianne Pothier, Carol Aylward, Rocky Jones, and Vincent Kazmierski.

Lynn Jones recalled thinking, "Oh my God. [T]he man's so blatantly racist. How can he be sitting on the Supreme Court?"[40] Sharon Jones remembered people "sucking in their breath. People couldn't believe what they were hearing."[41] Asian lawyer Chantal Tie, observing from the overflow room for one of the intervener groups, was "appalled."[42] Michelle Williams, then with the African Canadian Legal Clinic, was disheartened: "What kind of decision can you expect ... when the Chief Justice makes racist comments?"[43]

THE INTERVENERS

Because the Charter brought controversial new issues before the courts, judges had begun to allow interveners to offer expertise "beyond the narrow facts of the case."[44] The Women's Legal Education and Action Fund (LEAF) and the National Organization of Immigrant and Visible

Chief Justice Antonio Lamer and Justice Claire L'Heureux-Dubé on the bench. Lamer interrupted counsel with questions and expressed racist views in court, to Justice L'Heureux-Dube's displeasure in this case.

Minority Women of Canada (NOIVMWC) had been granted intervener status.[45] Both groups were concerned about abuse of women in positions of authority, especially women of colour.[46] Their joint factum emphasized that Judge Sparks was a "Nova Scotian Black woman and the only Black judge in that province at the time."[47]

When she rose to speak, LEAF counsel Yola Grant was still incensed over Chief Justice Lamer's racial stereotyping. She was relieved to notice that Justice Claire L'Heureux-Dubé, the senior female judge on the bench, had pivoted in her chair to demonstrate her displeasure.[48] "Yes!" Grant remembered thinking, "What [he] said is outrageous. It's not just me who is getting hot under the collar."[49] When Grant raised Lamer's remarks about racialized gambling, he was quick to reply, "It was a hypothetical."[50] Yet the LEAF lawyer was staggered by his "disrespectful" tone. "Chief Justice Lamer was just mouthing off – a lot of hot air. His behaviour was unbecoming of the office."[51]

Yola Grant identified as a member of a mixed-race Jamaican family raised "in a Black majority culture." She moved to Canada at sixteen,

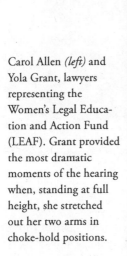

Carol Allen *(left)* and Yola Grant, lawyers representing the Women's Legal Education and Action Fund (LEAF). Grant provided the most dramatic moments of the hearing when, standing at full height, she stretched out her two arms in choke-hold positions.

obtained two science degrees at University of Toronto, graduated from Osgoode Hall law school, was called to the bar in 1989, and practised with the Ontario government.[52] Her co-counsel, Carol Allen, also from a mixed-race Jamaican family, graduated from Queen's law, was called in 1994, and practised as a sole practitioner in Toronto. LEAF had retained them both as its first African Canadian team to argue at the top court.[53] Allen was thrilled. "I had just been called to the bar. It was an amazing opportunity."[54] Grant had no qualms about her path-breaking role. Although this was her first appearance before the Supreme Court, she was confident. "I'm female, Black, tall, and I get a lot of 'you're intimidating' reactions. I don't need permission to enter the room."[55]

Then came one of the most dramatic moments in the hearing. Standing full height, Grant stretched out her two arms in choke-hold positions while stating: "The officer's own testimony indicated that he simultaneously held two Black youths in a choke hold, one of whom was handcuffed, and the other, the Appellant, the fifteen-year-old, was still straddling a mountain bike. Neither of them were in a position to escape readily."[56] Carissima Mathen, a LEAF staff lawyer of Indian origin seated in the courtroom, was riveted: "Yola's intervention was so important. She demonstrated this double headlock – two arms out, hooked as if over invisible necks. How was this a reasonable response to a kid on a bike who was being nosey?"[57] Grant recalled it with emotion later:

> [The officer] claims that RDS rode his bike so close to him that the bicycle wheel is between his legs. Somehow, he is intimidated by a 15-year-old child on a bicycle. With one in a choke-hold, he grabs the other one in a choke-hold – two choke-holds on the go. I tried to physically with my arms demonstrate to the court. This is the image the [trial] judge has, with two Black kids in choke-holds – *by the officer's own testimony!*[58]

It was April Burey's turn next, representing three additional interveners, the African Canadian Legal Clinic,[59] the Afro-Canadian Caucus of Nova Scotia,[60] and the Congress of Black Women of Canada.[61] Burey had moved with her parents and siblings from Jamaica to Nova Scotia where she completed her first law degree at Dalhousie, graduating with straight As as the class valedictorian. Called to the Ontario bar in 1985, she worked as a civil litigator with the federal Department of Justice in Toronto and then the Ontario Attorney General. In between, she completed a masters of law degree from Harvard where she studied with its first Black law professor, Derrick Bell.[62] Her family described her as a kind person, a skilled linguist, and an exceptional orator whose spirituality was at the core of her being. Colleagues described her as "brilliant," "articulate," "funny," "vivacious," "charismatic," "deeply spiritual," and "passionate about social justice."[63]

From the early 1990s, multiple sclerosis had compromised Burey's mobility, and she arrived at the courtroom in a wheelchair. The set-up

April Burey *(on the right)* with her sister Sharon. Burey, who had compromised mobility from multiple sclerosis, arrived at the courtroom in a wheelchair. Representing three Black interveners, she argued that the Nova Scotia courts had been wrong in requiring "formal proof" of racism, a practice that sanctioned the "conspiracy of silence" about racism.

was arranged for lawyers to stand when they addressed the court, and one judge complained that she was not visible from his sightline. After a flurry of commotion, she was allowed to speak while seated. Beside her at the counsel table was the clinic articling student, Jewel Amoah, another Black woman of Caribbean heritage. Amoah was impressed that two women with disabilities – Pothier and Burey – were counsel. She recalled her pride in the record number of Blacks in the room and the "glaring contrast" they posed to the "nine white judges."[64]

"This case involves a reverse triangle," Burey began. "Across this country, a common case is that of a white judge, a white police officer, and a Black accused in the middle. [But]here we have an African Canadian judge, an African Canadian accused, and a white police officer in the middle." It brought race "to the observable centre."[65]

She called the Nova Scotia courts wrong to require "formal proof" of racism. This practice sanctioned "the conspiracy of silence" about centuries-long racism against African Nova Scotians, including the "cruel and searing historical reality of slavery ... at its most vivid and horrifying." Burey's argument was steeped in religious spiritualism. "My personal belief is that Black Nova Scotians, like all Africans of the diaspora, are a people wandering in the wilderness, trying to prepare the way, trying to make straight in the desert a highway for their God."

She urged the judges to recognize "the moral and legal mandate of diversity" that "allows us all collectively to approach the knowledge and practical actualization of God."[66] Her final words were stirring: "This case is fundamentally about home. For centuries since our forcible enslavement from Africa, African Canadians have been seeking a place to call our own, a place to which we have a right, a place where our experiences, perspectives, and knowledge are included as valid and valuable to the greater whole."[67]

Southam News reporter Stephen Bindman captured the moment: "The nine white judges of the country's top court sat in mesmerized silence as the young black lawyer in a wheelchair preached for her people."[68] The other lawyers marvelled at Burey's soulful symbolism but worried about her lack of legal argument. Had the absence of judicial interruptions signalled respect or discomfort and disengagement?[69] Rocky Jones had no such qualms, and Lynn Jones called it an "absolutely dynamic" performance that spoke to the people of colour in the audience.[70] Years later, Michelle Williams added, "I believe April did what the spirit, her understanding of God, called her to do. [There is] something revolutionary in that choice. To take a different way of speaking that is reflective of the oral African tradition ... the call-and-response tradition of a Black church."[71] Carol Allen agreed. "The judges were hit with person after person representing Black people, a whole slew of agencies making essentially the same argument with different twists. There is security in that."[72] The diversity of approach offered a direct refutation of Lamer's assessment of racialized groups as monolithic units.

ORAL SUBMISSIONS FROM THE PROSECUTION

Robert Lutes had done a lot of thinking about how best to respond to Rodney Small's legal team. He believed focusing on race was counterproductive: "I didn't want it to be about race. I didn't see the need or the value for that. I saw the potential for negative outcomes. When you realize the importance of positive race relations, to me, the biggest goal for the *RDS* case was to make sure there was more positive than

Prosecutor Robert E. Lutes proved
to be a fair adversary. He believed
the focus on race was counterproductive and framed his case
around Donald Stienburg, the
police officer, instead.

negative [for] race relations."[73] Contrary to Adrian Reid's pointed attacks, Lutes "didn't really want Judge Sparks to be subject to criticism."
Nor did he want Donald Stienburg to suffer. "I felt it was unfair to the
police officer that this cloud would end up over his head. Stienburg
had no opportunity to clear his reputation." Lutes was also aware of
his own situation, a white male advancing the arguments:

> On a personal level, I told Jane, my wife, that I was privileged to do
> that case. I knew it was gonna be difficult. Presumptions are made about
> everybody. Because I'm white. Because I was a prosecutor. Because I'm
> a man. But I'm a lawyer, and I have a role to play. I was glad it was me,
> because I cared about the issues, and I cared about people.[74]

As he rose in court that morning, Lutes framed his case around
Donald Stienburg, the victimized police officer. "For all we know
Constable Stienburg may be the best officer on the force," he stated.
"I'm not saying he is or he isn't. I'm just saying that he needs to be
given an opportunity to respond."[75] It was an argument that the
Supreme Court would subsequently dismiss, indicating that Con-
stable Stienburg was not "on trial."[76]

Moving from the individual to the larger police force, Lutes continued. "Sometimes police do overreact," but "sometimes the community

and accused persons overreact to police."[77] "We are not here to say that racism does not exist – we all know that," he conceded. But no one should "stand up today and say uncategorically that police officers in Nova Scotia are racist." He challenged references to the Marshall report, demanding a "comprehensive literature search [with] a methodologist or a sociologist or whomever the other appropriate professional is to examine it, to test the study results." General studies might provide "a starting point" but did not implicate any particular officer.[78] Lutes sought to turn the damning findings of the Marshall report to his advantage. It had motivated the Halifax police to engage in "considerable" effort to "improve minority relations," and change had occurred since, upsetting the usefulness of "historical generalizations."[79]

Rocky Jones credited Lutes as a fair adversary, relieved that he chose not to argue "actual bias" but shifted to the less provocative "reasonable apprehension of bias." "[Lutes] was very senior and also incredibly fair," Jones explained. "He gave me so many tips on how to approach the case ... Bob Lutes was my mentor in that case."[80] Some litigators prefer the scorched earth strategy, but Lutes believed that professional civility was the wiser approach. Although his opponents would later characterize his presentation as "forceful," they agreed that he was not out to "make it difficult" for them.[81]

In his brief reply, Rocky Jones reminded the court that the discussion had addressed the harm to the white male officer but not to Rodney Small, now facing another trial, nor the Black female judge. "How can she sit on the bench," he queried, with police officers appearing before her, after the prosecutors insisted she was "racially biased against police?"[82] And with that, Chief Justice Lamer concluded the hearing. Everyone stood while the judges filed out.

COMPLAINT TO THE CANADIAN
JUDICIAL COUNCIL

The consternation caused by Chief Justice Lamer's questionable stereotypes was not easily quelled. The Chinese Canadian National Council (CCNC) and twenty other social-justice organizations filed a complaint

with the Canadian Judicial Council. They objected to Lamer's description of the Chinese "propensity to gamble" as a "matter of fact." False
stereotypes about Chinese gambling and criminality, rooted in the
nineteenth-century terror of a "yellow peril," had culminated in racist
head taxes and the *Chinese Exclusion Act*.[83] A Roma Advocacy Centre
spokesperson said it also "had a problem with Lamer's statements, even
if they were just oral arguments."[84] The groups suggested Lamer apologize and that all Supreme Court judges should undergo antiracism
training.[85] When the *Toronto Star* quoted the chief justice's comments
about Chinese "gamblers" and Roma "pickpockets" and reported that
his stereotyped comments took shots at ethnic groups, Lamer responded
with anger.[86]

In what the press described as "a spirited written response to *The
Star*," Lamer called the criticism "outrageous."[87] The racialized people
in his courtroom and the social-justice organizations who complained
now found their concerns reframed as his outrage over their critique.
It was a replication of the *RDS* case itself, in which the police turned
criticism of a questionable arrest of a Black youth into a racist attack
upon the officer. It was also an illustration of the escalation facing those
who voiced complaints about white racism.

In his letter to the *Star*, Chief Justice Lamer stressed that he "did not
mean any offence," repeating, "It was not in the least intended to offend
any group."[88] His proclamation of innocent intention was at odds with
legal rules that had long drawn a distinction between intent and harmful
impact in antidiscrimination law.[89] Lamer was on stronger ground when
he defended his remarks as "purely hypothetical examples of stereotypes,
not factual assertions."[90] In his *Star* letter, Lamer explained, "I put to
(the lawyer) various hypothetical stereotypes for the sake of argument,
to express my distaste for such stereotypes and to point out what I felt
was a flaw in her reasoning."[91] Jonas Ma, executive director of the CCNC,
replied that Lamer had missed the point. "Even giving hypothetical
examples of stereotypes can reinforce racist images," he explained.[92]

The *Toronto Star* editors were alarmed by the chief justice's anger.
When a staff reporter phoned him that evening, Lamer tried to alleviate
concern. "Let's start by saying I don't intend to sue anybody," he

quipped.[93] The *Star* published an apology one day later. The paper's white ombudsperson, Don Sellar, wrote a column describing Lamer as "under attack by the Chinese Canadian National Council and 20 other ethnocultural groups." The ombudsperson affirmed Lamer's words as spoken "hypothetically, the way judges often do when they test lawyers' arguments." Sellar even depicted Chief Justice Lamer as "the victim of a journalistic mugging."[94]

Undeterred, the CCNC pressed its complaint forward to the Canadian Judicial Council, which had the authority to investigate judicial misconduct and recommend penalties up to removal from office.[95] Established in 1971, the council was composed of the chief justices and associate chief justices of Canada's superior courts. Although the principle of judicial independence required that their misconduct be investigated by other judges, the inherent difficulties were clear. The chair of the council was none other than the chief justice of the Supreme Court of Canada, Antonio Lamer. The complaint was reviewed at first instance by Allan McEachern, who had jurisdiction because he was both council vice-chair and chair of the judicial complaints committee.[96] Recognizing the sensitivities involved, McEachern, the white chief justice of British Columbia, took the precaution of seeking an external review from a white Toronto lawyer.[97] It is unlikely this assuaged the fears of observers about the council's capacity to rule on a matter touching the top judge in Canada.

The complaint was dismissed three months later after McEachern concluded that the remarks could not be characterized as "misconduct." Chief Justice Lamer's comments were "hypothetical in nature," he wrote, made in the "specific context of a case" that concerned "matters of race and racial stereotypes in assessing the credibility of witnesses." Exchanges between counsel and judges were "often wide-ranging, probing and exploratory in nature."[98] The Montreal casino comments, the Roma pickpockets, and the false witnessing of "a certain ethnic group" passed without further scrutiny. Although there is a distinction between comments during oral submissions and a judicial decision, it was a light touch and a far cry from the critical eye trained upon Judge Sparks's words.

McEachern claimed to "understand the sensitivities that generated" the complaint and regretted that the "CCNC feels aggrieved by
the statements," but emphasized Lamer's unintentional motivation.
"[S]pirited argument between counsel and the Court can sometimes
create misunderstanding or cause hurt that is no less painful for its
being unintended," he added. "When this occurs, it is much to be
regretted, but judges must be free to test lawyers' submissions with
hypothetical questions" and "to engage in frank and wide-ranging
discussion."[99]

The blanket approval of hypotheses failed to inquire why Lamer
selected those particular ones, and what those choices signified about
his beliefs.[100] The council could have delved more deeply into the
stereotypes – that Chinese people gamble, that Roma people steal,
that "ethnics" lie on the stand – asking important questions: What is
the source of the presumption? Who is applying it? Who is it harming?
It failed to consider whether some hypotheses might be so offensive
they should not be used for jousting practice. According to the council,
frank and probing statements that advanced racial stereotypes were
open season. Jonas Ma's concerns that hypothetical racist stereotypes
fostered racism were dismissed.

10

The Supreme Court of Canada's "Gang of Five"

The sixty-four-page decision – four judgments from nine judges – was sufficiently tangled to baffle most readers. Even the order was bewildering. The dissenting judgment came first, then two middle decisions, with the majority ruling at the end.[1] Black lawyer Anthony Morgan later described himself as "frustrated, dismayed, and disheartened" as he tried to make sense of a "confusing" decision. He wondered if the "gymnastics had to do with discomfort about race."[2]

Justice Peter Cory attempted to clarify it in a postretirement judicial oral history interview. In the first two transcribed paragraphs below, he described two decisions from five judges.[3] The "Gang of Five" nickname surfaced in the early 1990s because the five judges often viewed issues similarly.[4] His third paragraph described the concurring decision that supported Judge Sparks most strongly – it will be considered in the next chapter.

> I wrote for the majority, and I said that [Judge Sparks's] remarks were unfortunate but when you looked at them in the total context of the case itself ... that they should not be taken as being an indication of bias. I said that they were unfortunate, they shouldn't be repeated, and certainly shouldn't have gone that far.

The Supreme Court of Canada judges who heard the *RDS* case in 1997. *Seated, left to right:* John Sopinka, Gérard La Forest, Antonio Lamer, Claire L'Heureux-Dubé, and Charles Gonthier. *Standing left to right:* Frank Iacobucci, Peter Cory, Beverley McLachlin, and John (Jack) Major.

[Jack Major said] "I would go further and say that they were so biased that there should be a new trial."

[Claire L'Heureux-Dubé and Beverley McLachlin] said it was quite alright, and this was a Black woman and it was simply an expression of her background and there was nothing improper about her remarks.

So that was the complete spectrum ... I think [the majority decision] was an attempt to deal with a very delicate situation in a way that was reasonable.[5]

Known as a judge who often took the middle road of consensus, Cory achieved his majority with a midpoint compromise.[6]

CORY'S MAJORITY DECISION: FROM INITIAL AGREEMENT TO THREE SEPARATE JUDGMENTS

Justice Cory's background was worlds apart from that of Judge Sparks. Born in Windsor, Ontario, to British parents, he had policing in his family. His father served with the North West Mounted Police on Vancouver Island before settling in Windsor to become personnel director for a chemical company. Cory's youthful recollections were of a comfortable middle-class home in an industrializing city that, in his opinion, "really wasn't racist at all."[7] "Thank God, we haven't that problem here," he would later say when discussing racist American jurors.[8]

He served as a Second World War RCAF bomber pilot at the age of seventeen, returned home to complete a bachelor of arts at the all-male Jesuit Assumption College, and graduated from Osgoode Hall law in a class of two hundred war veterans. His civil litigation practice at small Toronto firms covered administrative cases, municipal law, and white-collar crime. Well-connected through the Advocates' Society, the Lawyers' Club, and the Canadian Bar Association, he was also elected a Law Society bencher and County of York Law Association president. Cory was appointed a trial judge in 1974, to the Ontario Court of Appeal in 1981, and to the Supreme Court in 1989.[9]

Justice Peter Cory, known as a judge who often took the middle road, achieved his majority with a midpoint compromise. He stressed that Judge Sparks's comments about interactions between officers and non-white youth had been unfortunate, unnecessary, and close to the line.

Cory's explanation of the legal test for "reasonable apprehension of bias" attracted the support of six other colleagues.[10] Writing for a majority of seven, he began with "bias" – "a state of mind that is in some way predisposed to a particular result, or that is closed with regard to particular issues."[11] He added that "fairness and impartiality must be both subjectively present and objectively demonstrated to the informed and reasonable observer."[12] Next, he cautioned that "multicultural" Canada required a nuanced analysis:

> Canada is not an insular, homogeneous society ... [O]ur judges must be particularly sensitive to the need not only to be fair but also to appear to all reasonable observers to be fair to all Canadians of every race, religion, nationality and ethnic origin. This is a far more difficult task in Canada than it would be in a homogeneous society. Remarks which would pass unnoticed in other societies could well raise a reasonable apprehension of bias in Canada.[13]

Then he congratulated the Canadian judiciary for rising to the challenge:

> [Canadian judges] enjoy the respect of the vast majority of Canadians. That respect has been earned by their ability to conduct trials fairly and impartially ... Throughout their careers, Canadian judges strive to overcome the personal biases that are common to all humanity in order to provide and clearly appear to provide a fair trial for all who come before them. Their rate of success in this difficult endeavour is high.[14]

Possibly to explain how the judiciary could be performing so well in a multicultural society, he endorsed its changing composition. "Greater diversity" meant that "women and visible minorities" would bring "important perspectives" to judging. "True impartiality" did not require them to "discount" their "life experiences," Cory noted, but his platform was premised on a racially neutral setting: "A judge who happens to be black is no more likely to be biased in dealing with black litigants, than a white judge is likely to be biased in favour of white litigants."[15] He saw risks associated with judges who acted on racialized generalizations:

> [T]he judge must avoid judging the credibility of the witness on the basis of generalizations or upon matters that were not in evidence ... [I]t would not be acceptable for a judge to ... suggest that all police officers should therefore not be believed or should be viewed with suspicion where they are dealing with accused persons who are members of a different race. Similarly, it is dangerous for a judge to suggest that a particular person overreacted because of racism unless there is evidence adduced to sustain this finding.
>
> This does not mean that the particular generalization – that police officers have historically discriminated against visible minorities ... – is not true, or is without foundation. The difficulty is that reasonable and informed people may *perceive* that the judge has used this information as a basis for assessing credibility instead of making a genuine evaluation of the evidence.[16]

Up to this point, Cory's seven-person majority held firm. But as he moved to apply the bias test, he lost the support of every one of his colleagues except for Justice Frank Iacobucci, who, like Cory, characterized himself as a "centrist."[17] The other judges fanned out in two directions. Three felt the critique of Judge Sparks did not go far enough and wrote a dissent.[18] Four others formed a coalition to exonerate Judge Sparks.[19] Left writing only for himself and Iacobucci, Cory stressed that Sparks's comments about the interactions between officers and non-white youth had been "unfortunate" (four times), "troubling" (twice), "worrisome" (once), "inappropriate" (once), and "unnecessary" (once). In fact, he summed up, the remarks had "come very close to the line."[20]

In keeping with his middle-of-the-road perspective, however, Justice Cory concluded that, viewed as a whole, the remarks did not "taint her earlier findings of credibility" or meet the high threshold for "reasonable apprehension of bias." The Crown had failed to prove its case because Judge Sparks had given convincing reasons for finding Rodney

Small credible and for her reasonable doubt as to the veracity of Donald Stienburg. He indicated that her comments about race may have been a response to the prosecutor's suggestion that she should automatically believe the police officer.[21] Because four others agreed with his and Iacobucci's conclusion to dismiss the Crown's appeal, Cory regained a six-judge majority on the final result. Rodney Small was entitled to an acquittal.

JUSTICE JACK MAJOR'S DISSENT: NOT A QUESTION OF RACISM HERE

Writing for himself, Lamer, and Sopinka, Justice Jack Major led the dissent. In his view, Judge Sparks's comments had crossed the line seriously enough to quash the acquittal. His earlier interjections at the oral hearing foreshadowed this. When Rocky Jones stated that the case had "racial overtones," Major interrupted, "Isn't that stereotyping that seems so out of favour these days?"[22] It was a common response to assertions of white racism: to condemn all racial stereotypes as a blanket evil. If it was wrong for white officers to stereotype Black teenagers as dangerous, it was also wrong to assume that white officers overreact. Antiracism educators have observed that white people often meet challenges of racism by insisting that assumptions should never be drawn. Such inversions, they suggest, destabilize the initial claim, moving the conversation to a "more comfortable" place or ending the race discussion completely.[23]

Indeed, Justice Major's dissent asserted that *RDS* "should not be decided on questions of racism."[24] He characterized Judge Sparks's comments as "stereotyping all police officers as liars and racists" and criticized her for applying "this stereotype to the police officer in the present case." He added, "It would be stereotypical reasoning to conclude that, since society is racist, and, in effect, tells minorities to 'shut up,' we should infer that *this* police officer told *this* appellant minority youth to 'shut up.'" Major offered stereotypes about "prostitutes" as a parallel example:

Justice John (Jack) Major – writing for himself and Lamer and Sopinka – led the dissent. Of a British Canadian background, his dissent asserted that the case should not be decided on questions of racism.

If a judge in a sexual assault case instructed the jury ... that because the complainant was a prostitute he or she probably consented, or that prostitutes are likely to lie about such things as sexual assault, that decision would be reversed ... Our jurisprudence prohibits tying credibility to something as irrelevant as gender, occupation or perceived group predisposition.[25]

He emphasized that old legal rules requiring "corroboration" of women and children had been eliminated.[26] It was an aspirational view of courts staffed by racism-free judges administering neutral laws equally to people of all races, classes, and genders.

Yet by his own accounts, Justice Major was no stranger to judging based on unfair stereotypes. Reflecting upon his career after retirement, he recalled stories about a 1920s Alberta district court judge who had proclaimed, on the record, "It's a well-known fact that Ukrainians lie under oath."[27] He recalled a Calgary magistrate who also chaired the Calgary Police Commission, whose "pro-police" outlook meant he rarely found an officer untruthful or mistaken.[28] No complaints of judicial bias had emerged against either.

Like Peter Cory, Jack Major had a background vastly different from Sparks. He was born in Mattawa, Ontario, into a solidly middle-class home with parents of English and Scottish/Irish heritage. His father's work as a Canadian Pacific Railway station agent took the family to the northern Ontario towns of Levack, White River, and Espanola where Major attended Catholic schools.[29] He recalled that "it was a white culture in Canada," where he "hardly ever saw a Black person."[30] He attended an all-male Jesuit boarding school in Kingston and obtained a commerce degree from the Jesuits' Loyola College in Montreal. He followed his brother to the University of Toronto law school, graduating in the top half of the class of twenty-nine men, one woman, and no Blacks.[31]

Major followed his brother out west to practise in Calgary, where he found the legal culture "less elitist, less formal." There, his path dovetailed briefly with Sparks, who had transplanted herself to Alberta where she, too, sought more open vistas. Unable to get a job in a law firm, Sparks soon returned home. Unlike her, Major flourished. He articled with the largest law firm in Calgary (a firm founded by Prime Minister R.B. Bennett), was called to the Alberta bar in 1958, continued to practise with Bennett Jones, and made partner in 1966.[32]

His top-flight litigation practice included clients such as the Alberta government, the federal tax department, and physicians sued for negligence. He became senior counsel to the Calgary Police Services.[33] He was active in Conservative politics prior to his judgeship, although both he and Prime Minister Brian Mulroney insisted that top court appointments were not political. Mulroney appointed Major to the Alberta Court of Appeal in 1991 and elevated him to the Supreme Court of Canada the next year.[34] Chief Justice Lamer, somewhat suspicious of a business lawyer with no litigation expertise, was happy to discover that Major was a "team player," a "practical" judge with a "poker face" who was "witty as hell."[35]

Major's dissent submerged the issue of racial identity. He described Rodney Small as "a young person" – without racial designation. Sparks and Stienburg were equally raceless, although the latter was identified as being "of a different race" than the apparently raceless accused.[36] It was as if the dissent was cognizant of race only as a tension of opposites. The features of racial identity, the history of race discrimination, and the sociological, psychological, and cultural context that gives racial designation its force and meaning were absent.

This was in keeping with other Canadian jurists who refused to identify race even when the case revolved around racism. When Viola Desmond, a Black Halifax businesswoman, sought to protest racial segregation in Nova Scotia theatres in 1946, the judges rejected her claim without reference to her race, the race of the (white) theatre owner, the race of the (white) police officer who arrested her, or the race of the (white) magistrate who convicted her. Nor did the court acknowledge the theatre's racially segregated seating policy. Instead, the raceless litigants appeared to be sparring over a provincial taxation statute.[37]

The *RDS* dissent rested firmly on the absence of *evidence* of racism. The three dissenters had each made this plain at the oral hearing. Justice John Sopinka, known as Canada's leading expert on the law of evidence, emphasized that the question was "whether or not [the presumption] can be applied to the particular facts of the case."[38] Chief Justice Antonio Lamer focused on Officer Stienburg: "We have to decide whether *this one* was racist ... But we don't know which ones are unless they do things to reveal it, and the smarter ones don't."[39] Chief Justice Lamer's earlier career as criminal defence counsel was well known to have left him "street smart" about police misbehaviour.[40] Here, he sought words or deeds linked directly to racism. Justice Major also demanded evidence to "show racism on the part of the police officer." Questioning Rodney Small's lawyers at the oral hearing, he raised the bar for assertions of racism very high:

> Were there events where he acted in a racist way? What is there available by way of evidence other than things like studies which are general? What is the value of the studies of the population in general, looking at the conduct of a specific individual? How do you bring the results of [a] study down to a single individual policeman? You have to show evidence that something in his past, or somebody at the incident told it.[41]

Would it have made a difference if Judge Sparks had referred to the Marshall report in her initial decision, rather than in supplementary reasons, which were discounted because she concluded the trial before their delivery? Perhaps not. Neither side had raised the Marshall report or other race-and-policing studies at the trial, and Judge Sparks might have risked being overruled for independently resorting to this as evidence.[42] Crown appellate lawyer Robert Lutes had argued that statistical reports required vetting by experts subjected to rigorous cross-examination. He also warned that dated reports might not comport with reformed police practices. This left dim hope for lawyers attempting to provide foolproof evidence to back their submissions, even assuming they had funding to produce state-of-the-art research attested to by costly experts. How complex statistical studies might have fared in lower-level family courts, with their rough-and-ready approach to heavy dockets and frenetic pacing, is yet another mystery. Top court judges insisting on this evidence demanded a counsel of perfection that was out of reach with the realities of youth courts.

Justice Major's queries indicate that even an up-to-date, validated, general report might be inapplicable to a specific individual and incident. Where racism is hidden, indirect, and systemic, some questioned whether demanding such evidence placed an intolerable burden on a fifteen-year-old charged with a minor offence.[43] Ottawa criminal defence lawyer Michael Johnston observed that judges sometimes demand rigid compliance with evidentiary procedural rules, sometimes not. He described the *RDS* approach as "'show us the detailed expert evidence if you want to make the argument. You want to overturn our applecart? You follow all the rules.' The rule enforcement is selective based on whether the system likes your argument."[44] Others emphasized that the same courts that recognize the harmful effects of gun violence without evidence are loath to accept the harms of racism.[45] Still others described it as a perspective garbed in objectivity and neutrality, one that rested on the unstated presumption that there were no problems of racism in the Halifax police department and that race was irrelevant. That in itself was a generalization not based on evidence.[46]

Justice John Sopinka, known as Canada's leading expert on the law of evidence, emphasized that the question was whether the presumption of racism applied to the facts of the case.

Chief Justice Antonio Lamer, who was of mixed French Canadian and Irish heritage, demanded evidence that Officer Stienburg was racist.

Justice Sopinka suggested that Judge Sparks even had a responsibility to canvass other valid reasons for police overreaction: "[S]he doesn't try to find some legitimate explanation ... [W]hy would this person [Officer Stienburg] – what would this person's motive be to lie?"[47] Shifting the focus to the individual suggested that the dissenting judges understood racism as discrete, isolated acts of prejudice committed by specific people, rather than as complex, interconnected patterns. The discussion had slipped a long way from assessing an allegedly wrongful arrest. It was as though the police officer himself was under criminal charges for intentional racism. As critical race scholar Sherene Razack sarcastically appraised it, "The heroes of this story are innocent, white subjects."[48]

Sopinka's censure of Sparks resonated oddly with an earlier speech he gave to the Canadian Bar Association. Although he emphasized the importance of impartial judging, he also expressed concern that "demands for political correctness" might unduly restrict judges' free speech. The free speech he rose to defend was of the politically incorrect genre. "The over-zealous dissection of every word that drops from the bench, with a view of finding some indicia of political incorrectness ... may result in decisions that are politically correct but not legally and factually correct."[49] His defence of judges perceived "politically incorrect," a phrase then used to capture sexism, racism, ableism or homophobia, was not extended to Judge Sparks.

The queries voiced at the hearing all found their way into the dissenting judgment. Writing for the three, Justice Major summed up:

> Trial judges have to base their findings on the evidence before them ... The life experience of this trial judge, as with all trial judges, is an important ingredient in the ability to understand human behavior, to weigh the evidence, and to determine credibility ... It is of no value, however, in reaching conclusions for which there is no evidence ... Life experience is not a substitute for evidence ...
>
> [T]he appellant was entitled to call evidence of the police officer's conduct to show that there was in fact evidence to support either his bias or racism. No such evidence was called. The trial judge presumably called upon her life experience to decide the issue. This she was not entitled to do ... [T]he absence of evidence to support the judgment is an irreparable defect.[50]

Unlike Justice Cory's gentler admonishments, this was unfiltered censure.

MINORITY SUPPORT FOR JUDGE SPARKS

The two decisions written by Justices Cory and Major and signed by Justices Iacobucci, Sopinka, and Lamer, covered the views of the "Gang of Five." Two other judges forged a separate path. Writing together, Justices Claire L'Heureux-Dubé and Beverley McLachlin, the only two women on the court, penned a spirited defence of Judge Sparks. Two additional judges signed their names to that judgment: Justices Charles

Doherty Gonthier[51] and Gérard Vincent La Forest.[52] It made a minority of four.[53] But since all four joined Cory's end result – upholding Judge Sparks's acquittal of Rodney Small – the four were "concurring" justices, not "dissenting" like the Major-Lamer-Sopinka trio.[54] No wonder people were confused.

11

The Concurring Opinion
in Defence of Judge Sparks

Justices Claire L'Heureux-Dubé and Beverley McLachlin took pains to distance themselves from Justice Cory's chastisement of Judge Sparks. Dispensing with the usual diplomacy that judges adopt to temper their disagreements, they wrote:

> [W]e disagree with Cory J.'s position that the comments of Judge Sparks were unfortunate, unnecessary, or close to the line. Rather, we find them to reflect an entirely appropriate recognition of the facts in evidence in this case and of the context within which this case arose – a context known to Judge Sparks and to any well-informed member of the community.[1]

It was a sea change from the "Gang of Five," composed jointly by two women who had experienced gender discrimination themselves.[2]

L'HEUREUX-DUBÉ AND McLACHLIN:
TWO EARLY WOMEN JUDGES

L'Heureux-Dubé and McLachlin's backgrounds differed from Judge Sparks's, but they, too, entered the judiciary when it was overwhelmingly male. L'Heureux-Dubé was the second woman on the top court, and the first woman from Quebec. McLachlin was the third on that court, the first woman from western Canada.[3]

Descended from generations of French Canadians, L'Heureux-Dubé was born in Quebec City. She graduated from Laval, the last Canadian law school to admit women. Her class had two women out of fifty students. She was told that the law was no place for women and denied a scholarship because of her gender. McLachlin was born in Pincher Creek, Alberta, to parents of German and Polish heritage. She enrolled in law at the University of Alberta, feeling like "an imposter" when she joined with seven females and fifty-eight men in a classroom that was, in her words, "oozing male dominance." Despite top

A Quebecer schooled in cloistered convents, Claire L'Heureux-Dubé was called to the Quebec bar in 1952. Like Judge Sparks, she entered the judiciary when it was overwhelmingly male. She was the second woman appointed to the Supreme Court of Canada and the first woman from Quebec.

grades, she was passed over for law review editorship. The coveted spot went to a male student with lower marks.[4]

After her call to the bar in 1952, L'Heureux-Dubé's only job offer came from one of Quebec City's few Jewish lawyers. It signified, as one male classmate put it, the "general attitude" to "women *and* Jews." She received sexist treatment from judges, lawyers, and clients and was forced into family law, a practice disdained by many Catholic Quebecers who opposed divorce on religious grounds. Called to the Alberta bar in 1969, McLachlin found work in Alberta and British Columbia law firms but had to fight for her own office, endure sexist stereotypes and jokes, suffer hurtful gossip, and experience exclusion from men's-only clubs. She switched to teaching law at the University of British

An Albertan of German and Polish ethnicity, Beverley McLachlin graduated in 1968 and was called to the Alberta bar a year later. She found work in law firms but endured sexism in the office and exclusion from men's-only clubs.

Columbia.[5] Despite the challenges, both women were well placed when the pressure to move women into the judiciary intensified.[6]

Their appointments to the Supreme Court of Canada, in 1987 and 1989, respectively, came in the wake of a powerful feminist movement that advocated greater female participation after the introduction of the Canadian Charter. While some observers cheered, others raised public criticisms rarely voiced about male appointees. Commentators speculated that they were "not the most qualified" but picked simply because of their gender. Justice Lamer threatened to resign if L'Heureux-Dubé were appointed. Another judge refused to speak to her for the first three months because he said she was "on probation."[7] Some joked that McLachlin's meteoric rise had moved her through to the top court faster than most litigants.[8] "We felt isolated," explained L'Heureux-Dubé: "We were not part of the gang."[9]

When they wrote in favour of women's equality, it attracted exceptional critique. Misogynistic outbursts greeted L'Heureux-Dubé's decision that myths and stereotypes about sexual assault had no place in law.[10] National newspapers, radio talk shows, and male defence lawyers complained that her "radical feminist cant" had "hijacked" and "disgraced" the court. The conservative REAL Women of Canada's group demanded that the Canadian Judicial Council remove her from the bench because feminism was incompatible with judging. It made no charge against the male judge who signed the same decision. The complaint was dismissed after gruelling public debate.[11] The same REAL group demanded McLachlin's removal after she gave a speech suggesting that criminal laws against abortion and prostitution were "based on outdated sexual stereotypes and led to unfair and unequal treatment of women." The organization insisted her feminist ideology had undermined the integrity of the court. This complaint was also dismissed, but the personalized attacks over "feminist bias" must have given both women a shared understanding of how outsider judges could be singled out for condemnation.[12]

Some wondered if early women judges might vote together on gender issues. A 1998 study concluded that the first women on the Supreme Court were "more than twice as likely as their male colleagues to support equality claims under the *Charter*."[13] Yet women judges' perspectives could be unpredictable. Justices L'Heureux-Dubé and McLachlin both rejected sexist tax laws but split over cross-examination of sexual assault complainants.[14] Observers dubbed their *RDS* decision a "rare joint judgment," but in L'Heureux-Dubé's assessment, over time she and McLachlin came increasingly to share views regarding women's issues.[15]

Whether gender sensitivity would cross over to racism was less clear. Both sensed themselves to be outsiders by ethnicity – a Quebecer in a majority Anglo-Canadian country and an Albertan whose German birthname (Gietz) marked her apart in a postwar setting hostile to such ancestry. Yet L'Heureux-Dubé's schooling in cloistered convents in francophone Quebec gave her no exposure to racial diversity, and McLachlin's hometown "thought of itself as white and mostly Anglo-Saxon."[16] French Canadian and German ethnicity was on a different plane from African Canadian heritage. Both women were white vis-à-vis Canada's Black populations, in a country where antiracist activists had long critiqued the racism of women with white privilege. It was by no means obvious how the two women would rule on *RDS*. What they wrote may suggest less about race sensitivities than their sympathy with a judge attacked for bias in ways similar to complaints they withstood on gender.

THE CONCURRENCE: "JUDGES CAN NEVER BE NEUTRAL," MUST "STRIVE FOR IMPARTIALITY"

The two women distinguished between "impartiality," which was "required of all judges," and the illusory concept of "neutrality." The reality, noted L'Heureux-Dubé and McLachlin, was that "judges can never be neutral, in the sense of purely objective." They quoted the famous white male American judge, Benjamin Cardozo: "All their lives, forces which [judges] do not recognize and cannot name, have been tugging at them – inherited instincts, traditional beliefs, acquired convictions ... We may try to see things as objectively as we please. None the less, we can never see them with any eyes except our own."[17] According to L'Heureux-Dubé and McLachlin, the "impartiality" judges should strive for instead recognized that a judge's "own insights into human nature" properly influence findings of credibility and facts. What impartiality required was that judges make decisions "only after being equally open to, and considering the views of, all parties before them."[18]

L'Heureux-Dubé and McLachlin cited University of Toronto law professor Jennifer Nedelsky, who recommended the "enlarged mind" approach. "What makes it possible for us to genuinely judge, to move beyond our private idiosyncrasies and preferences, is our capacity to achieve an *enlargement of mind*," she wrote. "We do this by taking different perspectives into account."[19] It was an aspirational approach endorsed by the Canadian Judicial Council's *Commentaries on Judicial Conduct*: "True impartiality does not require that the judge have no sympathies or opinions; it requires that the judge nevertheless be free to entertain and act upon different points of view with an open mind."[20] Quoting both Nedelsky and the *Commentaries* with approval, Justices L'Heureux-Dubé and McLachlin wrote that Judge Sparks's oral reasons illustrated she had approached the case with an "open mind."[21]

But L'Heureux-Dubé and McLachlin noted that cases "do not arise in a vacuum," so awareness of social conditions furnished another essential precondition to impartiality. This could come from "testimony from expert witnesses" or "academic studies properly placed before the

Justice Claire L'Heureux-Dube's appointment to the Supreme Court in 1987 came in the wake of a powerful feminist movement and the introduction of the Charter of the Rights and Freedoms. Justice Lamer threatened to resign if she were appointed.

Justice Beverley McLachlin was appointed to the Supreme Court in 1989. Some joked that her meteoric rise had moved her to the top court faster than most litigants.

Court." Equally important was "the judge's personal understanding and experience of the society in which the judge lives and works."[22] These last words placed the two women in flat disagreement with Major, Lamer, and Sopinka, who had categorically rejected such notions.

In *RDS*, they added, the impartial judge would be "cognizant of the existence of racism in Halifax, Nova Scotia," as would any "reasonable person":

> The reasonable person ... must be taken to possess knowledge of the local population and its racial dynamics, including the existence in the community of a history of widespread and systemic discrimination against black and aboriginal people, and high-profile clashes between the police and the visible minority population over policing issues ... The reasonable person is cognizant of the racial dynamics in the local

community, and, as a member of the Canadian community, is supportive of the principles of equality.[23]

That meant Judge Sparks's contextual analysis was beyond reproach:

> Judge Sparks' oral reasons show that she approached the case with an
> open mind, used her experience and knowledge of the community to
> achieve an understanding of the reality of the case, and applied the
> fundamental principle of proof beyond a reasonable doubt ... In alerting
> herself to the racial dynamic in the case, she was simply engaging in the
> process of contextualized judging which, in our view, was entirely proper
> and conducive to a fair and just resolution of the case.[24]

Although legal theorists had been analyzing the broader concept of
"contextualism" since the advent of the Charter, this expanded its
application to judicial bias for the first time.[25]

NAMING RACISM, INTRODUCING EVIDENCE, AND THE BURDEN OF PROOF

The case would have offered a cleaner foundation if racism had been
named and litigated. Racism had never been overtly raised at trial.
Neither Rodney Small nor Rocky Jones used the word. African Nova
Scotians had little doubt about the reality of racism but knew that
voicing it was more likely to backfire than to assist. Yet as Justice
L'Heureux-Dubé had indicated at the earlier oral hearing, the consequences of silence were problematic. She questioned whether it was
"better for society" that no one spoke up about "issues of gender, of
racism" so that "nobody knows what's in the head of the person who
judges?"[26]

Legal experts were split. Some cautioned that the "prudent judge"
might prefer to remain silently "inscrutable" to avoid the appeals that
gave rise to *RDS*.[27] Justices Cory and Major made clear that they believed
such remarks were better left unsaid. Others argued that to bury race
would mask the (erroneous) operating assumption that Halifax police

treated Blacks and whites the same.[28] African Nova Scotian activists were demanding more overt recognition, emphasizing that Sparks's courageous words had given them a "sense of relief."[29] Unlike their colleagues, L'Heureux-Dubé and McLachlin gave judges licence to speak about racism in their courtrooms.

The demand for evidence of racism provoked further disagreement. At the hearing, L'Heureux-Dubé had argued that weeks-long trials "with experts on every side" were unrealistic.[30] Expert evidence was prohibitively expensive. The study of Canadian racism rarely attracted researchers with the requisite court credentials, and there were few traditionally qualified experts available to testify. In her Marshall Inquiry testimony, Esmeralda Thornhill described the very concept of expert evidence as problematic within a legal system premised on the invisibility of racism.[31] And as the dissenting judges had demonstrated, even the best studies could be dismissed for failure to tie the racism to a specific actor or event. L'Heureux-Dubé and McLachlin rebuffed their colleagues' insistence that judges should not draw conclusions about racial context without explicit evidence.

The women buttressed their decision on the Crown's failure to prove its case. Judge Sparks had found Rodney Small sufficiently believable to conclude that some of the officer's testimony was not credible. She was then left with a "reasonable doubt" as to Rodney's guilt. The two women took issue with Justice Major's misquoting of Sparks's words. He had written that she "in effect was saying" that she had "a suspicion that this police officer may have lied." L'Heureux-Dubé and McLachlin noted that "Judge Sparks did quite the opposite." She stated that she was "*not* saying Constable Stienburg had misled the court" and that she was "*not* saying that Constable Stienburg had overreacted," merely that he "*probably* overreacted."[32] They continued:

> At no time did Judge Sparks rule that the probable overreaction by Constable Stienburg was motivated by racism. Rather, she tied her finding of probable overreaction to the evidence that Constable Stienburg had threatened to arrest the appellant R.D.S. for speaking to his cousin ... [S]he had accepted the evidence that the other youth arrested that

day was handcuffed and thus secured when R.D.S. approached. This constitutes evidence which could lead one to question why it was necessary for both boys to be placed in choke-holds ... Her comments were based entirely on the case before her, were made after a consideration of the conflicting testimony of the two witnesses and in response to the Crown's submissions, and were entirely supported by the evidence.[33]

This portion of the decision echoed Cory's majority judgment. What followed was more dramatic:

While it seems clear that Judge Sparks *did not in fact* relate the officer's probable overreaction to the race of the appellant R.D.S., it should be noted that if Judge Sparks *had* chosen to attribute the behaviour of Constable Stienburg to the racial dynamics of the situation, she would not necessarily have erred. As a member of the community, it was open to her to take into account the well-known presence of racism in that community and to evaluate the evidence as to what occurred against that background.[34]

It was a full-fledged, forthright endorsement of judicial recognition that racism infected the Canadian legal system.

THE CONCEPT OF "IMPARTIALITY"

Legal academics point out that the demand for "impartiality" requires that judges behave "as though there might be a social and political consensus" about what "impartiality" and "bias" mean, yet there remains "intense confusion" over both terms.[35] One observer noted that we worry that some people are "too close" to rule justly, but others can be "too far" from the problem, lacking the "experience or knowledge" to render a fair decision.[36] Another suggested that "objectivity" as a norm was "inaccurate as a description," "incoherent as theory," "naïve as sociology and psychology," and "unachievable as method."[37] Critical race theory challenges the "myth" of objectivity and emphasizes that dominance and hierarchy are built into conceptions of judicial impartiality.[38] The world can look different depending on one's place in it.[39]

One year before the *RDS* trial, Corrine Sparks sat on the Canadian Bar Association task force that issued a report on equality, diversity, and accountability. One of its most significant conclusions was that a "white male view" was "not neutral."[40] Most people assume their own way of thinking is "just normal." But white men can find their perspectives "magnified by a culture that reflects their experience back to them," which helps explain why white male perspectives are often touted as "common sense."[41] Audrey Kobayashi, a Queen's professor of geography, race, and gender studies, pointed out that had the *RDS* courtroom been filled entirely with white people, including the judge, the police officer, and the accused, "the same issues of racialization would have applied." It was just unlikely anyone would have recognized them as such.[42] This may also explain why, despite several hundred years of decision making by white judges, Judge Sparks's case was the first judicial race bias complaint to reach the Supreme Court.[43] Discriminatory statements by white males can pass for normal. When antiracists and feminists try to explain their own sense of reality, their statements appear unconventional, aberrant, and askew.

DOUBLE STANDARDS OF ASSESSMENT

RDS was not the first case in Canadian legal history in which a challenge of racial bias might have been launched. George T. Denison, a white magistrate presiding over Toronto courtrooms from 1877 to 1921, described Jews as "neurotic," southern Europeans as "hot-blooded," the Chinese as "degenerate," and Indigenous peoples as "primitive." A supporter of the slave-holding American Confederacy, he depicted Blacks as "child-like savages" and referred disparagingly to the "Negro element" in his cases.[44] William Renwick Riddell, a white Ontario Court of Appeal judge from 1925 to 1945, served as president of the Canadian Social Hygiene Council, an organization that promoted eugenics to accelerate "racial improvement." In his academic writing, Riddell characterized Blacks as incompetent and uncivilized and

Indigenous people as having "savage appetites" in contrast to whites, whom he designated a "higher race."[45]

Other white male judges had expressed racist comments more recently, also without bias appeals. In 1982, Manitoba Court of Appeal justice Alfred Monnin, asked to rule on the exclusion of Indigenous witness testimony, said, "If I had to strike from the record the evidence of drunken Indians that I have heard over the past 25 years, there wouldn't be much left."[46] A 1991 study found "ingrained" racist assumptions in Northwest Territories' decisions: an overemphasis on alcohol use that reinforced "stereotypes of the 'drunken Indian,' improper victim blaming, and a minimization of the harm that sexual assault caused Indigenous women."[47] In 1994, Dalhousie law professor Wayne MacKay noted that some judges "exhibit[ed] racism and sexism" but found themselves "rarely criticized" despite "highly offensive" in-court comments.[48]

Multiple reports on systemic racism implicated judges. The 1989 Marshall Inquiry received complaints that some judges treated racialized minorities disrespectfully.[49] The inquiry heard that one judge had said privately to an attorney: "Don't get your balls caught in a vise over an Indian."[50] The 1995 *Report of the Commission on Systemic Racism in the Ontario Criminal Justice System* compiled more evidence of racist judges: "Most criminal defence lawyers know of judges who have a reputation for holding racist views, or being biased against certain groups (Jews, blacks, etc.)."[51] The 1999 Canadian Bar Association report, *Racial Equality in the Canadian Legal Profession,* disclosed accounts of "judges who seemed to show a bias in the courtroom against a lawyer or client from a racialized community."[52] A 1995 opinion column in the *Halifax Daily News* claimed that "[y]ou would not have to spend 10 minutes in a Nova Scotia court to find examples of white experience colouring judicial decisions."[53] Anthony Ross, a Caribbean-born Black lawyer who practised in Nova Scotia from the 1970s to the late 1990s, recalled "tons of stories about white lawyers and judges making anti-Black comments. None of them faced professional repercussions."[54]

The impunity of white male judges did not extend to Blacks. Challenged for race bias, the renowned Justice A. Leon Higginbotham

The Final Appeal

"Sparks will *fly*"

SUPREME COURT JUDGE UPHOLDS SPARKS DECISION

Following the decision, the Ontario *Law Times,* on 10 November 1997, published a cartoon in which one police officer reads a newspaper covering the Sparks decision while predicting that "Sparks Will Fly."

Jr., an African American judge of the United States Court of Appeals for the Third Circuit, refused to recuse himself in 1974.[55] His stirring words have resonated across borders and time:

> [B]lack lawyers have litigated in the federal courts almost exclusively before white judges, yet they have not urged that white judges should be disqualified on matters of race relations ... As do most blacks, I believe that the corridors of history in the country have been lined with countless instances of racial injustice ... Perhaps, among some whites, there is an inherent disquietude when they see that occasionally blacks are adjudicating matters pertaining to race relations. [P]erhaps that anxiety can be eliminated only by having no black judges sit on such matters [or] by having the latter bend over backwards to the detriment of black litigants and black citizens and thus assure that brand of "impartiality" which some whites think they deserve. [S]hould [black judges] be robots? ... Should they not tell the truth about past injustices?[56]

The controversy that greeted Judges Sparks and Higginbotham posed a marked contrast to the earlier reception accorded white judges David

Doherty and Paul Niedermayer. As Rocky Jones had pointed out to the top court, Doherty and Niedermayer were apparently impervious to bias complaints despite their clear statements about racism. An entrenched double standard ruled the day.

"CONTEXTUALIZED JUDGING"

Although legal realists argue that no judge makes decisions without contextual frameworks shaping his or her thinking, it was a Black female judge's unfamiliar reference to race that first brought the Supreme Court to speak of "contextualized judging" with regard to bias. The concept became explicit only when the life experience of an outsider judge stood out, different from the underlying perspectives of white judges. Once acknowledged at the Supreme Court, contextualized judging brought forth a flurry of discussion.

Some commentators pointed out several risks of using "historically contingent" and "culturally loaded" context to inform judicial decision making. While supporting the L'Heureux-Dubé-McLachlin decision, Dalhousie law professor Richard Devlin noted that "reality" was "much too complex" and "too messy" in our "deeply diversified society" to open up contextualization without incurring risks. He queried whether an "unguarded embrace of contextualism might be read as a licence for other judges to shoot from the hip."[57] Ignoring racism in a racist world could perpetuate discrimination, but recognizing race could potentially have the same effect.[58] For every African Canadian judge whose social context might include police harassment, would white upper-class judges, whose social context might include excessively polite police interactions, feel freer to accept police credibility? Would Chief Justice Lamer be positively encouraged to make specific reference to his "knowledge" of the tendencies of some racialized groups?

Dalhousie law professor Dianne Pothier advocated resolving this problem through the application of Charter values. Contextualized judging should always be "checked against *Charter* values, especially of equality," she wrote.[59] When judges use perspectives that reinforce racial imbalances, it is problematic. When judges use perspectives that

82 Thursday, October 2, 1997   The Chronicle-Herald   The Mail-Star

OPINION

All judiciary members bring experiences to jobs

Joan Jones

SOME TIME ago, I wrote about a well-publicized decision handed down by Judge Corrine Sparks. She had prefaced a decision to acquit a young black man with comments regarding the credibility of some white police officers when dealing with "non-whites."

The police fraternity and the legal community took her to task, implying that she had used her life experiences as an African Canadian when passing sentence. Her well-thought-out decision was subsequently reversed by the Chief Justice of the Nova Scotia Supreme Court trial division, Constance Glube. Chief Justice Glube ordered a new trial.

It is hard to believe that even the most impartial of white judges do not somehow bring to the bench the full baggage of their culture, upbringing and experiences. If it were otherwise, we would have judges without compassion, or empathy. They would, therefore, be no better than machines.

In the decision handed down last Friday, the Supreme Court of Canada agreed with the arguments put forward by Burnley (Rocky) Jones. They reinstated Judge Sparks' original decision to acquit.

The significance of this case, even before the outcome was known, had been felt across Canada. Prior to the Supreme Court giving its decision, this case had already become required reading for many Canadian first-year law students.

So important was this case that six groups were given intervenor status by the Supreme Court of Canada. It could well be the most important case regarding race that the Supreme Court has ever dealt with, outside the aboriginal context. Perhaps it will open the door for more progressive litigation in the field of race relations.

The point that the police fraternity is holding against Judge Sparks is the very same one that African Canadians have been voicing for generations: that members of the entire judicial system bring their race and culture with them on the job. In fact, had it not been for the white majority of this country acting on their biases and experiences, racism would have been eradicated from our society long ago.

The remarks made by Judge Sparks were but a public statement reflecting her own knowledge and experience. We frequently hear allegations of racial biases by police force members. Why would it be acceptable for some members of the judicial system to draw on their life experiences in carrying out their duties, but not for others?

The reality is that the Marshall inquiry has shown the glaring imbalance that exists in our courts. The elevation of Judge Sparks to the bench was but one small step in an attempt to correct this glaring disparity. Becoming the first female African Canadian judge made history then, and she is part of history again.

Requiring that she and other black judges leave their culture and experiences behind them in rendering decisions would all but defeat the purpose of their nominations. It would have the effect of asking them to leave their heritage, their "blackness," behind.

Another important consequence of the Supreme Court decision may well get lost in the shuffle. Mr. Jones, who, along with Dianne Pothier, defended the case in front of the court, is an African Nova Scotian lawyer. He is also a recent graduate of Dalhousie Law School. The current controversy surrounding the Indigenous Black and Mi'kmaq program of the law school would have had us believe that the program produced lower-quality graduates. Burnley Jones (whom I was once

married to) and many other African Canadian and Mi'kmaq lawyers are proving the disbelievers totally wrong.

Very few legal eagles, of any race, can put on their resumes that they have successfully argued and won in front of the highest court in the land - particularly after practising law for only four years.

If this had been the accomplishment of someone from the "old boys club," there is no doubt that many prestigious law firms would now be interviewing him to bring him into their fold.

Could it be that the members of the legal community bring the full baggage of their upbringing, culture, experience and biases when recruiting tomorrow's successful lawyers?

■ *Joan Jones is a metro-area human rights activist.*

On 2 October 1997, in the *Halifax Chronicle-Herald,* Joan Jones argued that "all judiciary members bring experiences to jobs." Although legal realists argue that no judge makes decisions without contextual frameworks, the Supreme Court first spoke of "contexualized judging" in issues relating to racism after Judge Sparks, a Black female judge, referenced race.

diminish racist imbalances, it is something quite different. Judge Sparks evaluated the evidence based on her concern about racist police responses. That is distinct from a judge who evaluates evidence based on a concern that Blacks have a propensity to commit more crime than whites. The former fosters an egalitarian justice system. The latter condones and replicates discrimination. As one media outlet jocularly put it, "some biases are more equal than others."[60]

There is a significant difference between egalitarian perspectives and those that reflect the racial dominance of whites. A bias complaint against a judge who espouses racist analysis is distinct from a bias complaint against a judge who espouses antiracist analysis. To critique both as biased is false parallelism.[61] As Australian law professor Reg Graycar noted, we must "draw a distinction between negatively stereotyping" and "constructively recognizing differences and disadvantage in a way that is sensitive to discrimination and inequality."[62] Justices L'Heureux-Dubé and McLachlin came closest to recognizing this when they indicated that the "reasonable person" who conducts the bias test would be "aware of the history of discrimination faced by disadvantaged groups" and supportive of "the *Charter's* equality provisions."[63] It was a distinction lost on the dissenting trio of judges.

Yet El Jones, Black antiracist activist, former Halifax poet laureate, and fifth chair of women's studies at Mount Saint Vincent University, was disheartened that the women judges did not also speak about the intersectionality of sexism and misogyny. El Jones wished they had addressed how white racism impacts Black *women*. She also emphasized that however important it was to take into account contextualized judging, *RDS* was framed individually, allowing a judge to take his or her own personal experience into account. "Nowhere does anyone talk about structural racism," she added. "It is individualized, no systemic solution there."[64]

Critical race theorist Audrey Kobayashi agreed. Emphasizing that impartiality and contextualized judging were only part "of the story," she wrote:

> The [majority] findings in *RDS* explode the concept of impartiality based on neutrality, which is a major step in recognizing that judicial rationality needs to respond to the context created by a diverse society. [B]ut there is no room for complacency, for in themselves these achievements do little to dismantle the huge wall of systemic racism that encloses our society ...
>
> Systemic racism requires a much more fundamental approach that challenges the basic premises of judicial rationality, addresses the inability of the law to address racism in its everyday manifestations, and asserts law's complicity in setting the boundaries in which racism flourishes. Substituting faces on the bench is not a sufficient measure of social change [when] *all* judgments are made within a racialized context. I do not only want to see discrimination removed from judicial appointments, I want to see the judiciary turned into a force against racism.[65]

12

Epilogue

THE WITNESSES

Rodney Small's first arrest was not his last. Rocky Jones warned him the police would be on the lookout and to steer clear of trouble. But the initial court reversals took a toll on the teenager. He admitted he "started to get involved with things I shouldn't have." In 1995, he pleaded guilty to drug trafficking and served two months in the Waterville youth correction facility. An after-school altercation with a student who called him the N-word resulted in another arrest. Then he dropped out of school.[1]

As he had threatened to do, Small left home before the final ruling and only heard about the decision en route to Toronto.[2] He returned in time to be feted at a victory party at Rocky Jones's home. Years later, he teared up when he remembered the celebration. "Rocky's family accepted me just like family. Joan and Sharon and all of his kids were all there. I knew I was a part of something bigger than just me."[3]

With the help of renewed religious faith, sympathetic teachers, and student support workers, he completed Grade 12 at Queen Elizabeth High and a bachelor of management degree from Dalhousie. An internship at the Black Business Initiative led him to cofound Common Good Solutions, an award-winning social enterprise service assisting young people to start new businesses.[4] The 5557 Cunard Street office

Rodney Small beside Burnley (Rocky) Jones's portrait, Dalhousie Law School, 2018.

had earlier housed Rocky Jones's law office and a community daycare that Rodney attended in his childhood. He volunteered with the 7th Step Society, an organization helping ex-offenders. He supported the Black Lives Matter movement in the wake of the police murder of George Floyd in Minneapolis in 2020, describing the traumatic video as devastating.[5] He protested gentrification's displacement of North End Blacks, a reminder of the forced destruction of Africville.[6]

Reflecting on the turnaround, Small added, "One thing I can tell you is statistically I'm not supposed to be where I am today. [M]any young men that I grew up with are either doing life in prison, or are six feet under the ground."[7] Crediting Jones, he mused: "Man, he was special. When I got convicted on drug charges, Rocky was still, 'Don't give up young fellow, there's more to you. There's something about you.'"[8] He felt similarly toward Judge Sparks. One of his proudest moments was hearing her speak at a Dalhousie law school event. Afterwards, he posed for a photograph with her beside a portrait of the late Rocky Jones.[9]

Donald Stienburg, the arresting officer, enrolled part-time at Dalhousie on top of his police shifts, then took a full semester away from the force between the trial and the final decision. He completed his science degree in 1996. His work ethic stood him in good stead in his career and he was promoted to staff sergeant. Decades later, he emphasized that he "harboured no ill will against Judge Sparks."

I would think a little differently now than then. The Supreme Court judges said her comments were unfortunate and it would have been nice if she hadn't singled me out, but it's water under the bridge. I think it's too bad this had to overshadow all those things she completed. It was more an argument about whether a judge should be able to draw from their experience. It's the same with police officers. Should we be able to draw from experience in making an arrest? It helps to know the courts wanted to straighten out a point of law. It's just really too bad it had to be on that case.[10]

The executive director of the Nova Scotia Police Association, Joe Ross, was harsher: "The judge's remarks were quite unfortunate at the time, but if the Supreme Court upheld the decision, it's really unfortunate."[11]

THE LAWYERS

Rocky Jones, the lawyer at the helm of Rodney Small's case, was fishing out west when the final decision arrived. He felt "amazed" and "pleased" that Sparks had been "vindicated."[12] He called it the "first case" where Blacks were "totally involved all the way through" and recognized "they could protect one of their own." And he commended Rodney Small: "This young kid had no idea what was going on, no idea how significant this was, around this really simple thing of him confronting a cop. Rodney Small, he is the hero of this story."[13]

Jones had little time to rest on his laurels. For six acrimonious years, he and Halifax lawyer Anne Derrick were forced to defend themselves against a costly defamation suit. A white female police officer alleged they damaged her reputation when they claimed she mistreated their clients, three Black teenage girls, because of their race. The case ricocheted from a devastating trial award against the two lawyers, a Nova Scotia Court of Appeal verdict reversal, and a top court denial of leave to appeal that terminated the officer's lawsuit. The stress sparked a heart attack that landed Jones in intensive care for a triple bypass.[14]

Rocky Jones was fishing out west when the final
decision arrived.

Shortly after the *RDS* decision, Jones left Dalhousie Legal Aid. He
worked for two years as counsel for the Canadian Union of Public
Employees and then opened his own law firm, practising criminal,
human rights, employment, and real estate law. Due to his penchant
for representing clients for free, there were some months when he had
trouble making rent.[15] Yet his community work never stalled. With
environmentalist Elizabeth May, he fought to clean up the Sydney Tar
Ponds. He was appointed to the Court Challenges board to distribute
funds for equality cases until the Conservative Harper government
dismantled the program. He advised Parks Canada on the need to
recognize Blacks with historical plaques and monuments. He helped
found Ujamaa, a Black organization to promote community-based
economic sustainability.[16]

Jones's support for Dalhousie's Indigenous Blacks and Mi'kmaq
(IB&M) Initiative never wavered. He recruited more students to enrol

and attended all of its events. Black law students embraced and celebrated him in return, spearheading efforts to commission a formal portrait of him, which was unveiled at the Twenty-Fifth IB&M Initiative Anniversary.[17] Jones was awarded an honorary doctorate by the University of Guelph in 2004 and the Order of Nova Scotia in 2010.[18]

El Jones recalled giving speeches about prison abolition and police brutality in her early years as a Black activist when she was labelled "crazy." She said Rocky's encouragement never faltered: "He would be in the back raising his fist, right on. He would identify young people, train you, nurture you. Dalhousie should have given Rocky $60,000 a year to give the occasional lecture and go about his work as he saw right. He should have had a faculty chair, a Senate seat."[19]

Despite mounting health concerns, Rocky Jones refused to slow his pace. He died in 2013, aged seventy-one, of cardiac arrest and organ failure. His funeral featured African drumming and Mi'kmaw chanting, in recognition of the bridges he had built between Blacks and Indigenous peoples. Judge Sparks was one of the speakers at his Dalhousie memorial service. George Elliott Clarke's homage made mention of *RDS*.[20]

Dianne Pothier, Rodney Small's co-counsel who made the compelling Charter argument at the Supreme Court, continued teaching at Dalhousie, where she was promoted to full professor. She litigated more volunteer cases for LEAF and the DisAbled Women's Network. She received the Frances Fish Women Lawyers Award and was inducted into the Bertha Wilson Honour Society. Her 2012 Canadian Bar Association President's Award ironically followed in the footsteps of Chief Justice Antonio Lamer, who received the award a decade earlier. Jack Major followed both of them in 2015. She published articles on equality and disability law, many cited with approval by Supreme Court judges. One of her best was the analysis of *RDS* she coauthored with Richard Devlin. She rejected the suggestion to let her name stand for appointment to the Supreme Court because it would "distract" from projects that mattered more. She died in Halifax in 2017, aged sixty-two, still engaged in equality litigation.[21]

Yola Grant, who spoke with such authority on behalf of LEAF at the Supreme Court, opened a law firm in Toronto, where she practised employment, labour, and human rights law with Black lawyer Kim Bernhardt and continued to volunteer as counsel for LEAF. In 2014, she was appointed associate chair of the Ontario Human Rights Tribunal. In 2020, she returned to practice, specializing in mediation, arbitration, and investigation. In 2021, she was awarded the Ontario Bar Association's Randall Echlin Mentorship Award for her promotion of racial diversity among adjudicators, particularly Black women and men.[22]

April Burey, who gave the stirring spiritual address at the Supreme Court, was invited to address the American NAACP on the significance of *RDS*.[23] An article she published later recalled the nine white able-bodied justices in their "staid black robes" emitting an "almost audible gasp" when they found themselves faced with a "colourfully clad, intently silent band of people of colour." She wrote:

> My personal engagement with the *RDS* case proved, at once, emotionally moving, physically demanding, and academically challenging. So intense was my effort, I remember being close to tears at the end of my oral presentation ... I find it difficult, even more than a year removed from my appearance ... to put into words my personal sense of disappointment, indignation and even outrage at the appeal of Judge Sparks' decision. I felt a tremendous sadness for what this case said about the state of racism in our country and for what Judge Sparks must have been personally enduring because of it.[24]

Two years and two months after the final *RDS* decision, April Burey died in Toronto.[25] An obituary column in the *Globe and Mail* designated her "one of Jamaica's most exuberant exports to Canada" and described the courtroom during her *RDS* intervention as "crowded with minority rights advocates, including April's own cheering section, who had driven up to Ottawa to watch her slay the dragons."[26]

Rick Miller, the Crown prosecutor at the Halifax trial, secured a permanent position with the Nova Scotia Public Prosecution Service, where he joined Adrian Reid, who had appealed the trial decision.[27] (Reid declined to be interviewed; he was promoted to deputy director in 2003, worked with the new mental health court, and retired in

2014.)[28] Years later, Miller remained convinced that *RDS* had "absolutely nothing to do with race." Watching it progress through the higher courts, he added, "Really, you sit back and marvel at it. I guess it took on a life of its own." He thought the Supreme Court decision misguided.

> One judgment suggested that a judge can take into consideration their own personal perspectives and experiences. And I'm thinking, well, okay, that's great, but if this was some old white guy on the bench who had said, "Well, geez, my experience with Black kids is they steal, assault, cheat," would the Supreme Court have upheld that? I mean, everybody would have been outraged. Maybe I'm misinterpreting things, but I thought it was an odd decision.[29]

Robert Lutes, who lost the prosecution case at the Supreme Court, was seconded to Ottawa by the Department of Justice to revise the *Young Offenders Act.* There, he helped design the 2003 *Youth Criminal Justice Act,* emphasizing reduced incarceration. He coauthored the definitive legal text on the new statute but never returned to the Prosecution Service. He volunteered with the 7th Step Society, where he crossed paths with Rodney Small once more, this time the two of them working in concert toward the successful re-entry of released prisoners.[30]

THE JUDGES

The year of the final *RDS* decision brought Chief Justice Glube, the first Nova Scotia judge to overturn Sparks's ruling, back to Dalhousie law school, where she and Judge Sparks were both honoured with the inaugural Frances Fish Award. Named after Nova Scotia's first female lawyer, the award recognized both women for their respective "firsts."[31] To have the two on the same platform must have carried more than a whiff of irony, but there was no overt evidence of it. Judge Sparks recalled that she had "no personal animus" toward her chief justice.[32] Her judicial colleagues recalled that Glube still believed she had decided

Connie Glube, the first judge to overturn Sparks's ruling, received the Order of Canada from Governor General Michaëlle Jean on 15 December 2006.

RDS correctly.[33] At another Dalhousie law school function, she had rebuked professor Richard Devlin for his legal article critical of her views. There were rumours she considered citing him for contempt.[34]

In 1998, Glube added to her list of firsts when she was elevated to become the first female chief justice of the Nova Scotia Court of Appeal.[35] She was named to the Order of Nova Scotia in 2005 and to the Order of Canada in 2006. She received honorary doctorates from Dalhousie, Mount Saint Vincent, and Saint Mary's. In 2009, the Nova Scotia branch of the Canadian Bar Association established the Constance R. Glube CBA Spirit Award to recognize the achievements of Nova Scotia women lawyers.[36]

In her last years, Glube became less defensive about her decisions, describing herself as stoic in the face of unhappy litigants and lawyers: "They appealed, and if I was overturned, I didn't mind."[37] At a retirement dinner for Claire L'Heureux-Dubé, she spoke openly of her admiration for the retiring judge's courage and added that, in retrospect, she regretted some of her own decisions.[38] Shortly before Glube's death, Dalhousie law dean Kim Brooks recalled discussing *RDS* with her. "You know," commented Glube, "I think I just got that one wrong."[39] Connie Glube died, aged eighty-four, in 2016.

Ted Flinn, the Nova Scotia appeal judge who overruled Judge Sparks, received an honorary doctorate from Saint Mary's University in 1998, two years before Glube. The citation praised his contributions to the Halifax community and his profession. He died in Halifax, aged sixty-six, in 2002.[40] Ronald Pugsley, Flinn's colleague who signed the decision to overrule Judge Sparks, was honoured with Dalhousie's Weldon Award for Unselfish Public Service in 1999. He predeceased his colleague Ted Flinn, after a sudden illness in 2000. His burial site in the Fairview Lawn Cemetery bears the epigraph: "By Your Decisions Will You Be Known."[41]

Gerald Freeman, the lone dissenting Nova Scotia judge, moved back home to Beach Meadows on Nova Scotia's South Shore at the fork of the Medway and Wildcat Rivers. There, he settled his voluminous library into a country cottage, devoting his retirement years to poetry, English literature, nature, and country living.[42] Interviewed the year before his death, he recalled little jubilation in Halifax when the Supreme Court reversed so many Nova Scotia judges on the issue of racial bias: "It wasn't much celebrated, no." But Freeman himself was "very pleased." "I knew that I was playing pretty fast digs then," he smiled, "and to be supported by the Supreme Court of Canada was a real feather in my hat, I thought."[43] Gerald Freeman died in 2020. His *Halifax Chronicle-Herald* obituary listed his *RDS* dissent as one of his most important decisions.[44]

In 2001, two years after his retirement, Supreme Court judge Peter Cory acknowledged that he had "forgotten [Judge Sparks's] exact words" but characterized them as "certainly racist with regard to white officers in a Black district." He added that he hoped that "she will never talk in that way again."[45] His comments went much further than anything in his 1997 decision. It may have been a lapse in memory, or it may simply reveal what he thought but did not state at the time. He died, aged ninety-four, in 2020.[46]

In a more recent interview from Calgary, the dissenting Supreme Court judge Jack Major seemed moved to learn about Judge Sparks's career challenges and Nova Scotia race history. He did not dispute that all judges were influenced by their upbringing: "I think judges consciously or otherwise make up their mind on their life experience. If you did a psychoanalysis, you'd find I think that somewhere growing up they encountered a situation that informed what they think." He also agreed that minority judges' experiences might factor into decision making:

> It seems to me so logical that a Black judge couldn't help but harbour some suspicion that a white police officer, most white police officers, don't give Blacks a fair deal. That seems just part of the society we lived in. You can have well-founded biases. I think that's what this judge [Connie Sparks] had. I didn't attach a whole lot of malice to what she said. I thought what she said was completely accurate. White officers did not treat Blacks or Indians and maybe Asians the same way as they treated white people. I think that it probably is less evident as we speak today, but I think it still occurs. I feel some sympathy for this judge, but from my perspective, she just expressed a valid opinion in the wrong place. What she said was true. But it wasn't in evidence.
>
> You may think I'm just being stubborn, but in a trial, you rely on evidence. If there had been evidence of systemic prejudice, I would have been on board, and I think John [Sopinka] and Tony [Lamer] would have too. Or if she had just said, "The police aren't always believable," if she had stopped there, it would have been all right. She should not have made those remarks.[47]

"I reread my reasons," he added, "and thought they were very good, although my colleagues didn't think much of them. I would rule the same way today."[48]

Claire L'Heureux-Dubé, whose Supreme Court decision supported Sparks, retired in 2002, showered with accolades for her decisions opposing discrimination against women and LGBT communities. *RDS* represented the high-water mark of her jurisprudential legacy on race.[49]

It was a position opposed to the fabled "Gang of Five" and reflected her visible animus toward Chief Justice Lamer, whose interjections at the oral hearing had been so disruptive.[50] In retrospect, she was most pleased that she and Justice McLachlin had been able to cosign the concurring opinion supporting Judge Sparks. "There were occasions where we were at odds with each other. But we were on *RDS* together."[51]

In 2000, Beverley McLachlin, the other Supreme Court judge to support Sparks, replaced Lamer as the first female chief justice of Canada, an achievement that vaulted past Connie Glube's distinction as the first female chief justice of a province. The appointment positioned her as chair of the Canadian Judicial Council and of the board of the National Judicial Institute, the organization devoted to the continuing education of judges.[52] As chief justice, she completed an instructional video for the judicial advisory committees that vetted applications for federal judgeships. Choosing *RDS* to illustrate the importance of judicial diversity, she described how a Black female judge acquitted a Black youth charged with assaulting a police officer. She explained that the judge noted in passing that police had been known to overreact and mislead when dealing with non-white groups. Without mentioning that five of the nine Supreme Court judges had criticized Sparks's racial remarks, McLaughlin endorsed contextual judging: "The issue on appeal was whether this showed bias. The Supreme Court rejected this argument, holding that the judge, as a member of the community, was entitled to take into account the well-known presence of racism in that community and to evaluate the evidence of what occurred against that background." With her last words, that "a final test of judging in a diverse society is the challenge of maintaining confidence in the justice system," she transformed *RDS* into a model of how to improve the Canadian justice system of the future.[53] Beverley McLachlin retired in 2017.

JUDGE CONNIE SPARKS

The challenges facing Judge Sparks intensified after the final *RDS* ruling. Venomous letters, mostly anonymous, arrived in the mail claiming that she should not be on the bench, that she should not have raised racism, that she should "know her place." The writers threatened her, her father, and her mother, and added that they could "find out where she lived."[54]

The lawyers and judges disgruntled with the reversal of the Nova Scotia rulings were also not quick to forget. Sparks's judicial colleague Sandra Oxner observed that "many people were surprised and strongly disagreed – some to the point of being infuriated."[55] Judge Pamela S. Williams, appointed to the Provincial Court in 2003, reflected back to what she thought of the reaction when she was still a lawyer: "The [Halifax] legal community for the most part was not in favour of the *RDS* decision. They saw themselves as quite a knowledgeable, intellectual, smart group of people who didn't see themselves as racist, so, therefore, they didn't see racism."[56]

The media added fuel to the fire. Black columnist Charles Saunders claimed that after Judge Sparks was "vindicated," those who "pilloried her" were "wiping egg off their faces."[57] Opposing columnist Harry Flemming retorted that the top court's six-to-three "mixed message" was no victory but a cautionary warning for Judge Sparks: "Her lip was outdistancing her brain. If she wishes to play journalist, sociologist, community activist, or political candidate ... let her resign from the bench and follow a better calling."[58]

In 1999, all the judges from the stand-alone Family Court were elevated to the newly created Unified Family Court, a division of the Nova Scotia Supreme Court.[59] All but one. Judge Sparks, the most senior woman and only Black, was omitted. It was in blunt contrast to Connie Glube, who had seen her career advance after *RDS*. The Liberal cabinet of Prime Minister Jean Chrétien made the appointments upon the advice of Justice Minister Anne McLellan, but rumours had it that local interference kept Judge Sparks out. Glube would have had some sway as chief justice, but observers suggested there were many others who weighed in as well.

El Jones, an African Nova Scotian antiracist activist, saw it as retribution for acknowledging racism: "People understood it would impact her career, that she would never be promoted."[60] Sparks's former law partner Douglas Ruck called it part of a pattern: "Many careers have been terminated as a consequence of somebody taking a principled stand."[61] Law professor Esmeralda Thornhill, then Dalhousie's Chair of Black Canadian Studies, wrote to McLellan of the "widespread disbelief and shock" in the African Canadian community over her "unfathomable" decision. That someone of Judge Sparks's "legal standing and public stature" had been treated so "discreditably" was "an earth-shattering shock."[62] Gerald Freeman did not disagree. "I know of no reason why [Judge Sparks] shouldn't have been appointed to the Unified Family Court," he said. "I can only suspect that it was the general prejudice that I didn't share. And I suspect it existed."[63]

African Nova Scotian social worker Robert S. Wright, familiar with Sparks's judging in Family Court, described himself as "livid":

> She was the senior judge on that court. She had extended generous assistance to many of the people who were appointed over her. Not only was she not appointed, but because Family Court disappeared in Halifax, she became a judge without a courtroom. *RDS* established that reasonable people are supposed to understand how racism works and be responsive to that – if you are police officer, prosecutor, judge. That challenges the entire system. As the implications of *RDS* continued to roll out, that maelstrom did not subside. It expanded. They were gunning for her.[64]

Because her initial appointment was to the Family Court, and not to the wider Provincial Court, Sparks could not simply shift to hearing cases in other courts. She was, indeed, "a judge without a courtroom."

There were petitions of protest from Dalhousie law school. Picketers showed up when McLellan next came to deliver a guest lecture.[65] Protesters gathered outside the Nova Scotia Supreme Court.[66] The African United Baptist Association held a press conference in protest. The entire provincial NDP caucus sent a complaint to Justice Minister McLellan. Questions were raised in the Canadian Senate, the House of Commons, and the Nova Scotia legislative assembly.[67] Gus Wedderburn of the Nova Scotia Black Lawyers Association called it "plain racism" that set back the cause "one hundred years."[68] The *Toronto Star* reported a "fireball of criticism" from Black lawyers, their associations,

Judge Sparks, ca. 1996.

and the "opposition caucus."[69] A campaign from Black elementary school students made headlines in the *National Post:* "Youngsters add voices. Only black jurist in court. Corrine Sparks left out in Nova Scotia restructuring."[70]

Judge Sparks kept her thoughts to herself when she was assigned to courtrooms outside of the Unified Family Court jurisdiction and required to drive to Truro, Kentville, Shubenacadie, and Windsor. She helped organize multiple national and international judicial education events, including workshops designed to bring African Nova Scotian communities and judges together to enhance reciprocal understanding.[71] She completed a Dalhousie graduate degree, a master's in law, in 2001.[72] Her 243-page thesis was titled "Africville: Reparation in the Paradoxical Legal Construction and Deconstruction of an African Canadian community."[73] She launched an innovative project with the law school to support African Nova Scotian and Indigenous lawyers interested in becoming judges. She sustained herself through religious faith, gardening, travel, and music, especially jazz festivals.[74]

Yet the indignities continued to mount. She was moved to a tiny office in an alcove storage area, where she was segregated from the other staff and judges. Lacking a proper office, forced to commute through all kinds of weather to far-flung courtrooms, she found her health suffering. Some of the other judges alleged that she was not working hard enough; one even monitored her dockets and court schedules. Although not all colleagues participated in the critiques, the general disrespect, derogatory comments, and insensitivity rendered the environment

toxic. Judge Sparks increasingly found judicial meetings too poison-
ous to attend. Then she discovered that, in her absence, the judges had
discussed her work schedule and her missed meetings, with one critic
suggesting that something should be done, that her judicial allowance
should be revoked.[75]

Concerned that her colleagues were pressuring her to quit, Judge
Sparks decided it was necessary to respond. She complained to her
chief judge about interference, bullying, and an infringement on her
judicial independence under the *Provincial Court Act* (PCA). She also
filed a complaint with the Human Rights Commission alleging that
three judicial colleagues had singled her out for differential treatment
because she was Black and female. She chose to do this away from
public view, telling no one, not even her parents. The PCA complaint
was settled when the chief judge attested that her work ethic and
professionalism were unquestionable. He admitted that her office
conditions were inadequate, advised that judicial allowances were ir-
revocable, and offered a seminar for the judges on respect in the
workplace. Judge Sparks withdrew the human rights complaint when
the commission advised her that she would have to name the chief
judge as a respondent due to his institutional responsibility. She did
not believe he personally deserved to become a respondent. She broke
her silence about these complaints only after her retirement in 2021.[76]

In contrast to the icy environment in the courthouse, tributes recognizing Judge Sparks's stature began to mount. Despite her reticence
over public recognition, the Canadian Association of Black Lawyers
(CABL) hosted an event in her honour one month after the final *RDS*
decision.[77] In 2002, she received an award from the Congress of Black
Women and in 2003 from the Elizabeth Fry Society.[78] When Dalhousie's
Black Law Students' Association created the Judge Corrine Sparks
Award to recognize students using legal education as a tool for change,
over two hundred guests arrived for the inaugural presentation. Rocky
Jones was in attendance, beaming with pride for Judge Sparks.[79] In
2008, she received the Touchstone Award from the Canadian Bar Association for promotion of equality in law.[80] More distinctions followed:
the Harry Jerome African Canadian Achievement Award for Excellence

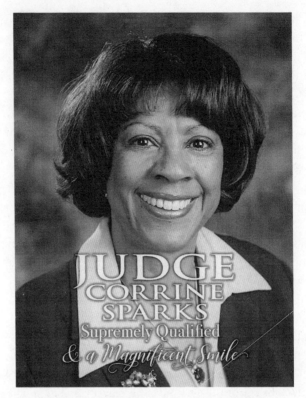

JUDGE
CORRINE
SPARKS
Supremely Qualified
& a Magnificent Smile

The program cover to celebrate Judge Corrine Sparks's
thirty years on the bench. The event, at Sparks's request,
included all African Nova Scotian judges appointed after
her. African drummers led a procession of seven judges
and guest speakers.

in Law in 2008, the Bertha Wilson Honour Society in 2015, the Weldon
Award for Unselfish Public Service in 2020, the appointment in 2021
as commissioner to the Land Titles Initiative to review African Nova
Scotian claims for clear title to their lands, and an honorary doctorate
from Mount Saint Vincent University in 2022.[81]

Although her well-deserved promotion never materialized, in 2018
organizers requested permission to celebrate her thirty years on the
bench. Sparks demurred, reluctant to become the centre of public

attention. Only when the plan was revised to include all the African Nova Scotian judges appointed after her did she consent. On 9 February 2018, African drummers led a procession of seven African Nova Scotian judges and guest speakers before a large and enthusiastic crowd of dignitaries, judges, lawyers, and community members.[82] African American journalist Evelyn C. White described it as an entrance marked by dignity, decorum, and protocol with a "definitive African influence." One of the new judges described herself as "speechless" at the auspicious occasion and chose to sing an acapella gospel song instead of spoken remarks. "I got the sense that the community there felt a sense of what had been accomplished, the meaning of Corrine Sparks and her position," added White. "It was awe-striking. It was a magnificent moment."[83]

Valerie Miller, the second Black female judge, appointed to the Tax Court of Canada in 2007, spoke that night to acknowledge that Judge Sparks's appointment had "inspired all visible minorities to dream large." Jean Whalen, the third Black female judge, appointed to the Provincial and Family Courts in 2009, asked the audience to think back to where they were when they first heard that Judge Sparks was appointed to the bench. It was a "historical moment" that opened up recognition that "all things are possible." Juanita Westmoreland-Traoré, the first Black judge in Quebec, who had travelled from Montreal, credited much of the growing diversity on the bench to Sparks's *RDS* decision. Although she knew that Sparks was "uncomfortable" talking about the case or the recriminations that followed, Westmoreland-Traoré emphasized that it was important to "bear witness" to her courage. She extolled Connie Sparks as "one of the most distinguished judges in our country."[84]

CONCLUSION

Rodney Small

An infinite number of conclusions could be drawn from *RDS*. To lay out the detailed dimensions – how it originated, who it implicated, how it was argued, how it was decided, what it left in its wake – is to invite diverse reflections. There is enough open space to think in multiple and different ways about what this case means.

My thoughts can be summarized briefly. I believe this case illustrates the failure of the legal system to examine police abuses of power. A case that began with a white officer in a minor skirmish with a Black teenager led to choke holds, handcuffs, and criminal charges of assaulting a police officer. *RDS* was first and foremost a case about policing. It should have attracted serious scrutiny over the interaction between the police and an African Nova Scotian youth. Some observers believed that the situation should have resulted in a criminal charge and policing complaint against the officer. That it somehow transformed itself into a complaint of racial bias against a Black judge is truly astonishing. The position the defence took at trial was that the policing was seriously out of proportion to the situation. That faded from view almost immediately. The pressing issue of racism and policing, a documented concern of long standing for the African Nova Scotian community, disappeared as the appellate courts and surrounding commentators trained their eyes on Canada's first Black female judge.

I think the case also unveils a legal system seriously unskilled in assessing racism. It exposes the insularity, white privilege, and white fragility of powerful lawyers and judges. That this was our first judicial race bias case suggests that Canada has run a mile from grappling with issues of racism. There was insufficient legal language available to tackle the complexities of racism and antiracism, and the distinctions between the two. *RDS* illustrates how supposedly neutral practices exacerbate inequalities within the web of rules, habits, and prejudices that make up our legal system. It is obvious that we can no longer take refuge in simplistic notions of "objectivity" and "bias," yet a sophisticated racial and gendered appreciation of the concepts remains elusive.

That *RDS* became a focal point for antiracist resistance allows us to recognize and applaud the courage and strength of the African Nova Scotian and broader African Canadian community, which continued to mount sustained pressure for change in the years that followed. Even as this book goes to press, the case has provided the inspiration for an impressive academic conference of thirty-one scholars, the majority of them racialized professors. "Locating RDS in the 21st Century" will be held at the University of Windsor Faculty of Law in September 2022. In a brilliant 2022 article, retired professor Esmeralda Thornhill has also offered a fresh appraisal of the burgeoning commentary on *RDS,* critiquing the dissection and probing that many writers have trained upon the multiple top court judgments as "gnawing away" at the significance of Judge Sparks's historic trial decision.[1]

The fuller narrative of the case also allows us to peer into the terrible costs of this battle for all the principal actors but primarily for Judge Sparks, Rodney Small, and Donald Stienburg. Too often we forget the personal pain and anguish that accompany legal milestones. Some observers might query whether the police officer suffered harm to the same degree as Rodney Small and Judge Sparks. While the harms may not have been parallel or equal, it is clear from Donald Stienburg's comments that he experienced harm. In my view, it would be wrong not to take account of all of the pain involved. We tend to single out individual "bad apples" when confronting race discrimination. While this frequently leaves systemic and institutional racism unaddressed and wider changes unimplemented, it also visits real harm upon all of the individuals connected to the event.

I continue to find it significant that it took 122 years for a race bias case to surface at the Supreme Court of Canada. Certainly, it was not for lack of racism on the bench in the earlier decades. Tracing the convoluted path that brought the case to the top court exposes the access-to-justice heights that had to be scaled.[2] Rodney Small, without funds or legal knowledge, had to find a skilled defence lawyer. The staff at the Black United Front had to provide the pivotal link to the Dalhousie Legal Clinic. Dalhousie's precarious clinic funding had been the cause of consternation just a few years earlier; fortunately for Rodney, it had survived intact.

Most legal-aid lawyers would have viewed *RDS* as a simple case and recommended that a youthful first offender plead guilty for a community-service order, which would have brought the case to a halt. Most lawyers would not have recognized the race dimensions of the arrest or risked the danger of raising racism. Rocky Jones was unusual, one of only a few Black lawyers and an antiracism crusader. How did Jones get to the Dalhousie Legal Clinic? He had come through Dalhousie's Indigenous Blacks & Mi'kmaq (IB&M) Initiative, which he had been instrumental in setting up in the aftermath of the Marshall Inquiry. Challenged to sign up himself, he had become a member of its first graduating class. Like most of the other early IB&M grads, his professional options were circumscribed. He was not hired by any Halifax law firm. He was working at the clinic.

The Blackness of the courtroom that morning contributed to an unbalancing of the customary racial hierarchies, discomfiting the white participants and opening the space for counsel and judge to speak about race. The only Black female judge in the country was sitting on the bench. Things might have terminated after the acquittal, but for the efforts of the white police and prosecutors to staunch the overt references to race. When the Nova Scotia Supreme Court reversed Judge Sparks's decision, things might have stopped again, but for Rocky Jones's insistence that the appeals continue.

Without funding from the Court Challenges Program and Dalhousie University, without the expertise of Dalhousie law professors and students, Jones would not have been able to carry on. Without the energy and organizing talents of Lynn Jones and her networks, and the generosity of the white law students who dispersed to the alternate viewing room, the audience that faced the Supreme Court judges on the day of oral arguments would not have resembled "a sea of Black faces." Had the case been heard a decade earlier, the antiracist and feminist intervener organizations that stepped in to strengthen the defence argument would not have existed. The formerly all-male Supreme Court had opened its doors to women only fifteen years earlier. Without the resistance of the two women judges, the final ruling might have gone the other way.

I am left with as many questions as answers. Was there something about Nova Scotia that made it an obvious venue for *RDS*? It would be wrong to suggest that anti-Black racism is more severe in Nova Scotia than in our other Canadian regions, any one of which could have furnished similar catalysts. But Nova Scotia was home to the oldest embedded Black communities, with centuries of settlement behind them, and its Black United Front, although in danger of imminent demise, was highly instrumental. Dalhousie housed the only Canadian law school with an enhanced admissions program for Blacks. The Nova Scotia judiciary boasted the first Black female judge. The province's political, economic, and cultural history had produced a cohesive, entrenched white hierarchy insistent upon defending itself from external critique. It was a potent mix for the protracted clash that occurred.

Was the decision too confusing, a missed opportunity for the legal recognition of racism? Or was it a helpful start, a stable foundation on which to move forward, a building block for the next foray? Given law's inherent conservatism, is incrementalism about all we can expect? And what if the judges had ruled differently, unanimously pronouncing Judge Sparks biased? With three different decisions, it would not have taken much for the dissent to carry the day. Would that have been disastrous for Black judges, lawyers, and communities? Or might it have proven a "useful loss"? Like the misogynistic *Murdoch* decision that provoked sweeping legislative reform of family law in the 1970s and '80s, might a negative decision have inspired wider political protest, resulting in a deeper overhaul of the judiciary and faster, more substantial change?[3]

Will greater racial diversity in the legal profession and the judiciary diminish discrimination? That Nova Scotia's most visible antiracist lawyer led Rodney Small's defence must offer some clue as to the significance of diversity. That Canada's first Black female judge recognized the race implications of Halifax police practices offers still more. That the only two female judges on the top court were the ones who wrote to endorse Judge Sparks's words affirms that assessment. That the first female chief justice, Constance Glube, rejected Judge Sparks's words recommends caution in drawing any firm conclusions. Inclusivity must surely be a step forward, but we need to recognize the pressures on outsiders to assimilate, and the grave risks they face, exacerbated because they are outsiders, when they deviate from traditional protocols. Are there ways to reduce the pressures on outsider lawyers and judges? What would it mean to *welcome* newcomers? Can racialized organizations that support their members with safe spaces for consultation and mentoring sustain themselves?

What factors continue to prevent the calling out of white racism within the legal system? Despite centuries of racial inequities, discussions about anti-Black racism have rarely registered inside our courts. Against all odds, *RDS* upended those silences, forcing police, lawyers, judges, academics, the media, and the wider society to debate racism. It catapulted the law into the centre of pained and tumultuous debates. Did *RDS* enhance free speech or contribute to greater silencing about claims of racism? For every lawyer or judge who draws strength from Judge Sparks's courage, many will have learned the lesson that voicing racism will invite retribution. Why is it so easy for whites to see what we often characterize as racism against us but not to recognize racism against racialized minorities? If whites have difficulty identifying race discrimination against minorities, and minorities are intimidated into silence, who counts as the "reasonable person" in assessing the "apprehension of bias"?

What forms of antiracism education might help solve these problems? Examining the issues through the lens of history has the benefit of allowing learners to grapple with challenging matters without feeling personally implicated. Conversely, historical approaches may leave audiences shrugging their shoulders at the suggestion that racism continues unabated. Some educational materials appear to be persuasive, others less so. Still others seem to generate the very hostility they are intended to defuse. Generic programs aimed at homogeneous audiences may prove ineffective for delivery to learners at different stages. Rigorous evaluation of educational initiatives will be essential in aiding antiracism educators to accomplish their objectives.

Did *RDS* effect actual legal change? Has its legacy helped to dismantle racism on the ground? One could chronicle some significant victories achieved at great cost since 1997, but to understand the complexities of our current situation would take many books. Historians typically examine the past, relieved that we can deal with stable pieces of evidence in a particular time frame. The demanding task of documenting the moving target of current jurisprudence and newly emerging sociolegal trends is probably best shouldered by others. For those who would prefer this narrative end with a definitive update on what courts have done following *RDS*, I regret to disappoint.

The impermanence of our legal, social, economic, and political worlds makes updates transitory. Movements toward race and gender equality are never straight-line trajectories up or down. Swelling waves of improvement meet troughs of backlash. What is clear is that the opportunities opened by *RDS* have the potential to move us forward. Whether the momentum materializes or continues, in what form, and for how long rests with all of us.

RDS is one of the most important legal decisions on race in Canadian history. Disrupting the "racelessness" that our legal system has long revered, it upended some of the silences about the race biases interconnecting law and society. This case compelled lawyers, judges, and communities to begin to wrestle with turbulent debates over policing, lawyering, and judging. The theatrical drama of the *RDS* trial and appeals was unprecedented for its time and remains unparalleled to date. *RDS* can rightly be acclaimed a watershed moment that will long outlast the principal actors involved.

It has left seeds of change in unexpected places. In a remarkable 2019 interview, retired Nova Scotia chief justice J. Michael MacDonald expressed the view that there was now a "positive duty on a trial judge to do what Judge Sparks did." He added: "It is mandatory to not only articulate the racist dynamics that are happening, but to educate yourself on them, if you are not familiar with them first-hand as Judge Sparks was."[4] The long-range impact of *RDS* awaits the verdicts of future generations, yet it is apparent today that judicial race bias, racism in policing, and racism within the larger legal system are open for transformation.

Chronology

1941   Burnley Allen (Rocky) Jones born, Truro, Nova Scotia.

1949   Nova Scotia Association for the Advancement of Coloured People (NSAACP) is established.

1953   Corrine Etta (Connie) Sparks born, Lake Loon, Nova Scotia, 13 August.

1961   Rocky Jones, age twenty, marries Joan Bonner in Oakville, Ontario.

1969   Black United Front (BUF) is established.

1971   Donald Marshall Jr., age seventeen, a Mi'kmaw from Membertou Reserve in Sydney, is wrongly convicted of murdering his African Nova Scotian friend, Sandy Seale, and sentenced to life imprisonment.

1974   Connie Sparks obtains a BA from Mount Saint Vincent University, age twenty-one.

       Rocky Jones obtains a BA from Dalhousie University, age thirty-three.

1977   Constance Glube appointed the first woman to the Nova Scotia Supreme Court.

1978   Rodney Darren Small born in Halifax, 3 July.

1979   Connie Sparks obtains an LLB (bachelor of laws) from Dalhousie University, Faculty of Law, age twenty-six.

1980   Connie Sparks called to the Nova Scotia bar, 19 February.

       Connie Sparks practises law as in-house lawyer in Calgary, later returning to Halifax to open a practice with Helen Foote.

1981   Connie Sparks begins law practice with the firm of Ruck & Mitchell, Halifax.

1982   Constance Glube appointed chief justice of Nova Scotia, the first woman in Canada.

1983   Donald Marshall Jr.'s wrongful conviction overturned by Supreme Court of Nova Scotia (Appeal Division), in a decision continuing to cast blame on Marshall.

1986   Appointment of the Royal Commission on the Donald Marshall, Jr., Prosecution, 28 October.

1987   Corrine E. Sparks, age thirty-four, sworn in to the Nova Scotia Family Court, the first African Nova Scotian judge in the history of the province, and the first Black female judge in Canada, 25 March.

1989   *Report of the Royal Commission on the Donald Marshall, Jr., Prosecution.*

        Inauguration of the Indigenous Blacks & Mi'kmaq (IB&M) Initiative to encourage Indigenous Black and Mi'kmaw admissions at Dalhousie Law School.

        Rocky Jones enters Dalhousie law school, age forty-nine, one of three Black students in the IB&M first cohort.

        Cole Harbour High School brawl between Black and white students creates public furor.

1991   Racial disturbance in downtown Halifax involving physical violence and property damage leads to charges of racially motivated mistreatment on part of Halifax police. The "three nights of fury" draw national and international headlines and result in a provincial inquiry.

1992   Rocky Jones graduates with an LLB from Dalhousie law school, age fifty-one, and is selected as valedictorian of the class.

        Judge Sparks appointed to the Canadian Bar Association's Task Force on Gender Equality in the Legal Profession.

1993   Altercation between Rodney Small, age fifteen, and Constable Donald Stienburg, age twenty-eight, 17 October.

        Arrest of Rodney Small and release on his own recognizance, 17 October.

        Information laid with three criminal charges against Rodney Small under ss. 270(1)(a), 270(1)(b), and 129(a) of the Criminal Code, 10 November.

        First appearance in Youth Court, Rodney Small enters a plea of "not guilty," 7 December.

        Rocky Jones called to the bar, age fifty-two.

        Canadian Bar Association releases the *Report of the Task Force on Gender Equality in the Legal Profession,* of which Judge Sparks is a member.

1994   Rodney Small's trial in Nova Scotia Youth Court, Halifax, 2 December.

        Reasons for judgment of Judge Corrine E. Sparks, Halifax Youth Court, 2 December.

        Press seeks access to tape of proceeding at hearing before Judge Sparks, 7 December.

Judge Sparks rejects request for access to the tape, December 17.

Notice of appeal of Rodney Small's acquittal filed with Nova Scotia Supreme Court by Attorney General of Nova Scotia, 22 December.

1995   Supplementary reasons for judgment of Judge Corrine E. Sparks, 13 January.

Rocky Jones and Anne Derrick (a Halifax lawyer) denounce the strip search of three school-age African Nova Scotian girls conducted by a white female police officer, 5 April. (Carol Campbell, the white female police officer, brings suit for damages for defamation against Rocky Jones and Anne Derrick in October.)

Constance Glube, chief justice of the Supreme Court of Nova Scotia, quashes Rodney Small's acquittal, sending the case back for a new trial before a different judge. Hearing and oral decision 18 April; reasons for judgment, 27 April.

Ian H. Palmeter, associate chief justice of the Supreme Court of Nova Scotia, grants the appeal of Judge Sparks's order to deny the press access to the tape recording of the trial. Written reasons, 12 May.

Notice of appeal of Rodney Smith's case to Nova Scotia Court of Appeal, 18 May.

Judgment of the Court of Appeal of Nova Scotia (Justices Pugsley, Flinn, and Freeman and reasons for judgment, 25 October).

Notice of application for leave to appeal to Supreme Court of Canada by Rodney Small, 20 December.

1996   Application for leave to appeal to Supreme Court of Canada granted, 6 May.

Castor Williams, second Black judge in Nova Scotia, appointed to Nova Scotia Provincial Court.

1997   Supreme Court of Canada oral submissions from counsel, 10 March.

Supreme Court of Canada decision, *R.D.S. v. Her Majesty the Queen,* 26 September.

Complaint about Chief Justice Lamer's racial stereotyping comments filed by the Chinese Canadian National Council with the Canadian Judicial Council, 28 October.

1998   Canadian Judicial Council releases text of letter closing file on complaint about Chief Justice Lamer, 23 January.

1999   Creation of Unified Family Court in Nova Scotia. Protests ensue over nonelevation of Judge Sparks.

2001   Judge Sparks receives LLM (masters of laws) degree from Dalhousie Law School.

Trial of the racial defamation action against Rocky Jones and Anne Derrick based on 1995 statements results in a finding of liability with damages and costs awarded against them totalling $315,000.

2002   Nova Scotia Court of Appeal reverses trial award of damages for defamation against Rocky Jones and Anne Derrick.

2013   Rocky Jones, age seventy-one, dies on 29 July of organ failure.

2016   Constance Glube, retired chief justice of the Supreme Court of Nova Scotia, age eighty-four, dies on 15 February.

2018   Celebration of thirty years of African Nova Scotian judges, Halifax.

2020   Gerald B. Freeman, retired Court of Appeal justice, age eighty-nine, dies on 1 June.

2021   Judge Sparks, age sixty-eight, retires, 31 December 2021. She was subsequently appointed a Land Titles Initiative commissioner, a land ownership adjudicator assisting residents to obtain clear title in historic African Nova Scotian communities.

Notes

ACKNOWLEDGMENTS

1 Interview with Joan Jones, Halifax, 15 August 2018.

INTRODUCTION

1 *R. v. S. (R.D.),* [1997] 3 S.C.R. 484.

2 Nell Irvin Painter, *The History of White People* (New York: W.W. Norton, 2010); Constance Backhouse, *Colour-Coded: A Legal History of Racism in Canada, 1900–1950* (Toronto: University of Toronto Press, 1999).

3 The *New York Times* explains that it capitalizes "Black" when it describes people and cultures of African origin, because it signifies a race and a culture rather than a colour: Nancy Coleman, "Why We're Capitalizing Black," *New York Times* (5 July 2020) A2. The earliest printed appeal for capitalizing "Negro" appears in an 1878 editorial by Ida B. Wells in the *Chicago Conservator,* which she owned and edited: Margaret Busby, ed., *Daughters of Africa: An International Anthology of Words and Writings of Women of African Descent from the Ancient Egyptian to the Present* (New York: Ballantine, 1994) at 150–51. Terminology of choice has shifted over time and place, for example, Negro, coloured, Black, Person of Colour, BIPOC.

4 Interview with George Elliott Clarke, Toronto, 6 September 2019. Robin W. Winks, a Yale University historian, published the original text in 1971; it was republished as *The Blacks in Canada: A History,* 2nd ed. (Montreal/Kingston: McGill-Queen's University Press, 1977).

5 Constance Backhouse, *Petticoats and Prejudice: Women and Law in Nineteenth-Century Canada* (Toronto: Women's Press, 1991).

6 Constance Backhouse, *Colour-Coded: A Legal History of Racism in Canada, 1900–1950* (Toronto: University of Toronto Press, 1999) is an earlier contribution.

7 Two proceedings before the Nova Scotia Supreme Court and one before the Nova Scotia Court of Appeal have no transcripts. Because the first involved a successful media-access lawsuit, all were covered by the press.

8 Judges are traditionally not prepared to speak publicly about their decisions, but several of the fifteen judges involved agreed to interviews after their retirement.

9 Unless otherwise indicated, all interviews were conducted by Constance Backhouse.

10 Patricia Monture-Angus, *Thunder in My Soul* (Halifax: Fernwood, 1995) at 210. I thank Evelyn C. White, the author of *Alice Walker: A Life* (New York: W.W. Norton, 2004), for her insight into the importance of attempting to temper such damage. Interview with Evelyn C. White, Halifax, 22 May 2018.

11 The Commission, *Royal Commission on the Donald Marshall, Jr., Prosecution,* 7 vols. (Halifax: Province of Nova Scotia, 1989).

12 *R. v. Ipeelee,* [2012] 1 S.C.R. 433.

13 The Canadian Judicial Council (and its counterpart provincial judicial councils) is composed of judges who assess such complaints internally. In the 1990s, the judicial councils began to receive complaints alleging racial and gender bias, religious bias, conflicts of interest, inappropriate or insensitive language, and undue delay in rendering judgments. Among the allegations of racial or anti-Semitic misconduct against federally and provincially appointed judges prior to *RDS* were the Donald J. Marshall Jr./Nova Scotia Court of Appeal complaint (1990); the NWT Minister of Justice/Bourassa J. complaint (1990); the Taylor/Whealy J. complaint (1994, 1998); the Théberge/Bienvenue J. complaint (1996); the Twinn and Ermineskin Tribal Council/Muldoon J. complaint (1997).

14 Early research into judicial council oversight includes Richard Devlin and Sheila Wildeman, "Introduction: Disciplining Judges – Exercising Statecraft" and "The Canadian Judicial Council's (Elusive) Quest for Legitimacy," in Richard Devlin and Sheila Wildeman, eds., *Disciplining Judges: Contemporary Challenges and Controversies* (Northampton, MA: Edward Elgar, 2021) 1, 49; Richard Devlin and Adam Dodek, *Regulating Judges: Beyond Independence and Accountability* (Northampton, MA: Edward Elgar, 2016); Martin Friedland, *A Place Apart: Judicial Independence and Accountability in Canada* (Ottawa: Canadian Judicial Council, 1995); A. Wayne MacKay, "Dispensing Justice in Canada: Exaggerating the Values of Judicial Independence" (1991) 40 UNBLJ 273; Naiomi Metallic, "Judicial Independence: A Licence to Discriminate?" [unpublished paper, 2008, copy in possession of the author].

CHAPTER 1: THE TRIAL

1 Trial transcript, Nova Scotia Youth Court, 2 December 1994, in *Rodney Darren Small [R.D.S.] v. Her Majesty the Queen* (N.S.) (Criminal) (By Leave), Supreme Court of Canada, Library and Archives Canada (LAC), RG 125, vol. 5231, file 25063A [hereafter *RDS* LAC]. There were four preliminary appearances involving the not-guilty plea and a rescheduled trial due to an absent Crown witness.

2 Interviews with Rodney D. Small, Halifax, 9 June and 14 August 2018. The *Young Offenders Act* prohibited the publication of names or identifying information about the accused to avoid affixing young people with permanent records for minor crimes.

3 Section 270(1)(a) of the *Criminal Code,* R.S.C. 1985, c. C-46, provided: "Every one commits an offence who assaults a public officer or peace officer engaged in the execution of his duty or a person acting in aid of such an officer." Section 270(1)(b) provided: "Every one commits an offence who assaults a person with intent to resist or prevent the lawful arrest or detention of himself or another person." The maximum punishment for either offence was five years' imprisonment. Section 129(a) provided: "Every one who resists or wilfully obstructs a public officer or peace officer in the execution of his duty ... is liable to imprisonment for a term not exceeding two years."

4 Interviews with Rodney Small.

5 *Ibid.*; *RDS* LAC.

6 Burnley "Rocky" Jones and James W. St.G. Walker, *Burnley "Rocky" Jones: Revolutionary* (Black Point, NS: Roseway, 2016).

7 Interviews with Rodney Small.

8 R.S.C. 1985, c.Y-1. At the time of trial, Youth Court was bifurcated in Nova Scotia. Young people under sixteen were tried in Family Court, while sixteen- and seventeen-year-olds were tried in adult Provincial Criminal Court. The Act covered youths between twelve and seventeen; children under twelve could not be charged. The maximum sentence was two years followed by one year probation, except for murder, which could elicit three years with two years of conditional supervision (s. 20; *Criminal Code,* ss. 717–18). Court records could only be retained for five years. Trials were held in open courtrooms, usually with few observers. Section 132 authorized judges to bar people from the courtroom if their presence seriously prejudiced the accused or their exclusion was in the interest of public morals or the proper administration of justice. The media was prohibited from reporting information about the victim or offender if it identified the youth (Part 6). The right to a lawyer was guaranteed; if necessary, the state would provide funding (s. 25(4)). Lee Tustin, *Caught in the Act: A User's Guide to the Youth Justice System and Young Offenders Act* (Don Mills, ON: Addison-Wesley Publishers, 1994).

9 Lacking statistical race breakdowns, impressionistic observations from provincial and family court judges remain the available evidence.

10 Rodney described a chance encounter outside the courthouse with family friend Robert Fraser, who "always kind of looked out for me." Fraser asked Rodney what was wrong. "If he hadn't asked, I wouldn't have asked him to come to court with me. I trusted him and said, 'I'm afraid.' In most cases, I would not admit I was afraid – that's my facade." Interviews with Rodney Small.

11 Interview with Connie Sparks, Halifax, 17 August 2018. Halifax-born Marva Welch was one of two African Nova Scotian court reporters. Ray Lawrence was apparently the only African Nova Scotian deputy sheriff.

12 The Commission, *Royal Commission on the Donald Marshall, Jr., Prosecution*, vol. 1, *Findings and Recommendations* (Halifax: Province of Nova Scotia, 1989) at 151, 154.

13 Interview with Judge Sparks. Judge Micheline Rawlins, appointed in 1992 to the Ontario provincial court in Windsor, the second Black female judge in Canada, indicated that she had "never lived to see the day where I had an all-Black courtroom." Interview with Micheline Rawlins, Windsor, 7 October 2019.

14 Interviews with Rodney Small. Others familiar with the Halifax police force were less complimentary.

15 *Ibid.*; James W. St.G. Walker, "A Black Day in Court: 'Race' and Judging in *R. v. R.D.S.*" in Barrington Walker, ed., *The African Canadian Legal Odyssey: Historical Essays* (Toronto: University of Toronto Press, 2010) 437 at 439.

16 *RDS* LAC, at 18–24. The transcript refers to "Mr. R." and "Mr. S." I have substituted "N.R." and "R.D.S." to prevent confusion.

17 *Ibid.* at 26.

18 *Ibid.* at 33–35.

19 *Ibid.* at 36–37.

20 Jones and Walker, *Burnley "Rocky" Jones,* at 196.

21 Walker, "Black Day in Court," at 443. Jones had lived through shifting terminology, from "Negro," a term associated with slavery; to "Coloured," a word linked to the segregationist American south; to "Black," which was aligned with "Black Power"; to "African Nova Scotian," which emphasized global connections with the mother continent: Jones and Walker, *Burnley "Rocky" Jones,* at 104.

22 Walker, "Black Day in Court," at 443, noting that the judge also made this observation later.

23 *RDS* LAC, at 38, 43, 46, 49, 51.

24 *Ibid.* at 53–54.

25 Interview with Jim Walker, Waterloo, 8 August 2018, recalling discussions with Jones while preparing the memoir.

26 *RDS* LAC, at 55.

27 Walker, "Black Day in Court," at 439.

28 Interviews with Rodney Small.

29 *RDS* LAC, at 58–59.

30 Interviews with Rodney Small.

31 *RDS* LAC, at 61–62.

32 *Ibid.* at 62.

33 *Ibid.* at 63–64.

34 *Ibid.* at 66–68.

35 *Ibid.* at 59–75. Jones argued that even if Rodney's bicycle had touched Stienburg, an assault required "an intentional application of force." None had been proven. He complained that the police had issued three charges from the minor incident of allegedly running into an officer's leg.

36 *Ibid.* at 76–78. Miller resisted the claim of overcharging, noting that it was "normal practice" to have charges in the alternative.

37 *Ibid.* at 80–81A.

38 *Ibid.* at 89–93. She indicated that two of the three counts seemed duplicative, arising out of the same incident.

39 Interview with Sherry Bernard, Halifax, 17 July 2019, recounting the recollection of the court reporter.

40 Interviews with Rodney Small; Evelyn C. White, "Judge Corrine Sparks," *Pamphlet for the 30th Anniversary Celebrating African Nova Scotian Judges* (Halifax: Delmore "Buddy" Daye Learning Institute, 2018).

CHAPTER 2: THE PEOPLE

1 Interview with Donald Stienburg, Halifax, 28 September 2018; interview with Chris Giacomantonio, Halifax, 15 July 2019.

2 Interview with Donald Stienburg.

3 *Ibid.*

4 Interviews with Rodney D. Small, Halifax, 9 June and 14 August 2018.

5 Interview with Richard (Rick) B. Miller, Halifax, 17 August 2018.

6 Interview with Donald Stienburg.

7 Interview with Richard Miller.

8 *Ibid.*; Burnley "Rocky" Jones and James W. St.G. Walker, *Burnley "Rocky" Jones: Revolutionary* (Black Point, NS: Roseway, 2016) at 196–97.

9 *Ibid.* at 196.

10 Interview with Donald Stienburg.

11 Interview with Richard Miller.

12 Interview with Donald Stienburg.

13 *Ibid.*

14 Jones and Walker, *Burnley "Rocky" Jones,* at 196.

15 Interview with Richard Miller.

16 Judith Fingard, Janet Guildford, and David Sutherland, *Halifax: The First 250 Years* (Halifax: Formac, 1999); Paul A. Erickson, *Historic North End Halifax* (Halifax: Nimbus, 2004); Paul A. Erickson, *Halifax's North End: An Anthropologist Looks at the City* (Hantsport, NS: Lancelot Press, 1987).

17 Interviews with Rodney Small. Denise Small had one additional adoptive son, Michael Carver.

18 *Ibid.* Cain's conviction for second-degree murder came when Rodney was about eight. After Cain served eighteen years of a life penalty, new evidence was produced, the conviction was reduced to manslaughter, and he was released on time served.

19 *Ibid.*

20 *Ibid.*

21 *Ibid.*

22 *Ibid.*

23 Ta-Nehisi Coates, *Between the World and Me* (New York: Random, 2015).

24 Interviews with Rodney Small.

25 Jones and Walker, *Burnley "Rocky" Jones,* ch. 1; Richard F. Devlin, "Begun in Faith, Continued in Determination" in Adam Dodek and Alice Woolley, eds., *In Search of the Ethical Lawyer: Stories from the Canadian Legal Profession* (Vancouver: UBC Press, 2016) 81 at 83.

26 Jones and Walker, *Burnley "Rocky" Jones,* chs. 1–2.

27 *Ibid.*; Reakash Walters, "Against Amnesia, African Nova Scotia Women's Generational Leadership in Civil Rights Organizing, 1950–1979" (2020) 32 CJWL 383.

28 Interview with Jim Walker, Waterloo, 8 August 2018; Jones and Walker, *Burnley "Rocky" Jones,* chs. 2–3, and the afterword by George Elliott Clarke; interview with Vince Kazmierski, Ottawa, 31 July 2018.

29 Interview with David Woods, Halifax, 6 June 2018.

30 Jones and Walker, *Burnley "Rocky" Jones,* chs. 2–3, and afterword.

31 George Elliott Clarke, "Rocky Jones Remains a Guiding Force," *Halifax Daily News* (9 April 1988) 13.

32 Jones and Walker, *Burnley "Rocky" Jones,* chs. 4–9; Wendie L. Poitras, "Rocky and Joan: A History of Sacrifice," *The Coast* (5 July 2018), online: <https://www.thecoast.ca/halifax/rocky-and-joan-a-history-of-sacrifice/Content?oid=15826432>.

33 I owe this quote to one of the anonymous reviewers of the manuscript, with acknowledgment and thanks for such a striking observation.

34 Alan Story, "Why the Dreams for Justice Do Not Die" *Toronto Star* (24 January 1987) B5; Jones and Walker, *Burnley "Rocky" Jones,* chs. 5–8; James W. St.G. Walker, "A Black Day in Court: 'Race' and Judging in *R. v. R.D.S.*" in Barrington Walker, ed., *The African Canadian Legal Odyssey: Historical Essays* (Toronto: University of Toronto Press, 2012) 437 at 440.

35 Spencer Sparks was born in Weymouth Falls, Digby County, of Black Loyalist heritage. Helen Sparks (whose birth name was also Sparks) was born in Lake Loon, Halifax County. Her Black Refugee heritage can be traced to the arrival of Winslow Sparks between 1815 and 1818. Interview with Judge Sparks, Halifax, 17 August 2018; Kevin Podgursky, "A Genealogy Report for Lavone Sparks," 30

April 2008, copy in possession of the author; Evelyn C. White, "Judge Corrine Sparks," *Pamphlet for the 30th Anniversary Celebrating African Nova Scotian Judges* (Halifax: Delmore "Buddy" Daye Learning Institute, 2018); Sharon Melson Fletcher, "Corinne [sic] Sparks Biography," *Contemporary Black Biography: Profiles from the International Black Community,* vol. 53 (Farmington Hills, MI: Thomson Gale, 2006) at 150.

36 Interview with Judge Sparks.

37 In referring to Judge Sparks, I have chosen to use the first name she prefers – "Connie" – instead of her birth name, "Corrine Sparks." When referring to legal documents that use "Corrine Sparks," I have reverted to her legal birth name. See explanatory comment in the Introduction.

38 *Ibid.*

39 Interview with Delvina Bernard, Halifax, 15 August 2018. On the wider context of racism that motivated mothers to be strict with their children, see Paula Giddings, *When and Where I Enter: The Impact of Black Women on Race and Sex in America* (New York: William Morrow, 1984), one of Judge Sparks's favourite books.

40 Pamphlet for Sparks third family reunion, 11–14 August 2016. "You have to have coping mechanisms in this life; no one glides through it. For me it has been my faith. I am very grateful that I was raised in a Christian home": Fletcher, "Sparks Biography," at 152.

41 Interview with Judge Sparks. The theatre position was prized because whites rarely hired African Nova Scotians in visible storefront jobs. Eventually a few light-complexioned girls were hired in preliminary efforts to reduce racist employment barriers. Interview with Delvina Bernard.

42 Interview with Judge Sparks.

43 *Ibid.*; Fletcher, "Sparks Biography," at 151; White, "Judge Corrine Sparks."

44 The Nova Scotia Association for the Advancement of Coloured People had convinced the president of Mount Saint Vincent University to create spaces for a few young African Nova Scotian women, beginning in 1969. Interview with Senator Wanda Thomas Bernard, Ottawa, 28 August 2019.

45 White, "Judge Corrine Sparks"; Fletcher, "Sparks Biography"; Walker, "Black Day in Court," at 474.

46 Interview with Judge Sparks.

47 Henry Sylvester Williams, from Trinidad and the first known Black to enrol at Dalhousie law in 1892, dropped out after first year because of racism (including an assault by a white student in the library) but was admitted to the English bar in 1902. Halifax-born James Robinson Johnston was the first Black to graduate in 1898. Several Caribbean-born Blacks followed. One of them, Frederick Allan Hamilton, graduated in 1923 and practised in Sydney. George Webber Roache Davis, the second Nova Scotia–born Black, graduated in 1952. Donald Oliver graduated in 1964; Wayne Kelsie, in 1972; Caribbean-born Anthony

Ross and Hobartson Augustus James (Gus) Wedderburn, in 1973 (both practised in Nova Scotia); Kenneth David Crawford, in 1975; Antigua-born Castor Henry F. Williams, in 1976 (practised in Nova Scotia); and Douglas G. Ruck, in 1977. Records of two Black women survive: Caribbean-born Marlene I. King (later Nourbese Philip) began law at Dalhousie in 1971 but completed her degree in 1973 at Western University; Irene A. Healey graduated in 1976. See Justin Marcus Johnston, *James Robinson Johnston: The Life, Death and Legacy of Nova Scotia's First Black Lawyer* (Halifax: Nimbus, 2005); J. Barry Cahill, "Constructing an 'Imperial Pan-Africanist': Henry Sylvester Williams as a University Law Student in Canada" in Walker, *African Canadian Legal Odyssey*, at 84; Philip Girard and Jeffrey Haylock, "Stratification, Economic Adversity, and Diversity in an Urban Bar" in Constance Backhouse and W. Wesley Pue, eds., *The Promise and Perils of Law* (Toronto: Irwin Law, 2009) 75; George Elliott Clarke, Council on African Canadian Education, and Nova Scotia Department of Education, African Canadian Services Division, *The Times of African Nova Scotians: A Celebration of Our History, Culture and Traditions*, vol. 2 (Halifax: Effective Publishing, 2008) at 26; Bridglal Pachai, *Blacks* (Halifax: Formac, 1997) at 56; Bridglal Pachai and Henry Bishop, *Historic Black Nova Scotia* (Halifax: Nimbus, 2006) at 54–75, 72.

48 Interview with Douglas Ruck, Halifax, 16 July 2019. The law dean repeatedly confused the two of them, even though White was five foot six and Ruck was six foot three and one had a "hefty Afro" and the other did not.

49 Interview with Judge Sparks; White, "Judge Corrine Sparks," pamphlet; Jane Doucet, "History in the Making," *Hearsay: The Schulich School of Law Alumni Magazine* 40 (24 July 2019) at 20. "Law school experience was decried as a lonely and alienating experience for Women of Colour. Apart from being shunned and ostracized from participation in study groups and social events, students reported being questioned, directly and indirectly, about their right to attend law school": Task Force on Gender Equality in the Legal Profession, *Touchstones for Change: Equality, Diversity and Accountability* (Ottawa: Canadian Bar Association, 1993) at 33. Sparks added that a lot of men from the African diaspora also dropped out.

50 Interview with Wayne MacKay, Halifax, 15 August 2018.

51 Correspondence from Leon Trakman to the author, 25 July 2018.

52 Interview with Judge Sparks. Doug Ruck had graduated earlier.

53 Constance Glube, Sandra Oxner, and Jean Whalen were others. "The city hired us when nobody else would. It had trouble finding lawyers to represent it": interview with Sandra Oxner, Toronto, 21 June 2019.

54 Interview with Judge Sparks.

55 Born in 1955 in Halifax and raised in Dartmouth, Foote graduated from St. Mary's University, and from Dalhousie law in 1979. She articled in New Glasgow, was called to the bar in 1980, and practised out of her home until she partnered with Sparks. Another group of three women claimed to be the first

all-female firm, but Foote explained that a newspaper photograph of herself and Sparks demonstrated that their firm had opened first. Interview with Helen Foote, Halifax, 16 July 2019; interview with Judge Sparks; email from Judge Sparks, 14 May 2020.

56 Sparks credited her board appointment to the backing of Nova Scotia cabinet minister Tom McInnis. Interview with Judge Sparks.

57 Born in Halifax in 1950, Ruck graduated from King's College and then Dalhousie law in 1977. He articled with Gus Wedderburn, a Caribbean-born Black. Then, after time as a sole practitioner, Ruck joined white lawyer Blair Mitchell. The Ruck & Mitchell firm operated two offices, Mitchell in Halifax and Ruck in Dartmouth. In 1985, Ruck suffered a serious illness that kept him out of practice for seven years. He later became a civil litigator in employment, labour, administrative, and human rights law, as well as a labour adjudicator/mediator. Interview with Douglas Ruck.

58 White, "Judge Corrine Sparks," pamphlet; Fletcher, "Sparks Biography."

59 Interview with Douglas Ruck.

60 A Dalhousie law graduate from 1964, Oliver learned much later that his raises were consistently less than those of his white lawyer colleagues. Interview with Donald Oliver, Halifax, 27 October 2019; Donald Oliver, *A Matter of Equality: The Life's Work of Senator Don Oliver* (Halifax: Nimbus, 2021). Oliver recalled that a lawyer in another firm once sent him legal papers with an attached note: "Take this to the N ...": Stephen Kimber, "Profile of Senator Donald H. Oliver QC" *Halifax Daily News* (15 May 1995), available from Stephen Kimber. His autobiography later substituted "spook" for the N-word (Oliver, *A Matter of Equality*, at 107).

61 Premier Gerry Regan appointed Sandra Oxner in 1971, making her the first female provincial court judge in Atlantic Canada. Born in Halifax in 1941, she held a BA from King's College (1961) and a Dalhousie law degree (1965). Called to the bar in 1965, she practised from 1965 to 1971, until her judicial appointment. Interview with Sandra Oxner, Toronto, 21 June 2019; R.E. Kimball, *The Bench: The History of Nova Scotia's Provincial Courts* (Halifax: Province of Nova Scotia, 1989) at 208–10.

62 The first-known Canadian Black judge, George Ethelbert Carter, was appointed to Ontario provincial court in 1979: "Trailblazing Judge George Ethelbert Carter Embodied Ethics" *Globe and Mail* (15 June 2018), online: <https://www.theglobeandmail.com/canada/article-trailblazing-judge-george-ethelbert-carter-embodied-ethics/>. Grenadian-born Julius Isaacs (1989, Ontario Supreme Court) and Romain Pitt (1994, Ontario Superior Court) were the first two Blacks appointed to superior courts in Canada: "Canada's First Black Chief Justice Dies" *Toronto Star* (20 July 2011), online: <https://www.thestar.com/news/canada/2011/07/20/canadas_first_black_chief_justice_dies.html>; "Romain W.M. Pitt"

Globe and Mail (4 May 2020) online: <https://www.legacy.com/ca/obituaries/theglobeandmail/name/romain-pitt-obituary?pid+196135392>. Castor Williams was the second Black Nova Scotia judge. Born in Antigua, Williams worked with the civil service there, a bank, a credit union, and as a noncommissioned officer in the West India Regiment. He obtained a BA in political science and economics and graduated from Dalhousie law in 1976. He practised in his own solo firm until he was appointed a Dartmouth Crown attorney in 1992. His 1996 appointment to the Nova Scotia Provincial Court made him the first Black at that level of court in Nova Scotia. (Sparks's appointment was to the stand-alone Family Court.) Assistant Chief Provincial Court Judge Joseph Kennedy described Williams as a "significant man from a significant community and some would say, I suppose, it is due time." Williams had reached the short list and been passed over three times before: Amy Smith, "Judges' Appointments Timely" *Halifax Chronicle-Herald* (9 March 1996) A7; "McDonough Rebukes Grits for Lack of Black Judges on Provincial Court Bench" *Halifax Chronicle-Herald* (11 January 1995), clipping, SMU Archives; "Retired Judge Castor Williams Dies" *Halifax Chronicle-Herald* (24 May 2019), online: <https://www. saltwire.com/nova-scotia/news/retired -judge-castor-williams-dies-315566/>.

63 White, "Judge Corrine Sparks."

64 *Ibid.*; interview with John Buchanan, Halifax, 30 July 2018.

65 "Programme for Dinner Tribute to The Honourable Judge Corrine E. Sparks BA, LLB," 28 March 1987, Dartmouth Inn Regency Room; White, "Judge Corrine Sparks."

66 Bertha Wilson et al., *Touchstones for Change: Equality, Diversity and Accountability* (Ottawa: Canadian Bar Association, 1993). Judge Sparks's report, Women of Colour in the Legal Profession, was included as an appendix.

CHAPTER 3: A BLACK HISTORY OF NOVA SCOTIA

1 In *Toward Freedom: The AfricCanadian Experience* (Toronto: Umbrella, 1996), Ken Alexander and Avis Glaze note (at 58) that roughly fifty thousand slaves escaped via the Underground Railroad to Canada.

2 Afua Cooper, *The Hanging of Angelique: The Untold Story of Slavery in Canada and the Burning of Old Montreal* (Toronto: Harper Collins, 2006) at 68; Harvey Amani Whitfield, ed., *Black Slavery in the Maritimes: A History in Documents* (Peterborough, ON: Broadview Press, 2018); Harvey Amani Whitfield, *North to Bondage: Loyalist Slavery in the Maritimes* (Vancouver: UBC Press, 2016). A slave shackle, with an enslaver's initials, unearthed near the Bay of Fundy, is held in a local museum: interview with Afua Cooper, Halifax, 22 May 2018.

3 Afua Cooper et al., *Report on Lord Dalhousie's History on Slavery and Race* (Halifax: Dalhousie University, 2019) at 7.

4 Constance Backhouse, *Colour-Coded: A Legal History of Racism in Canada, 1900–1950* (Toronto: University of Toronto Press, 1999) at 257–58. A British ship transported a six-year-old from Madagascar or Guinea as the property of David Kirke. The boy was sold to French clerk Olivier Le Baillif (also called Olivier Le Tardiff) and transferred to Guillaume Couillard. In 1633, he was baptized Olivier Le Jeune. He remained in New France all his life: Dorothy W. Williams, "Olivier Le Jeune," *Canadian Encyclopedia* (23 January 2020), online: <https://www.thecanadianencyclopedia.ca/en/article/olivier-le-jeune>.

5 Although slavery was legal in French and British Canada, Nova Scotia courts occasionally freed some who petitioned for freedom: D.G. Bell, J. Barry Cahill, and Harvey Amani Whitfield, "Slavery and Slave Law in the Maritimes" in Barrington Walker, ed., *The African Canadian Legal Odyssey: Historical Essays* (Toronto: University of Toronto Press, 2012) at 363; Philip Girard, Jim Phillips, and R. Blake Brown, *A History of Law in Canada,* vol. 1 (Toronto: University of Toronto Press, 2018) at 202–15; Robin W. Winks, *The Blacks in Canada: A History,* 2nd ed. (Montreal/Kingston: McGill-Queens University Press, 1977) at 1–60; Cooper, *Hanging of Angelique,* at 70–73, 104; Kenneth Donovan, "Slaves and Their Owners in Ile Royale, 1713–1760" (1995) 25:1 Acadiensis 3; Harvey Amani Whitfield, *Biographical Dictionary of Enslaved Black People in the Maritimes* (Toronto: University of Toronto Press, 2022); Karlyn Smadz Frost, "Planting Slavery in Nova Scotia's Promised Land, 1759–1775" in Michele A. Johnson and Funke Aladejebi, eds., *Unsettling the Great White North: Black Canadian History* (Toronto: University of Toronto Press, 2022) at 53; Natasha Henry, "Where, Oh Where, Is Bet? Locating Enslaved Black Women on the Ontario Landscape" in Johnson and Aladejebi, eds., *Unsettling the Great White North* at 85. At least 266 individuals were enslaved in Île-Royale from 1713 to 1758, and by 1750 there were at least 50 enslaved Blacks in Halifax: George Elliott Clarke, Council on African Canadian Education, and Nova Scotia Department of Education, African Canadian Services Division, *The Times of African Nova Scotians: A Celebration of Our History, Culture and Traditions,* vol. 1 (Halifax: Delmore "Buddy" Daye Learning Institute, 2014) at 17–18.

6 William C. Wicken, *The Colonization of Mi'kmaw Memory and History, 1794–1928* (Toronto: University of Toronto Press, 2012); L.S.F. Upton, *Micmacs and Colonials: Indian-White Relations in the Maritime Provinces, 1713–1867* (Vancouver: UBC Press, 1979). James W. St.G. Walker, *The Black Loyalists: The Search for a Promised Land in Nova Scotia and Sierra Leone, 1783–1870* (Toronto: University of Toronto Press, 1992) notes at 40 that the 1767 Nova Scotia census listed 104 enslaved persons out of a population of 3,022.

7 Sir John Wentworth, whose notorious relationship with a Black woman in East Preston resulted in the birth of several children, claimed ownership of nine men, six women, and four children in 1784: Whitfield, *North to Bondage,* at 56; Sylvia Hamilton, "Naming Names, Naming Ourselves: A Survey of Early Black

Women in Nova Scotia" in Peggy Bristow, Dionne Brand, Linda Carty, Afua P. Cooper, Sylvia Hamilton, and Adrienne Shadd, eds., *"We're Rooted Here and They Can't Pull Us Up": Essays in African Canadian Women's History* (Toronto: University of Toronto Press, 1994) 13 at 17.

8 Cooper et al., *Report on Lord Dalhousie's History*; Shirley Tillotson, "How (and How Much) King's College Benefitted from Slavery in the West Indies, 1789–1854" [unpublished, 6 May 2019], online: <https://ukings.ca/wp-content/uploads/2021/01/202001TillotsonKingsSlaveryIndirectConnections_Secure.pdf>.

9 T. Watson Smith, "The Slave in Canada," *Collections of the Nova Scotia Historical Society for the Years 1899–98,* vol. 10 (Halifax: Nova Scotia Printing Co., 1899).

10 "Sale by Auction by Mr. Hill" *N.S. Gazette and Weekly Chronicle* (4 July 1786).

11 Girard, Phillips, and Brown, *History of Law in Canada,* at 203; Margaret Conrad, ed., *They Planted Well: New England Planters in Maritime Canada* (1988); Margaret Conrad, *Making Adjustments: Change and Continuity in Planter Nova Scotia, 1759–1800* (1991); *Intimate Relations: Family and Community in Planter Nova Scotia* (1995); Margaret Conrad and Barry Moody, *Planter Links: Community and Culture in Planter Nova Scotia* (2001), all published in Fredericton, New Brunswick, by Acadiensis Press.

12 Winks, *Blacks in Canada,* at 51; Carrie M. Best, "That Lonesome Road" in George Elliott Clarke, ed., *Fire on the Water: An Anthology of Black Nova Scotian Writing,* vol. 1 (Lawrencetown Beach, NS: Pottersfield Press, 1991) at 122.

13 Clarke et al., *Times of African Nova Scotians,* vol. 2, at 12. Mattieu da Costa, a multilingual Black man who spoke both French and Mi'kmawísimk (the Mi'kmaw language), arrived at Annapolis Royal with fur trader Pierre du Gua and explorer Samuel de Champlain: William Inglis Morse, *Pierre Du Gua, Sieur de Monts* (London: Quaritch, 1939) at 51.

14 Nova Scotia "offered refuge to at least 3,000 Black Loyalists" of an estimated thirty thousand Loyalists: Walker, *Black Loyalists,* at 18, 32; Hamilton, "Naming Names," at 21; Judith Fingard, Janet Guildford, and David Sutherland, *Halifax: The First 250 Years* (Halifax: Formac, 1999) at 26.

15 Girard, Phillips, and Brown, *History of Law in Canada,* at 212–13.

16 *King v. Jesse Gray,* Record of Court of Sessions at Shelburne, Minutes (7 July 1791), Nova Scotia Archives, RG 60 F9.4.

17 Walker, *Black Loyalists,* chs. 2–4; Hamilton, "Naming Names," at 19–22; Fingard, Guildford, and Sutherland, *Halifax,* at 26.

18 The Black Loyalists' former occupations included field hand, blacksmith, cooper, tailor, carpenter, sailor, and baker. Tagged the Ethiopian Regiment, the soldiers sewed the inscription "Liberty to Slaves" on their uniforms: Walker, *Black Loyalists,* chs. 1–3 and 6; Winks, *Blacks in Canada,* ch. 2; Clarke et al., *Times of*

African Nova Scotians, vol. 2, at 12; Evelyn C. White, email communication, 26 February 2020.

19 Winks, *Blacks in Canada,* at 78–95; John N. Grant, *The Maroons in Nova Scotia* (Halifax: Formac, 2002). White commissioner Alexander Ochterloney "took five or six of the most attractive Maroon girls to his bed ... keeping a 'seraglio' for his friends": Theophilus Chamberlain (surveyor) to Governor Wentworth (20 June 1798) Colonial Records Office, 217/69. Governor Wentworth and Maroon Sarah Colley also left descendants: Bridglal Pachai, *The Nova Scotia Black Experience through the Centuries* (Halifax: Nimbus, 2007) at 90.

20 Harvey Amani Whitfield, *Blacks on the Border: The Black Refugees in British North America, 1815–1860* (Burlington: University of Vermont Press, 2006); Winks, *Blacks in Canada,* ch. 5.

21 George Ramsay, 9th Earl of Dalhousie, to Lord Bathurst (29 December 1816) Nova Scotia Archives, RG 1, vol. 112, at 1–5.

22 Winks, *Blacks in Canada,* at 128.

23 The Pro-slavery Almon and Johnston families received five hundred pounds for people enslaved in the Caribbean: Cooper, *Report on Lord Dalhousie's,* ch. 7.

24 Winks, *Blacks in Canada,* at 298–313, 434–45; Michelle Y. Williams, "African Nova Scotian Restorative Justice: A Change Has Gotta Come" (2013) 36 Dal LJ 425. Canadian immigration agents discouraged West Indian arrivals: "[I]t is the opinion of the Department that we don't want the West Indian n***** [and] every obstacle is to be put in their way": W.L. Barnstead to L.M. Fortier (30 June 1914), LAC, Immigration Branch Records, RG76-566-810666-1.

25 Interview with Michelle Williams, Halifax, 5 June 2018; interview with Angela Simmonds, Halifax, 9 April 2018.

26 Interview with Afua Cooper. Carrie Best also notes the erasure of Indigenous and diverse ethnic communities: *That Lonesome Road* (New Glasgow, NS: Clarion, 1977) at 163–65.

27 Hamilton, "Naming Names," at 22. Simeon Perkins, a white merchant from Liverpool, described ten days of violence: "[A]n Extraordinary mob or Riot has happened in Shelburne. Some thousands of People Assembled with Clubs and Drove the Negroes out of Town": Clarke et al., *Times of African Nova Scotians,* vol. 2, at 12. A Shelburne bylaw forbade "Negro Dances and Negro Frolicks": Stephen Kimber, *Loyalists and Layabouts: The Rapid Rise and Faster Fall of Shelburne, Nova Scotia, 1783–1792* (Toronto: Anchor, 2002) at 202.

28 "An Account of the Life of Mr. David George (c. 1743–1810) told to Brother John Rippon" in Clarke, *Fire on the Water,* vol. 1, at 36–37; Cooper, *Report on Lord Dalhousie's History,* at 35.

29 James (John) Mitchell, capital case file (1880–89), LAC, RG 13, vol. 1417, file 146A; George Elliott Clarke, "White Judges, Black Hoods" (2016) 41:2 Can L Libr Rev 10 at 14.

30 Best, "Lonesome Road," at 123; Sarah-Jane Mathieu, *North of the Color Line: Migration and Black Resistance in Canada, 1870–1955* (Chapel Hill: University of North Carolina Press, 2010) at 110–16.

31 Fingard, Guildford, and Sutherland, *Halifax,* at 139.

32 David Steeves, "Maniacal Murder or Death Dealing Car: The Case of Daniel Perry Sampson, 1933–35" in Walker, *African Canadian Legal Odyssey,* at 228–29.

33 "Local Groups Would Oppose Klan" *Halifax Chronicle-Herald* (8 December 1980) 11; Gordon Delaney, "KKK Material Not Hate Literature – Police" *Halifax Chronicle-Herald* (3 November 1992).

34 Backhouse, *Colour-Coded,* at 251; Colin A. Thomson, *Born with a Call: A Biography of Dr. William Pearly Oliver, C.M.* (Cherry Brook, NS: Black Cultural Centre for Nova Scotia, 1986) at 7–11; Walker, *Black Loyalists,* at 386–88; Winks, *Blacks in Canada,* at 286 and ch. 12. In 1983, the last segregated school in Nova Scotia, in Guysborough District, closed its doors: Clarke et al., *Times of African Nova Scotians,* vol. 1, at 13. Judge Sparks's uncle describes the Black school he attended in an oral history interview: Municipality of Digby, The Elder Transcripts, "Bill Sparks," YouTube (19 May 2016), online: <https://youtu.be/3qSfYMMrME8>.

35 Black Learners Advisory Committee (NS), *BLAC Report on Education: Redressing Inequality – Empowering Black Learners,* vol. 2 (Halifax: BLAC, 1994); Carol Aylward, "Adding Colour – A Critique of 'An Essay on Institutional Responsibility': The Indigenous Blacks and Micmac Programme at Dalhousie Law School" (1995) 8:2 CJWL 470 at 481.

36 Robyn Maynard, *Policing Black Lives: State Violence in Canada from Slavery to the Present* (Halifax: Fernwood, 2017) at 213.

37 Thomson, *Born with a Call,* at 104, quoting William Pearly Oliver.

38 Maynard, *Policing Black Lives,* at 213. Suzanne Morton, "Separate Spheres in a Separate World: African-Nova Scotian Women in Late-19th-Century Halifax County" (1993) 22:2 Acadiensis 61 at 70: "[T]he racist policies of the Halifax school board prohibited access to education beyond grade seven."

39 Philip Antiba Goff, Matthew Christian Jackson, Brooke Allison Lewis Di Leone, Carmen Marie Culotta, and Natalie Ann DiTomasso, "The Essence of Innocence: Consequences of Dehumanizing Black Children" (2014) 106:4 J Personality and Social Psychology 526; Robin Bernstein, *Racial Innocence: Performing Childhood and Race from Slavery to Civil Rights* (New York: New York University Press, 2011); Kristia Hemming, *The Rage of Innocence: How America Criminalizes Black Youth* (New York: Pantheon, 2021), noting that Black children are seen as threatening, predatory, sexually deviant, and immoral, dehumanized like criminals to establish boundaries of whiteness before they reach adulthood.

40 Black Learners Advisory Committee, *BLAC Report on Education,* vol. 2, at 20; Maynard, *Policing Black Lives,* at 218.

41 Winks, *Blacks in Canada,* at 423–27, 452; Mathieu, *North of the Color Line,* at 62, 81–92.

42 The Commission, *Royal Commission on the Donald Marshall, Jr., Prosecution,* vol. 4, *Discrimination against Blacks in Nova Scotia* (Halifax: Province of Nova Scotia, 1989) at 14.

43 Backhouse, *Colour-Coded,* at 251; Winks, *Blacks in Canada,* at 325.

44 Clarke et al., *Times of African Nova Scotians,* vol. 2, at 28–29; Africville Genealogical Society, eds., *The Spirit of Africville* (Halifax: Formac, 1992); Paul Erickson, *Historic North End Halifax* (Halifax: Nimbus, 2004) at 128; Winks, *Blacks in Canada,* at 452.

45 Don Oliver, *A Matter of Equality: The Life's Work of Senator Don Oliver* (Halifax: Nimbus, 2021) at 12, recounting the experience of his father.

46 Winks, *Blacks in Canada,* at 419–20; *Halifax Chronicle* (27–30 October 1937) 9.

47 Winks, *Blacks in Canada,* at 325; Calvin Lawrence, *Black Cop* (Toronto: Lorimer, 2019) at 16–17. Whether the curfews were set through municipal bylaws or imposed extralegally by white residents and authorities is still unclear.

48 In the 1920s, white Nova Scotian Henry Bannon advocated legislation to disenfranchise Blacks, bar them from political office, and ban interracial marriage: Mathieu, *North of the Color Line,* at 168–69; Walker, *Black Loyalists,* at 55; Winks, *Blacks in Canada,* at 286, 325; Bridglal Pachai, *Blacks* (Halifax: Nimbus, 1997) at 16.

49 James W. St.G. Walker, *The Black Identity in Nova Scotia: Community and Institutions in Historical Perspective* (Halifax: Black Cultural Centre for Nova Scotia, 1985) at 8. Steeves, "Maniacal Murder," describes the murder conviction in 1933–34 of an African Nova Scotian man on circumstantial evidence by all-white jurors. Although some of them admitted prejudice prior to their empanelment, the white judge dismissed multiple challenges for cause. There were two threatened lynchings before the final hanging.

50 Calvin W. Ruck, "The Rejection of Black Volunteers" in Clarke, *Fire on the Water,* vol. 1, at 151–57. All-Black battalions were "put to work hauling waste and dismembered remains in European battlefields known to be peppered with land mines": Mathieu, *North of the Color Line,* at 20.

51 Mathieu, *North of the Color Line,* at 169. Until 1969, some Nova Scotian cemeteries denied Blacks burial: Winks, *Blacks in Canada,* at xiii; Lindsay Ruck, *Winds of Change: The Life and Legacy of Calvin W. Ruck* (Lawrencetown Beach, NS: Pottersfield Press, 2014) at 103–4.

52 George Elliott Clarke, *Directions Home: Approaches to African-Canadian Literature* (Toronto: University of Toronto Press, 2012) at 46–52; Walker, *Black Loyalists,* at 66–80.

53 Backhouse, *Colour-Coded,* ch. 7; Anna-Maria Galante, "Ex-mayor Lewis Broke New Ground" *Halifax Chronicle-Herald* (19 February 1993) 7; Ruck, *Winds of Change,* at 110; Mathieu, *North of the Color Line,* at 21, 169.

54 Candace Bernard and Wanda Thomas Bernard, "Learning from the Past/ Visions for the Future: The Black Community and Child Welfare in Nova Scotia" in Brian Wharf, ed., *Community Work Approaches to Child Welfare* (Toronto: University of Toronto Press, 2002) at 116–28; Maynard, *Policing Black Lives,* ch. 7.

55 Although the orphanage was a tribute to the survival efforts of the Black community, it followed a strict disciplinary regimen and was chronically under-funded. In 2014, the province settled a class action from claimants who had been abused as children there, a case with parallels to many other Canadian children's facilities. See Wanda Taylor, *Nova Scotia Home for Colored Children: The Hurt, the Hope and the Healing* (Halifax: Nimbus, 2015); Charles R. Saunders, *Share and Care: The Story of the Nova Scotia Home for Colored Children* (Halifax: Nimbus, 1994).

56 Ruck, *Winds of Change,* at 55; Maynard, *Policing Black Lives,* at 77; Black Learners Advisory Committee, *BLAC Report on Education,* vol. 2, at 27.

57 Africville Genealogical Society, *The Spirit of Africville,* at 74; Thomson, *Born with a Call,* at 16–18, 84; African Canadian Legal Clinic, *Anti-Black Racism in Canada: A Report on the Canadian Government's Compliance with the International Convention on the Elimination of All Forms of Racial Discrimination* (Toronto: African Canadian Legal Clinic, 2002).

58 Haliburton's Sam Slick opines that "N*****rs ... those thick skulled, crooked shanked, flat footed, long heeled, woolly headed gentlemen, don't seem fit for much else but slavery": Clarke, *Directions Home,* at 23.

59 Ted Rutland, *Displacing Blackness: Planning, Power, and Race in Twentieth-Century Halifax* (Toronto: University of Toronto Press, 2018); Paul A. Erickson, *Halifax's North End* (Hantsport, NS: Lancelot Press, 1986) at 68–73; Africville Genealogical Society, *The Spirit of Africville.*

60 Tina Loo, *Moved by the State: Forced Relocation and Making a Good Life in Postwar Canada* (Vancouver: UBC Press, 2019).

61 Rutland, *Displacing Blackness,* at 8–9, 162–64.

62 George Elliott Clarke, Book Review of *The Blacks in Canada: A History* by Robin W. Winks, (2000) 30:1 American Rev Can Studies 93 at 93–94.

63 Backhouse, *Colour-Coded,* ch. 7; Thomson, *Born with a Call,* at 77.

64 Pachai, *Blacks,* at 49 credits the NSAACP with the 1955 *Fair Employment Practices Act* and the 1959 *Fair Accommodations Act.*

65 Thomson, *Born with a Call,* ch. 5; Thomas H. Raddall, *Halifax – Warden of the North* (Halifax: Nimbus 2010) at 333–4; interview with Stephen Kimber, Halifax, 15 July 2019.

66 Williams, "African Nova Scotian Restorative Justice," at 425–26; interview with Michelle Williams, Halifax, 5 June 2018.

67 I thank an anonymous reviewer for reminding me that African Nova Scotians prefer the term "settl*ed* people" as distinct from "white settl*er* colonists," due to their forced migration from Africa to North America.

68 Donald Clairmont and Dennis W. Magill, *Nova Scotian Blacks: An Historical and Structural Overview* (Halifax: Dalhousie University, 1970); Suzanne Morton and Donald Wright, "Black History in Atlantic Canada: A Bibliography" (2021) 50:1 Acadiensis 223.

CHAPTER 4: RACE AND POLICING IN NOVA SCOTIA

1 Interviews with Rodney D. Small, Halifax, 9 June and 14 August 2018.

2 The Commission, *Royal Commission on the Donald Marshall, Jr., Prosecution,* vol. 4, *Discrimination against Blacks in Nova Scotia* (Halifax: Province of Nova Scotia, 1989); Calvin Lawrence, *Black Cop* (Toronto: Lorimer, 2019) at 49. Records linking crime and Blackness date to the transatlantic slave trade when enslaved people who escaped were criminalized for theft. In nineteenth-century Canada, Blacks were disproportionately convicted of violence, prostitution, and drug offences: Robyn Maynard, *Policing Black Lives: State Violence in Canada from Slavery to the Present* (Halifax: Fernwood, 2017) at 4, 40. Between 1864 and 1873, Black women (3 percent of the Halifax population) accounted for 40 percent of incarcerated women, mostly for prostitution offences: Judith Fingard, "Jailbirds in Mid-Victorian Halifax" in Peter Waite, Sandra Oxner, and Thomas Barnes, eds., *Law in a Colonial Society: The Nova Scotia Experience* (Toronto: Carswell, 1984) 81 at 90.

3 Don Oliver, *A Matter of Equality: The Life's Work of Senator Don Oliver* (Halifax: Nimbus, 2021) at 45. Oliver was then a summer student at the paper, prior to becoming a path-breaking African Nova Scotian lawyer and Canadian senator.

4 Murray Barnard, "For Negroes in Halifax, Black Power versus Ping-Pong," *Maclean's* (1 November 1967) 1.

5 Drummond's uncle, Delmore "Buddy" Daye, was a Halifax boxing champion, public servant, and community activist. *The 4th Estate* reporter was African Canadian Frank Fillmore: Craig Marshall Smith, *The Journey Continues: An Atlantic Canadian Black Experience* (Dartmouth: Black Green and Red Educational Products, n.d.) at 106; Craig Marshall Smith, *You Had Better Be White by Six A.M.: The*

African-Canadian Experience in the Royal Canadian Mounted Police (Yarmouth, NS: CMS Publishing, 2007).

6 Interview with Evangeline Cain-Grant, Toronto, 20 December 2019; Carol A. Aylward, "Take the Long Way Home: *R.D.S. v. R.* – The Journey" (1998) 47 UNBLJ 249 at 272; Smith, *You Had Better Be White*, at 47; Charles R. Saunders, *Black and Bluenose: The Contemporary History of a Community* (Lawrencetown Beach, NS: Pottersfield Press, 1999) at 13–31.

7 Africville Genealogical Society, ed., *The Spirit of Africville* (Halifax: Formac, 1992) at 85; Saunders, *Black and Bluenose*, at 209.

8 Interview with Evangeline Cain-Grant; John Spears, "Prosecutors Showed No Racial Bias, N.S. Court Rules" *Toronto Star* (21 October 1989); Peter McLaughlin, "Probe into Brawl Was Not Racially Biased – Judge" *Halifax Daily News* (24 March 1990) 5; Bridglal Pachai, *The Nova Scotia Black Experience* (Halifax: Nimbus, 2007) at 320. Born in New Glasgow in 1950, Potts completed law at Dalhousie, was admitted to the bar in 1975, and appointed Halifax Crown prosecutor in 1979. She was the second woman appointed to the Provincial Court in 1988: R.E. Kimball, *The Bench: The History of Nova Scotia's Provincial Courts* (Halifax: Province of Nova Scotia, 1989) at 137, 208–9.

9 Interview with Mark Knox, Halifax, 16 July 2019; Andrea MacDonald, "Judge Recommends Chemical Castration," Ottawa Women's Centre (5 August 2004), online: <http://www.ottawamenscentre.com/news/20040805_chemical_castration.htm>; Blair Rhodes, "Cesar Lalo Victim Calls for Nova Scotia Government to Settle Suit" *CBC News* (14 November 2014), online: <https://www.cbc.ca/news/canada/nova-scotia/cesar-lalo-victim-calls-for-nova-scotia-government-to-settle-suit-1.2835961>; Blair Rhodes, "Ex-probation Officer Who Abused Children Dies" *CBC News* (21 September 2019), online: <https://www.cbc.ca/news/canada/nova-scotia/cesar-lalo-death-ottawa-lawsuit-1.5291917>.

10 Smith, *You Had Better Be White*, at 23, 46. Interview with Scot Wortley, University of Toronto criminologist, Toronto, 28 November 2019: "White criminality is viewed as individual pathology. They become anomalies; they don't represent whites. For Black persons, it is characterized as their whole community's problem. As a white person, one doesn't watch media depictions of crime and sit there saying, 'I hope it's not a white person.'"

11 Saunders, *Black and Bluenose*, at 78–80.

12 Barry Dorey, "Task Force Denies Bias in Pimping Investigation" *Halifax Chronicle-Herald* (23 January 1993) A3.

13 Davene Jeffrey, "Spurr on Hotseat for Alleged Racist Joke" *Halifax Chronicle-Herald* (22 June 1991), n.p.

14 Interview with Jean Whalen, Halifax, 14 July 2019.

15 JoAnn Sherwood, "Spurr Chooses Not to Appeal Police Commission Penalty" *Halifax Chronicle-Herald* (31 October 1991) n.p.

16 Cathy Nicholl, "Bar Beating, Police Action Caused Rioting, Says Youth" *Halifax Daily News* (20 July 1991) 5.

17 *Ibid.*; Saunders, *Black and Bluenose,* at 111–13. Interview with David Woods, African Nova Scotian artist and organization leader, Halifax, 6 June 2018: "I know a number of guys beaten up by bouncers and sent to the hospital. But the public image is Blacks beating up other people. About two hundred whites showed up with bats. The police came and arrested the Blacks."

18 Peter Hays, "Black-White Divisions Very Real, Meeting Told" *Halifax Daily News* (20 July 1991) 5.

19 *Ibid.*

20 Saunders, *Black and Bluenose,* at 113–15.

21 Interview with Anthony Ross, Toronto, 26 May 2019.

22 Susan LeBlanc and Bruce Erskine, "Riot Reports Worlds Apart" and "Trust Perceived to Be Key to Improved Black-Police Relations" *Halifax Chronicle-Herald* (20 December 1991) 1, A2; K. Cox, "Halifax Police under Fire for Probe of Racial Brawl" *Globe and Mail* (20 December 1991) A8; Aylward, "Take the Long Way Home," at 267–68.

23 Jennifer L. Eberhardt, *Biased: Uncovering the Hidden Prejudice That Shapes What We See, Think, and Do* (New York: Penguin, 2019) at 48.

24 *Ibid.* at 84.

25 *Ibid.* at 296.

26 The three Black civilian members were Mayann Francis and the Reverends Donald Skeir and Calvin Symonds. Report of the Incident Review Committee of the Halifax Police Department (17 December 1991); Aylward, "Take the Long Way Home," at 267–68; Smith, *You Had Better Be White,* at 22; Saunders, *Black and Bluenose,* at 111–17; Smith, *The Journey Continues,* at 159.

27 Interview with Robert S. Wright, Halifax, 14 February 2020.

28 Charles Saunders, "Two Wrongs Make Two Wrongs" *Halifax Daily News* (21 December 1991).

29 Charles Saunders, "Police Fail to Protect Victim" *Halifax Daily News* (4 November 1991) 14; Rob Roberts, "HPD Chief to Review Taped Arrest" *Halifax Daily News* (4 November 1991) 3.

30 Peter Hays, "Irked Judge Blasts Crown for Prosecution of Mahlangu; Charge Should Never Have Been Laid" *Halifax Chronicle-Herald* (28 May 1992).

31 Bruce Erskine and Barry Dorey, "Police Knew of Supremacist Camp" *Halifax Chronicle-Herald* (6 November 1992) A7.

32 Dolly E. Williams, "It Can Happen Here" *Halifax Daily News* (1 June 1992) 13.

33 Donna-Marie Sonnichsen, "Man Jailed for Threatening Officers Gets into Shoving Match with Deputies" *Halifax Chronicle-Herald* (13 July 1993).

34 Barry Dorey, "Cops, Kids at Odds" *Halifax Chronicle-Herald* (29 September 1993).

35 Malcolm Dunlop, "Charges Filed against Three Police Officers" *Halifax Chronicle-Herald* (14 April 1994); Aylward, "Take the Long Way Home," at 268.

36 Kevin Cox, "N.S. Warned Not to Ignore Racism Complaints at Jail" *Globe and Mail* (29 January 1994); Randy Jones, "Jail Union Denies Racism Charges" *Globe and Mail* clipping, SMU Archives, Lynn Jones Collection, 2016.002.1, box 5, series 3, subseries 4, file 1.

37 Prepared in 1968, the report was not made public until 1994. Smith, *You Had Better Be White,* at 56–57; Saunders, *Black and Bluenose,* at 80–82; David M. Tanovich, *The Colour of Justice: Policing Race in Canada* (Toronto: Irwin Law, 2006) at 58; Burnley "Rocky" Jones and James W. St.G. Walker, *Burnley "Rocky" Jones: Revolutionary* (Halifax: Roseway, 2016) at 148.

38 Lawrence, *Black Cop,* at 50–51, 60.

39 *Ibid.* at 11, 52–54, 68–71, 137–38. Calvin Lawrence, "Two Perspectives on Defining Systemic Racism in the RCMP" *CBC News* (15 June 2020), online: <https://youtu.be/fzMQbUGuQLk>.

40 Interviews with Donald Clairmont, Halifax, 16 August and 28 September 2018.

41 Scot Wortley, *Halifax N.S.: Street Checks Report* (Halifax: NS Human Rights Commission, 2019).

42 Interview with Scot Wortley, Toronto, 28 November 2019.

43 S. Baldwin, C. Hall, C. Bennell, B. Blaskovits, and C. Lawrence, "Distinguishing Features of Excited Delirium Syndrome in Non-fatal Use of Force Encounters" (2016) 41 J Forensic and Legal Medicine 21. Although the study focused on delirium, the data demonstrated the rarity of force in police-public interactions generally. Data drew from urban, suburban, rural, and remote communities for the years 2012 to 2015. The recipients of force were predominantly male (90.9 percent), had a mean age of thirty-two, and were violent (65.9 percent). Interview with Craig Bennell, Ottawa, 10 September 2019.

44 Interview with David Tanovich, Windsor, 7 October 2019.

45 Tanovich, *The Colour of Justice,* at 13–14, 24–27; interview with David Tanovich.

46 Interview with Craig Bennell.

47 Interview with Scot Wortley. The Commission, *The Report of the Commission on Systemic Racism in the Ontario Criminal Justice System* (Toronto: Queen's Printer for Ontario, 1995) found that with discretionary charges (e.g., obstructing justice) there was a greater prospect of race discrimination. Co-chair Judge David P. Cole noted, "In Toronto, if you're young and poor and Black and male, you are much

more likely to come to the attention of the police." Interview with David P. Cole, Toronto, 11 June 2019.

48 Acquaintances who visited Marshall in prison advised him that Roy Ebsary was the murderer. Marshall wrote to Ebsary, who wrote back with a virtual confession that Marshall forwarded to the RCMP: Michael Harris, *Justice Denied: The Law versus Donald Marshall* (Toronto: Macmillan, 1986).

49 Commission on Systemic Racism, *The Report,* vol. 1 at 15–18, 113–27.

50 Submission of the Nova Scotia Attorney General and the Department of the Attorney General; Ed Ratushny, *The Conduct of Public Inquiries* (Toronto: Irwin, 2009) at 70.

51 Cliff Boutilier, "Judge Denies Making Racist Remark" *Halifax Daily News* (6 January 1985) 1.

52 Commission on Systemic Racism, *The Report,* vol. 1 at 19–23. The court was then named the Nova Scotia Supreme Court (Appeal Division), and its judges were Chief Justice Ian M. MacKeigan, Gordon L.S. Hart, Malachi C. Jones, Angus L. Macdonald, and Leonard L. Pace, all white males. Chief Justice MacKeigan was found to have influenced Department of Justice officials to shift the onus to Marshall "to prove his own innocence" at the subsequent royal commission inquiry. That Leonard Pace (attorney general during the trial) sat on the appeal was found to be highly improper: M.E. Turpel/aki-Kwe, "Further Travails of Canada's Human Rights Record: The Marshall Case" in Alex Denny and Joy Mannette, eds., *Elusive Justice: Beyond the Marshall Inquiry* (Halifax: Fernwood, 1992) 79 at 89.

53 Attorney General Thomas J. McInnis, who had a hand in Judge Sparks's appointment, launched the CJC inquiry, explaining that faith in Nova Scotia's highest court had been "shaken." Pace resigned for health reasons, and MacKeigan retired, allowing both judges to escape discipline. The all-white disciplinary panel was composed of Chief Justices Allan McEachern, Guy A. Richard, and James Laycraft, plus lawyers Rosalie Abella and Daniel Bellemare. It concluded that the judges had "seriously mischaracterized the evidence" but declined to recommend their removal from office. Canadian Judicial Council, *Report to the Canadian Judicial Council of the Inquiry Committee Established Pursuant to Subsection 63(1) of the Judges Act at the Request of the Attorney General of Nova Scotia* (August 1990).

54 Newfoundland Chief Justice T. Alexander Hickman, Quebec Associate Chief Justice Lawrence A. Poitras, and Ontario Justice Gregory T. Evans QC were the three white judges who presided.

55 Donald Clairmont and Ethan Kim, "Getting Past the Gatekeepers: The Reception of Restorative Justice in the Nova Scotian Criminal Justice System" (2013) 36 Dal LJ 359 at 370.

56 The 1978 study on summary conviction first-time offenders showed 23 percent of whites discharged and 77 percent sentenced. No Blacks were discharged; all were sentenced: A.K. Warner and K.E. Renner, "Research on the Halifax

Criminal Courts: A Technical and Conceptual Report" (1978), cited in Philip Girard, Jim Phillips, and Barry Cahill, eds., *The Supreme Court of Nova Scotia, 1754–2004* (Toronto: University of Toronto Press, 2004) at 187–88; Commission on Systemic Racism, *The Report,* vol. 7 at 47–48.

57   Commission on Systemic Racism, *The Report,* vol. 7 at 66–73.

58   Jones and Walker, *Burnley "Rocky" Jones,* at 184–85.

59   Commission on Systemic Racism, *The Report,* vol. 7 at 56–63.

60   Jones and Walker, *Burnley "Rocky" Jones,* at 185. A 1995 Nova Scotia Barristers' Society report found problems persisted. While 70 percent of white males were hired back after articles, and 28.9 percent of white women were hired back, no articling students from racialized communities were hired back: Canadian Bar Association, *Racial Equality in the Canadian Legal Profession* (Ottawa: Canadian Bar Association, 1999) at 19; Editorial, "Judicial Equality Marching Far Too Slowly" *Halifax Chronicle-Herald* (23 February 1996).

61   Commission on Systemic Racism, *The Report,* vol. 1 at 17, 26, 49–50.

62   *Ibid.*, vol. 4 at 182–90; vol. 1 at 148–50, 193.

63   Eva Hoare, "Chief Denies Racism Played Role in Search" *Halifax Chronicle-Herald* (7 April 1995) 1; Aylward, "Take the Long Way Home" at 268.

64   Aylward, "Take the Long Way Home," at 272; Saunders, *Black and Bluenose,* at 128–29.

65   Interview with Craig Bennell.

66   Interview with Afua Cooper, Halifax, 22 May 2018.

67   Interview with Carolann Wright-Parks, Toronto, 23 August 2018.

68   Interview with Wanda Thomas Bernard, Ottawa, 28 August 2019; Robin DiAngelo, *White Fragility: Why It's So Hard for White People to Talk about Racism* (Boston, MA: Beacon, 2018).

CHAPTER 5: THE INITIAL FALLOUT

1   Trial transcript, Nova Scotia Youth Court, 2 December 1994, in *Rodney Darren Small [R.D.S.] v. Her Majesty the Queen* (N.S.) (Criminal) (By Leave), Supreme Court of Canada, Library and Archives Canada (LAC), RG 125, vol. 5231, file 25063A [hereafter *RDS* LAC].

2   Ibram X. Kendi, *How to Be an Antiracist* (New York: Random House, 2019) at 9–54.

3   *Campbell v. Jones,* [2001] N.S.J. No. 373 (T.D.); *Campbell v. Jones,* [2002] N.S.J. No. 450 (C.A.). See "Epilogue," ch. 12, this book, for more details. On the hostile response of many judges when racism is raised: David M. Tanovich, "The Charter of Whiteness: Twenty-Five Years of Maintaining Racial Injustice in the Canadian Criminal Justice System" (2008) SCLR 655.

4 Interview with Donald Stienburg, Halifax, 28 September 2018. All the words in this paragraph, including the emphasis, are from his interview.

5 *Ibid.*

6 Interviews with Donald Clairmont, Halifax, 16 August and 28 September 2018.

7 Interview with Donald Stienburg; Eva Hoare, "Complaint Launched over Judge's Remarks" *Halifax Chronicle-Herald* (13 December 1994) A7.

8 Interviews with Donald Clairmont.

9 Interview with Richard (Rick) B. Miller, Halifax, 17 August 2018. Miller also believed that Rodney Small made threatening statements to Stienburg in the heat of the moment but concluded that none were admissible because the youth had not yet been cautioned.

10 *Ibid.*

11 *RDS* LAC, twice at 30, once at 31, 50, and 80.

12 Judge Sparks noted that the ride-along witness was not there to corroborate Stienburg. Miller interrupted: "Your Honour, that's the person who I advised earlier was in the hospital ... in a coma." "I see, okay, thank you Mr. Miller," Judge Sparks replied: *ibid.* at 80.

13 Interview with Rick Miller.

14 *Ibid.*

15 Eva Hoare and Barry Dorey, "Top Cop Considers Action against Judge" *Halifax Chronicle-Herald* (10 December 1994) A4; Barry Dorey, "Cop Complains about Judge's Remarks" *Halifax Chronicle-Herald* (9 December 1994) A3; Eva Hoare, "Halifax Police Chief to Complain about Remarks from Judge" *Halifax Chronicle-Herald* (13 December 1994) n.p.; Barry Dorey, "Lawyer Claims Newspaper 'Racist'" *Halifax Chronicle-Herald* (22 December 1994) n.p.

16 Interview with Barry Dorey, Ottawa, 10 May 2019.

17 *Young Offenders Act*, R.S.C. 1985, c. Y-1, s. 44(1).

18 Extracts of the unreported oral decision appear in *The Halifax Herald v. Her Honour Judge Corrine E. Sparks and CBC Corp.*, S.H. No. 112742 (12 May 1995) at 5; Barry Dorey, "Paper Denied Access to Court Tape" *Halifax Chronicle-Herald* (17 December 1994) A3; editorial, "The Young Offenders Act and the Public Interest" *Halifax Chronicle-Herald* (23 December 1994) n.p.

19 Halifax-born in 1929, with a Dalhousie law degree in 1953, Palmeter practised in Halifax from 1954 to 1985. He had a QC and served on the Nova Scotia Barristers' Society council and Dalhousie's board of governors. An elder in the Presbyterian Church, a mason, and the commodore of a sailing club, he belonged to the Halifax Club and the Ashburn Golf Club. President of the Halifax Young PCs and the Halifax federal PC Association and campaign manager for Robert Stanfield, he was appointed by Conservative premier John Buchanan to

the County Court in 1985 and elevated to the Nova Scotia Supreme Court in 1993: "Palmeter, Ian Harold Morton" in Charles E. Haliburton, *A Biographical History of the Judges of Nova Scotia, 1754–2004* (Kentville, NS: Gaspereau Press for the Judges of Nova Scotia, 2004) at 93; "Palmeter, The Hon. Ian Harold Morton," *Canadian Who's Who* (Toronto: University of Toronto Press, 1988) vol. 23 at 651.

20   For details on the misconduct complaint against Judge John R. Nichols, see ch. 6, this book.

21   *Dartmouth/Halifax County Regional Housing Authority v. Sparks* (1992), 112 N.S.R. (3d) 389. Irma Sparks, a Black single mother of two children, challenged legislation that gave fewer eviction rights to public-housing tenants than to private-sector tenants. Palmeter found no *prima facie* equality violation. The Nova Scotia Court of Appeal overruled him, finding a discriminatory impact on single-female parents on social assistance, many of whom were Black: *Sparks v. Dartmouth/Halifax County Regional Housing Authority* (1993), S.C.A. No. 02681.

22   *Halifax Herald v. Sparks,* Supreme Court of Nova Scotia (written decision 12 May 1995) S.H. No. 112747 at 19–27.

23   Interview with Donald Stienburg.

24   Correspondence with Jennifer Stairs, Executive Office of the Nova Scotia Judiciary, 28 March 2019. There is no surviving record of an appointment of a disciplinary review committee. Judicial complaints and chief judges' correspondence are not public documents. A Judicial Council composed of Nova Scotia's chief justice, chief justice of the Supreme Court Trial Division, the Nova Scotia Barristers' Society president, a County Court judge, and a Provincial Court judge heard complaints against provincially appointed judges. Council proceedings were not public. R.E. Kimball, *The Bench: The History of Nova Scotia's Provincial Courts* (Halifax: Province of Nova Scotia, 1989) at 19–20.

25   Rob Roberts, "Apartheid without the Guns" *Halifax Daily News* (26 January 1987) 7.

26   Clarke was appointed chief justice in 1985 on the heels of the *Marshall Report.* Interview with Tom McInnis, Ottawa, 1 November 2018.

27   Interview with former premier John Buchanan, Halifax, 30 July 2018. At the banquet after Sparks's swearing in, Morris cited the challenging history of Black Nova Scotians as his motivation.

28   Halifax-born Morris graduated in political science from Dalhousie and worked as a journalist for the *Halifax-Chronicle* and the Ottawa Parliamentary Press Gallery. He was elected MP, Halifax mayor, and MLA (challenged unsuccessfully by Rocky Jones, who ran for the NDP): George Elliott Clarke, "Rocky Jones Remains a Guiding Force" *Halifax Daily News* (9 April 1988) 13; *Halifax Chronicle-Herald* (4 January 2003) 13; J. Murray Beck, *Politics of Nova Scotia,* vol. 2, *Murray*

to Buchanan, 1896–1988 (Tantallon, NS: Four East Publications, 1988); obituary, *Halifax Herald* (5 January 2003).

29 Interview with Tom McInnis. Morris was criticized for pulling funding from the Black United Front in 1983 for alleged financial mismanagement and later attempting to merge it with the Black Cultural Centre. He was convicted in 1988 for disclosing the social welfare records of a Black welfare-rights activist who had led a disruptive demonstration of single mothers and their children through the legislature; he then lost his cabinet post: Alan Jeffers, "Black United Front Official Rasheed Removed as Organization's Signing Authority" *Halifax Chronicle-Herald* (14 January 1984); Robert Devet, "How Dare You! Brenda Thompson on Welfare Activism in the Eighties" *Nova Scotia Advocate* (14 March 2017), online: <https://nsadvocate.org/2017/03/14/how-dare-you-brenda-thompson-on-welfare-activism-in-the-eighties/>.

30 Morris oversaw the closure of the open dump in Halifax's North End, worked to reduce homelessness, supported Black community leader Calvin Ruck when he campaigned to stop white barbers from refusing service to Blacks, and was the prime mover in locating new facilities for the Family Court. Morris's executive assistant, George Borden, was an African Nova Scotian who served with the Royal Canadian Air Force, cofounded the Black Hall of Fame, and worked with the Black United Front: Alex Cook, "George Borden, Champion of Black Canadian Military History, Has Died," online: <https://www.cbc.ca/news/canada/nova-scotia/george-borden-champion-black-canadian-military-history-1.5827022>; obituary, "Graham Leo Downey, 1st African Nova Scotian councillor, dead at 76," online: <https://www.cbc.ca/news/canada/nova-scotia/graham-leo-downey-1st-african-nova-scotian-councillor-dead-at-76-1.3220459>; Lindsay Ruck, *Winds of Change: The Life and Legacy of Calvin W. Ruck* (Lawrencetown Beach, NS: Pottersfield Press, 2014) at 61–64; Obituary of George Borden, "Serviceman Championed Contributions of Black Canadians in the Military" *Globe and Mail* (29 December 2020) B15.

31 Interview with Judge Sparks, Halifax, 17 August 2018. The following Black lawyers were then practising in Nova Scotia: Davies Bagambiire, Ken Crawford, George Davis, Wayne Kelsie, Cheet Mondayah, Donald Oliver, Anthony Ross, Doug Ruck, Connie Sparks, Gus Wedderburn, Cass Williams, and another male lawyer originally from Antigua (name unknown). Anthony Ross indicated that he turned down an earlier appointment overture. Interview with Anthony Ross, Toronto, 26 May 2019.

32 Family Court, established under provincial statute in 1963 to exercise the powers of a juvenile court and a provincial magistrate, was administered by the Nova Scotia Minister of Public Welfare (later renamed Minister of Social Services). Its jurisdiction included dependent parents, wives' and children's maintenance,

legitimacy and maintenance proceedings for children of unmarried parents, child employment, child neglect, truancy, misbehaviour prosecutions under the education statute, the federal *Juvenile Delinquents Act,* and certain assault charges under the Criminal Code: Timothy T. Daly, "A History of the Nova Scotia Family Court" in Kimball, *The Bench,* at 143–49.

33 Interview with Sandra Oxner, Toronto, 21 June 2019.

34 Interview with Judge Sparks; Evelyn C. White, "Judge Corrine Sparks" (2018) [unpublished, Halifax: Delmore "Buddy" Daye Learning Institute]. The appointment occurred a few months later, when Sparks was age thirty-four.

35 Interview with Anthony Ross.

36 Interview with Canadian senator Tom McInnis, formerly Nova Scotia minister of education (emphasis is his).

37 Interview with John Buchanan. Halifax-born Terry Richard Boyd Donahoe graduated from Dalhousie law in 1967 and practised with Ian Palmeter's firm before becoming an MLA: obituary, "Nova Scotians Mourn Death of Former MPP," online: <https://www.theglobeandmail.com/news/national/nova-scotians-mourn-death-of-former-mpp/article18256776/>.

38 Thomas Johnson McInnis completed Dalhousie law in 1976, practised property and commercial law before becoming a Conservative MLA, served in cabinet from 1978 to 1993, and was appointed to the Canadian Senate in 2012. He was one of few politicians to acknowledge racism: Gordon Delaney, "Racism Reaches beyond CJ System – AG" *Halifax Chronicle-Herald* (22 March 1990) C5. Interview with Tom McInnis, and his official website.

39 Interview with John Buchanan; White, "Judge Corrine Sparks." John MacLennan Buchanan graduated from Dalhousie law in 1958, practised in Halifax, was elected MLA in 1967, lost in 1974 to Liberal premier Gerald Regan, and led the Conservatives to victory in 1978, becoming premier until 1990 (the longest continuously serving premier in Nova Scotia history) and a Canadian senator from 1990 to 2006: J. Murray Beck, "John Buchanan," *Canadian Encyclopedia* (18 February 2018), online: <https://www.thecanadianencyclopedia.ca/en/article/john-buchanan/>.

40 Interview with Tom McInnis.

41 Interview with John Buchanan.

42 *Ibid.*

43 Interview with Douglas Ruck, Halifax, 16 July 2019.

44 Interview with Helen Foote, Halifax, 16 July 2019.

45 Daly, "A History of Nova Scotia Family Court," at 149.

46 Interview with Helen Foote.

47 Interview with Marva Welch, Halifax, 2 October 2018.

48 Interview with Evelyn C. White, Halifax, 22 May 2018.

49 Margaret Thornton, "Otherness on the Bench: How Merit Is Gendered" (2007) 29 Sydney L Rev 391.

50 *Ibid.*; Constance Backhouse, *Claire L'Heureux-Dubé: A Life* (Vancouver: UBC Press, 2017); Constance Backhouse, *Two Firsts: Bertha Wilson and Claire L'Heureux-Dubé at the Supreme Court of Canada* (Toronto: Second Story Press, 2019).

51 Interview with Delvina Bernard, Toronto, 15 August 2018. Robert S. Wright, an African Nova Scotian sociologist, described what it took for Blacks to achieve a similar reputation among whites. He used the outdated terminology of "Negro" ironically and deliberately: "There are two classes of people working for change. Angry 'Negroes' who run into the street and burn stuff down and reasonable 'Negroes' who get asked how to put the fire out. Those who count ourselves among the reasonable Negroes should not be confused. Our phones would never ring without the angry Negroes. But don't get me wrong. Underneath every reasonable Negro is a raging Negro who has through whatever means developed the skill to be bilingual, bicultural, to know how to talk to white people, how to do 'two-eyed seeing' as Indigenous people call it." Interview with Robert S. Wright, Halifax, 14 February 2020.

52 Interview with Delvina Bernard.

53 Both prosecution and defence counsel agreed, and the courts concurred, that Sparks was "functus" once she delivered her oral decision and failed to reserve. Notice of Appeal, "The Queen v. Rodney Darren Small" (22 December 1994), *R. v. R.D.S.,* [1995] N.S.J. No. 184 at 2–5.

54 Judge Corrine E. Sparks, "Supplementary Reasons for Judgment," at 4–6, included in Supreme Court of Canada, LAC, RG125, vol. 5231, file 25063A.

55 Interview with Arleen Huggins, Toronto, 13 May 2019; interview with Carolann Wright-Parks, Toronto, 23 August 2018; interview with Juanita Westmoreland-Traore, Montreal, 21 October 2018; interview with Robert E. Lutes, Halifax, 28 May 2018. For further analysis of the supplementary reasons, see "The Supreme Court of Canada's 'Gang of Five'" ch. 10, this book.

CHAPTER 6: THE APPEALS
BEGIN IN NOVA SCOTIA'S SUPREME COURT

1 Interview with Richard (Rick) B. Miller, Halifax, 17 August 2018.

2 *Manual on Appeals to the Court of Appeal,* forwarded by Denise Smith, Deputy Director, NS Public Prosecution Service, 5 June 2019. Smith declined an interview; email 6 June 2019.

3 Interview with Judge Jean Whalen, Halifax, 19 July 2019.

4 Notice of Appeal, "The Queen v. Rodney Darren Small" (22 December 1994).

5 *R. v. R.D.S.*, [1995] N.S.J. No. 184 at 3–4 [hereafter NSSC 1995].

6 Interview with Donald Stienburg, Halifax, 28 September 2018.

7 John Demont, "Regan Acquitted," *Maclean's* (28 December 1998); Stephen Kimber, *"Not Guilty": The Trial of Gerald Regan* (Toronto: Stoddart, 1999) at 263; Stephen Kimber, *Aphrodisiac: Sex, Politics, Power and Gerald Regan* (Cork: BookBaby, 2016) at 393; interview with Donald Clairmont, Halifax, 16 August 2018. Denise Smith, head of the Public Prosecution Service, email, 24 April 2018, noted that Reid, then retired, declined to be interviewed.

8 Demont, "Regan Acquitted."

9 NSSC 1995 at 4.

10 Barry Dorey, "Halifax Teenager Will Be Retried; Judge's Possible Bias against Police Triggers New Trial" *Halifax Chronicle-Herald* (19 April 1995).

11 NSSC 1995 at 4.

12 She documented the Crown's unusual assertion: "The Crown submits that this creates an appearance of unfairness. The Crown goes further and alleges that the remarks exhibit real bias": NSSC 1995 at 4.

13 *Ibid.* at 4–5.

14 *Ibid.* Rick Miller set a new trial date of 30 October 1995, but it was pre-empted by the appeal. Interview with Rick Miller; "Rocky Jones Plans an Appeal" *Halifax Daily News* (26 October 1995) 4.

15 "Sparks Did Make Mistakes" *Halifax Daily News* (7 May 1995) 21.

16 Allison Lawlor, "Obituary, Constance Glube: Canada's First Female Chief Justice Made History" *Globe and Mail* (15 February 2016), online: <https://www. theglobeandmail.com/news/national/constance-glube-nova-scotias-first-female -supreme-court-judge-dies-aged-84/article28759964/>.

17 "Sam Lepofsky Passes – Asst. Crown Attorney" *Ottawa Citizen* (23 October 1956) 7, describes her father as prominent in legal and Progressive Conservative circles. Her mother, Pearl Slonemsky Lepofsky, was a stenographer. After a business career, Richard Glube joined Dalhousie's faculty of business.

18 Interview with Connie Glube, Halifax, 28 October 2014. On the pipelines to graduate school built by Harvard-trained law professors for their award-winning law students, see Philip Girard, *Bora Laskin: Bringing Law to Life* (Toronto: University of Toronto Press, 2005).

19 Interview with Chief Justice Glube.

20 Philip Girard and Jeffrey Haylock, "Stratification, Economic Adversity, and Diversity in an Urban Bar: Halifax, Nova Scotia, 1900–1950" in Constance Backhouse and W. Wesley Pue, eds., *The Promise and Perils of Law: Lawyers in Canadian History* (Toronto: Irwin Law, 2009) 75 at 90–99.

21 *Ibid.*

22 Obituary, "Leonard Arthur Kitz," online: <https://www.legacy.com/ca/ obituaries/theglobeandmail/name/leonard-kitz-obituary?pid=189823243>. In

1955, he was elected Halifax's first Jewish mayor. See Charles E. Haliburton, *A Biographical History of the Judges of Nova Scotia, 1754–2004* (Kentville, NS: Gaspereau Press for the Judges of Nova Scotia, 2004) at 85, for year of call.

23 Interview with Chief Justice Glube.

24 *Ibid.*; Lawlor, "Obituary, Constance Glube." Connie Sparks articled with the Halifax City legal department two years after Glube left.

25 She was an original member of the congregation that her father-in-law helped found in 1957: "Constance Rachelle Glube Obituary," *Digital Memory*, online: <https://www.dignitymemorial.com/obituaries/halifax-ns/constance -glube-6803915>; "Constance Glube, 1st Female Chief Justice of a Canadian Court, Dead at 84," online: <https://www.cbc.ca/news/canada/nova-scotia/ constance-glube-first-woman-supreme-court-dead-1.3448762>; Joel Jacobson, "Constance Glube" *Canadian Jewish News* (15 February 2016), online: <https:// thecjn.ca/news/canada/constance-glube-was-canadas-first-female-provincial -chief-justice/>.

26 Informal conversations with Chief Justice Glube, Halifax, 2005.

27 Obituary, "Leonard Arthur Kitz"; Girard and Haylock, "Stratification," at 96–97.

28 Her appointment raised to 3.3 percent the Jewish judges named to the Nova Scotia higher courts in the twentieth century: R. Blake Brown and Susan S. Jones, "A Collective Biography of the Supreme Court Judiciary of Nova Scotia, 1900–2000" in Philip Girard, Jim Phillips, and Barry Cahill, eds., *The Supreme Court of Nova Scotia, 1754–2004* (Toronto: University of Toronto Press, 2004) 204 at 212–13. Justice Dubinsky presided over Donald J. Marshall's trial, in which Marshall was wrongfully convicted.

29 Interview with Chief Justice Glube.

30 Girard, Phillips, Cahill, *Supreme Court of Nova Scotia,* caption on photo, opposite 271.

31 Brown and Jones, "A Collective Biography," note at 213–14 that by 1995, 88 percent of the federally appointed judges were still male. Margaret Jane Stewart, called to the bar in 1979, was appointed to the Family Court (1985) and the Supreme Court (1992). Elizabeth Ann Roscoe, called to the bar in 1974, was appointed to the Family Court (1984), the Supreme Court Trial Division (1989), and the Appeal Division (1992). Haliburton, *A Biographical History of Judges of Nova Scotia,* at 129, 305.

32 Brown and Jones, "A Collective Biography," at 213–14.

33 Interview with Wayne MacKay, Halifax, 15 August 2018.

34 Constance Backhouse, *Two Firsts: Bertha Wilson and Claire L'Heureux-Dubé at the Supreme Court of Canada* (Toronto: Second Story Press, 2019).

35 Interview with Chief Justice Glube.

36 *Ibid.*

37 "Probably a part of me would have wondered how, as a woman, she was not able to see another type of discrimination." Interview with Michelle Williams, Halifax, 5 June 2018, speaking of her earlier thoughts while a lawyer at Toronto's African Canadian Legal Clinic.

38 Interview with Chief Justice Glube.

39 While acknowledging Laskin's extraordinary life and career, Girard compares him to civil rights activist Frank R. Scott, noting that "from his unassailable position in the Canadian elite," Scott could "commit any number of *faux pas* without losing his social capital; for a Jew, however, one false step could prove fatal." Girard, *Bora Laskin,* at 266–68.

40 Glube obituary, *Digital Memory*; "Constance Glube, 1st Female Chief Justice." Once appointed, she insisted on cutting ties with external organizations to maintain judicial independence. Yet she stayed on as honorary chair, Canadian Mental Health Association (NS region), Neptune Theatre treasurer, and Halifax Heritage Foundation board member: Haliburton, *A Biographical History of Judges of Nova Scotia,* at 85.

41 When the comment was published, Judge Nichols denied having said it, then reconsidered and admitted the statement: Alan Story, "Shooting Acquittal Angers Digby County Blacks" *Halifax Daily News* (3 January 1986) 10; Alan Story, "Judge's Comments on Blacks to Be Probed" *Toronto Star* (10 January 1986); Canadian Press, "Star Seeks Access to Witnesses" *Halifax Chronicle-Herald* (9 April 1986); Alan Jeffers, "Cloud Hangs over Judiciary" *Halifax Chronicle-Herald* (25 April 1986) 3. The other three members of the five-person panel, the first since the council's establishment in 1980, were Chief Justice Lorne Clarke, Provincial Court judge Charles O'Connell, and Nova Scotia Barristers' Society president Robert Huestis.

42 Responses from police representatives who wished not to be identified. Charles Saunders, *Black and Bluenose: The Contemporary History of a Community* (Lawrencetown Beach, NS: Pottersfield Press, 1999) refers at 74 to an "unidentified officer" who claimed that police were reluctant to enforce the law in Black areas "because department officials will leave them twisting in the breeze if charges of racism arise."

43 "HRP Deputy Chief Burbridge Announces Retirement" *Halifax.ca* (13 February 2012), online: <https://www.halifax.ca/home/news/hrp-deputy-chief-burbridge-announces-retirement>.

44 Marla Cranston, "Judge Said Too Much, Higher Court Rules" *Halifax Daily News* (20 April 1995) 5.

45 Charles Saunders, "Speaking Out Can Be Hazardous" *Halifax Daily News* (7 May 1995) 17. The article references assault charges filed by two Black men who claimed police used excessive force in a racialized interaction. The men

withdrew the charges because they could not find a lawyer. Burbridge was criticizing Darryl Gray, an African Nova Scotian minister who supported the claims.

46 Sylvia Hamilton and Claudie Prieto, dirs., *Black Mother Black Daughter* (Ottawa: NFB, 1989).

47 Interview with Senator Wanda Thomas Bernard, Ottawa, 28 August 2019.

48 Interview with Carolann Wright-Parks, Toronto, 23 August 2018.

49 Interviews with Rodney D. Small, Halifax, 9 June and 14 August 2018.

50 "What people said at the time was she was not soft on Black youth who were coming in front of her." Interview with Richard Devlin, Halifax, 9 March 2018. Officer Donald Stienburg said he had heard differently from colleagues: interview with Donald Stienburg.

51 Interview with Robert S. Wright, Halifax, 14 February 2020.

52 Interview with Carolann Wright-Parks; interview with Joan Jones, Halifax, 4 June 2018.

53 Interview with George Elliott Clarke, Toronto, 6 September 2019.

54 Interview with Carolann Wright-Parks.

55 Interview with Sherry Bernard, Halifax, 17 July 2019.

56 Interview with Lynn Jones, Halifax, 4 June 2018.

57 Interview with Sylvia Parris-Drummond, Halifax, 8 March 2018.

58 Interview with Delvina Bernard, Toronto, 15 August 2018.

59 Interview with Senator Wanda Thomas Bernard.

60 Interview with Michelle Williams.

61 Interview with Afua Cooper, Halifax, 22 May 2018.

62 Interview with Jalana Lewis, Toronto, 23 August 2019. Raised in Halifax's North End, Lewis graduated from Dalhousie law in 2013 and was called to the Ontario bar in 2015.

63 Interview with Juanita Westmoreland-Traoré, Montreal, 21 October 2018.

64 Neither the NDP government that appointed Montreal-born Rawlins nor Rawlins herself realized she was the second Black female judge at the time. Interview with Judge Micheline Rawlins, Windsor, 7 October 2019.

65 Interview with Judge Hugh Fraser, Ottawa, 18 September 2019. Fraser was appointed to provincial court in 1993.

66 Interview with Judge Sparks.

67 Interview with Denise Dwyer, Toronto, 26 July 2019. Dwyer added that she was not representing her organization in this comment.

68 Interview with Arleen Huggins, Toronto, 13 May 2019.

69 Interview with Elizabeth Adjin-Tettey, Victoria, 20 February 2020.

70 A retired Black judge from the Washington, DC, area mentioned the case to Judge Sparks at an international gathering. She was surprised to discover she was speaking to the woman at the centre of the challenge. Interview with Judge Sparks, Halifax, 8 December 2021.

71 Joan Jones, "Marshall Inquiry Lessons Have Yet to Be Learned" *Halifax Chronicle-Herald* (18 May 1995) B2.

72 Reakash Walters, "Against Amnesia: Black Women's Leadership in the Halifax Civil Rights Movement (1950–1979)" (2020) 32 CJWL 383. Joan Jones died in Halifax, 1 April 2019.

73 Jones, "Marshall Inquiry Lessons."

74 Interview with Joan Jones.

75 Supreme Court of Canada, Library and Archives Canada, RG 125, vol. 5231, file 25063A, p. 6.

CHAPTER 7: NOVA SCOTIA COURT OF APPEAL

1 Richard F. Devlin, "We Can't Go on Together with Suspicious Minds: Judicial Bias and Racialized Perspective in *R. v. R.D.S.*", (1995) 18 Dal LJ 408 at 422, found only one earlier case, where the white judge was exonerated of race bias despite "unfortunate" remarks about business corruption in Pakistan: *Pirbhai Estate v. Pirbhai,* [1987] B.C.J. No. 2685 (BCCA). The Supreme Court of Canada refused leave to appeal in 1988. *Arthurs v. The Queen,* [1974] S.C.R. 287, involved facts of overt racism, where the trial judge urged the jury to disregard the defence counsel's reference to the accused's race (both defence counsel and accused were Black), adding, "[I]t makes no difference whether a man is black, white, yellow, or red, they are all entitled to the same consideration." The Supreme Court upheld the trial judge's charge, stating that "[r]acial overtones are only of importance in the event that they result in a charge in which racial prejudice is manifested."

2 *R. v. R.D.S.,* [1995] N.S.J. No. 444 [hereafter NSCA 1995].

3 *Ibid.* at paras. 18, 22, 37. The court briefly rejected that the decision was based on credibility prior to the disputed comments (para. 19). It rejected that the concept of substantive equality under the Charter should frame Sparks's remarks because it was not raised in the court below (para. 45) and because the lower court had not applied "an inappropriate equality approach" (para. 46).

4 Barry Dorey, "Decision Reserved in Attempt to Have Teen's Acquittal Stand" *Halifax Chronicle-Herald* (14 October 1995).

5 Marla Cranston, "Judge's Police Remarks Echo Reality, Court Told" *Halifax Daily News* (14 October 1995) 6.

6 Interview with Mark Knox, Halifax, 16 July 2019; interview with Robert E. Lutes, Halifax, 4 June 2018.

7 Dorey, "Decision Reserved."

8 "Blind Justice, Bias Uneasy Partners" *Halifax Daily News* (28 October 1995) 21.

9 Charles E. Haliburton, *A Biographical History of the Judges of Nova Scotia, 1754–2004* (Kentville, NS: Gaspereau Press for the Judges of Nova Scotia, 2004).

10 "Flinn, Edward J. (Ted)," in *ibid.* at 135. Press coverage of his appointment described him as "another well-known Halifax Liberal lawyer": "Grits Accused of Patronage in Judicial Appointments" *Halifax Chronicle-Herald* (6 April 1995) A6; "Edward John Flinn: Doctor of Laws," Saint Mary's University, online: <https://smu.ca/academics/archives/edward-john-flinn.html>.

11 "Pugsley, Ronald Newton" in Haliburton, *A Biographical History of the Judges of Nova Scotia,* at 131; obituary, Ronald Newton Pugsley, *Globe and Mail* (9 May 2000), online: <https://www.legacy.com/ca/obituaries/theglobeandmail/name/justice-pugsley-obituary?pid=189712473>; tribute by Senator Donald H. Oliver, *Debates of the Senate (Hansard),* 36th Parl., 2nd Sess., vol. 138, issue 53 (9 May 2000). Pugsley and Oliver had been law partners at Stewart McKelvey.

12 Reference to the white detective accused of a shoddy investigation is in *Royal Commission on the Donald Marshall, Jr., Prosecution: Digest of Findings and Recommendations* (December, 1989) 3. On Nichols, see ch. 6, this book.

13 *Marshall Reference* (1983), 57 N.S.R. (2d) 286.

14 R. Blake Brown and Susan S. Jones, "A Collective Biography of the Supreme Court Judiciary of Nova Scotia, 1900–2000" in Philip Girard, Jim Phillips, and Barry Cahill, eds., *The Supreme Court of Nova Scotia, 1754–2004* (Toronto: University of Toronto Press, 2004) 204 at 223.

15 Girard, Phillips, Cahill, *Supreme Court of Nova Scotia,* at 188–90; interview with Senator Tom McInnis, Ottawa, 1 November 2018.

16 Nell Irvin Painter, *The History of White People* (New York: W.W. Norton, 2010), notes at 72–90 that Johann Fredrich Blumenbach, who invented the term, based his nineteenth-century research on a collection of skulls and his belief that Mount Caucasus produced "the most beautiful race of men." Painter describes the decision to label English-speaking white people after a "troublesome, mountainous, borderland just north of Turkey" as bizarre.

17 *The Committee for Justice and Liberty v. The National Energy Board,* [1978] 1 S.C.R. 369 at 394.

18 *Metropolitan Properties Ltd. v. Lannon,* [1968] 3 All E.R. 304 at 310.

19 Robert F. Reid and Hillel David, *Administrative Law and Practice,* 2nd ed. (Toronto: Butterworths, 1978) at 231.

20 NCCA 1995 at para. 31.

21 Devlin, "Suspicious Minds," at 418–21; Richard F. Devlin and Dianne Pothier, "Redressing the Imbalances: Rethinking the Judicial Role after *R. v. R.D.S.*" (1999) 31 Ottawa L Rev 1. Bruce P. Archibald, "The Lesson of the Sphinx" (1998) 10 C.R. (5th) notes at 58: "Courts posit the existence of 'reasonable person'

standards as if these are a sociologically realizable possibility. Yet we know that social, political, and economic differences, some of which may be linked to race, religion, nationality and ethnic origin, make this kind of consensus difficult, if not impossible to achieve."

22 NSCA 1995 at paras. 37–41.

23 *Ibid.* at paras. 42–43.

24 The Freemans were with the first New England settlers in Liverpool, home-steading on Mi'kmaw lands from which the French had been removed in the Acadian exodus: Viva E. Freeman, *Freeman Families of Nova Scotia and Their Ancestors and Descendants and Allied Families: A Genealogy* (Tustin, CA: Freeman Family Trust, 1986); *A History of Settlement of Queen's County Nova Scotia* (Halifax: Formac, 1996), volume held in Justice Freeman's personal library.

25 Interview with Justice Gerald Freeman, Beach Meadows, Queen's County, Nova Scotia, 13 August 2019. Justice Freeman explained that the "Black community in Queen's County was largely ignored" but that he was close friends with Reginald Warrington, a brother of Tiger Warrington, a Canadian boxing champion from the town's most prominent Black family. Nearby Shelburne County, with its history of racist violence, contained the historically segregated community of Birchtown, home of the largest Black Loyalist settlement.

26 *Ibid.* Freeman's partners included Anne Crawford, Ken Jones (also a Con-servative member of the Legislative Assembly), and Carl Milford.

27 *Ibid.*

28 Freeman was elevated in 1990, replacing Justice Ian MacKeigan, who retired before the Canadian Judicial Council review concluded. There was a hierarchy between the two levels of court, with the county courts lacking "prestige" and bearing "a clear badge of inferiority"; for almost a century, federal government policy prevented promotion to the Supreme Court: Girard, Phillips, Cahill, *Supreme Court of Nova Scotia,* at 149, 221.

29 Haliburton, *A Biographical History of the Judges of Nova Scotia,* at 127; interview with Justice Gerald Freeman.

30 NSCA 1995 at paras. 48, 50, 61.

31 *Ibid.* at para. 54.

32 *Ibid.* at paras. 57, 60.

33 *Ibid.* at paras. 59, 61.

34 *Ibid.* at paras. 59, 63–66.

35 *Ibid.* at paras. 62–63, 68.

36 Interview with Gerald Freeman.

37 Interview with Valerie Miller, Halifax, 20 May 2021.

38 Dorey, "Decision Reserved" *Halifax Chronicle-Herald* (14 October 1995); Barry Dorey and Davene Jeffrey, "Boy's Retrial to Go Ahead" *Halifax Chronicle-Herald* (26 October 1995).

39 These committees worked with the newly established National Judicial Institute, which had commenced a study of social context judicial education in 1994. Rosemary Cairns Way and T. Brettel Dawson, "Taking a Stand on Equality: Bertha Wilson and the Evolution of Judicial Education in Canada" in Kim Brooks, ed., *Justice Bertha Wilson: One Woman's Difference* (Vancouver: UBC Press, 2009) 278 at 286.

40 Interview with Helen Foote, Halifax, 16 July 2019.

41 Interview with Ruth Goba, Executive Director of the Black Legal Action Centre, Toronto, 18 February 2020.

42 Thurgood Marshall, who graduated first in his law class at Howard University and won twenty-nine of the thirty-two cases he argued as a lawyer before the Supreme Court, was belittled as neither bright nor hard-working, as someone who watched TV during the day, as the lazy, passive puppet of a white ideological ally, Justice William Brennan. Clarence Thomas was depicted as a "dim bulb in a brightly lit room," as a puppet of Anton Scalia who never asked questions during oral argument because he was sleeping, lazy, or did not know what to ask: Stephen L. Carter, "Thurgood Marshall," *New York Times Magazine* (18 July 2021) 21–26; Corey Robin, *The Enigma of Clarence Thomas* (New York: Henry Holt, 2019) at 10–11; Kevin Merida and Michael Fletcher, *Supreme Discontent: The Divided Soul of Clarence Thomas* (New York: Broadway Books, 2007), chs. 11 and 14.

43 Evelyn C. White, "Judge Corrine Sparks," *Pamphlet for the 30th Anniversary Celebrating African Nova Scotian Judges* (Halifax: Delmore "Buddy" Daye Learning Institute, 2018) at 2.

44 Interview with Sylvia Parris-Drummond, Halifax, 8 March 2018.

45 Born in St. Kitts, Ross completed a bachelors of education at St. Francis Xavier University, a law degree at Dalhousie, and was admitted to the Nova Scotia bar in 1973. Interview with E. Anthony Ross, Toronto, 26 May 2019.

46 Interview with Sherry Bernard, Halifax, 17 July 2019.

47 Interview with Robert S. Wright, Halifax, 14 February 2020.

48 Interview with Heather McNeill, Halifax, 16 August 2018.

49 Interview with Shawna Paris-Hoyte, Halifax, 14 August 2019. Paris-Hoyte added that she was speaking personally, and not representing her organization.

50 Interview with Delvina Bernard, Toronto, 15 August 2018.

51 *Ibid.*

52 Interview with Dianne Carter, Toronto, 29 July 2019.

53 Interview with Evelyn C. White, Halifax, 22 May 2018.

54 She emphasized that her support came from her mother, her aunt in Boston, her pastor, and a close friend at the Human Rights Commission. Interview with Judge Sparks, Halifax, 8 December 2021.

55 Interview with Sylvia Parris-Drummond.

56 Interview with Delvina Bernard.

CHAPTER 8: GENDER MATTERS

1 Kimberlé Williams Crenshaw, "Mapping the Margins: Intersectionality, Identity Politics, and Violence against Women of Color" (1993) 43 Stan Law Rev 1241; Kimberlé Williams Crenshaw *Critical Race Theory: The Key Writings That Formed the Movement* (New York: New Press, 1995); Nitya Duclos, "Disappearing Women: Racial Minority Women in Human Rights Cases" (1993) 6 CJWL 25; Emily Carasco, "A Case of Double Jeopardy: Race and Gender" (1993) 6 CJWL 142; Shelina Neallani, "Women of Colour in the Legal Profession: Facing the Barriers of Race and Sex" (1992) 5 CJWL 148. Ibram X. Kendi, *How to Be an Antiracist* (New York: Random House, 2018) notes at 188–89: "Women are a gender. Black people are a race. When we identify Black women, we are identifying a race-gender. When a policy produces inequalities between race-genders, it is gendered racism."

2 S. Baldwin, C. Hall, C. Bennell, B. Blaskovits, and C. Lawrence, "Distinguishing Features of Excited Delirium Syndrome, Non-fatal Use of Force Encounters" (2016) 41 J Forensic and Leg Medicine 21. Although the study focused on delirium, it also reported on gender in 10.9 million police-public interactions from 2012 to 2015.

3 Jennifer Eberhardt, *Biased: Uncovering the Hidden Prejudice* (New York: Viking, 2019); Neil Gross, "Prejudice Is Blind" *New York Times* (28 April 2019) 16.

4 Antiracist educator Anthony Morgan emphasized the vulnerability of Black children in a racist society: "Blackness is embedded in this inherent sense of threat. [The officer] is not seeing a child. He sees a man. He's encircled by Black men. Nobody male in that space was being read as a child": interview with Anthony Morgan, Toronto, 6 September 2019. Tera Eva Agyepong, *The Criminalization of Black Children* (Chapel Hill: University of North Carolina Press, 2018); Monique W. Morris, *Pushout: The Criminalization of Black Girls in Schools* (New York: New Press, 2016).

5 Don Clairmont and Ethan Kim, "Getting Past the Gatekeepers: The Reception of Restorative Justice in the Nova Scotian Criminal Justice System" (2013) 36 Dal LJ 359 at 369–70.

6 Gwendolyn L. Gerber, *Women and Men Police Officers: Status, Gender, and Personality* (Westport, CT: Praeger, 2001). El Jones thought a white female officer would not have behaved differently, pointing to the defamation lawsuit a white female officer brought against Rocky Jones and Anne Derrick. Interview with El Jones, Halifax, 15 October 2019.

7 Interviews with Rodney Small, Halifax, 9 June and 14 August 2018.

8 Interview with Donald Stienburg, Halifax, 28 September 2018.

9 Interview with Richard (Rick) B. Miller, Halifax, 17 August 2018.

10 Burnley "Rocky" Jones and James W. St.G. Walker, *Burnley "Rocky" Jones: Revolutionary* (Black Point, NS: Roseway, 2016); interview with Jim Walker, Waterloo, 8 August 2018; Reakash Walters, "Against Amnesia: Black Women's Leadership in the Halifax Civil Rights Movement" (2020) 32 CJWL 383.

11 Interview with Delvina Bernard, Halifax, 15 August 2018.

12 Her graduating class photograph shows 134 students: 93 males and 41 females. Dalhousie University Faculty of Law Archives, 1979.

13 Donald Oliver, who graduated in 1964, knew of no Black female graduates from 1955 to 1964. Caribbean-born Marlene I. King (later Nourbese Philip) began at Dalhousie in 1971 but graduated from University of Western Ontario law in 1973. "I.A. Healy" (incorrectly spelled without the "e") appears in the 1976 graduating class photograph but is also included on the list of missing photos in 1977. Either way, she appears to have been first; Elizabeth Sanford, Assistant to the Dean, Dalhousie Law School, email 28 May 2020. April Burey followed in 1983, Jean Whalen in 1984, Valerie Miller in 1985, and Carol Aylward in 1989. Dalhousie Faculty of Law Archives, 1971–93, composite photographs; emails from Judge Sparks, 14 and 15 May 2020; email from Donald Oliver, 15 May 2020.

14 Interview with John Buchanan, Halifax, 30 July 2018.

15 Jacqueline Mullenger, Nova Scotia Barristers' Society (email 22 July 2020), confirmed that Irene A. Healey was called 12 April 1977, never practised in Nova Scotia, and lived in Ottawa. Judge Sparks believed Healey was not from Nova Scotia.

16 Those who followed Sparks's call prior to the Indigenous Blacks and Mi'kmaq (IB&M) Initiative included Jean Whalen (1985), Valerie Miller (1986), and Cynthia Thomas (1991). Never called to the Nova Scotia bar, Burey practised in Ontario. Jacqueline Mullenger, Nova Scotia Barristers' Society (email 22 July 2020), confirmed there was no record of other Black females before 1993 but cautioned that the Barristers' Society did not ask questions about race.

17 Constance Backhouse, *Petticoats and Prejudice: Women and Law in Nineteenth-Century Canada* (Toronto: Women's Press, 1991), ch. 10.

18 Barry Cahill, "Everybody Called Her Frank: The Odyssey of an Early Woman Lawyer in New Brunswick" (2011) 2 J of New Brunswick Studies 55, online: <http://stu-sites.ca/jnbs/en/index.aspx>.

19 King's family moved to Alberta to escape racist violence and arson in Oklahoma. She graduated from the University of Alberta law school in 1953, the only female and only Black. She articled in Calgary, was called to the Alberta bar in 1954, practised with the Department of Citizenship in Ottawa, and then worked with the YMCA in the United States: Rachel K. Bailie, "Minority of One: Violet King's Entry into the Legal Profession" (2012) 24:2 CJWL 301.

20 The first Indigenous female, Roberta Jamieson, graduated from University of Western Ontario law in 1976. Backhouse, *Petticoats and Prejudice,* at 326.

21 Interview with Senator Tom McInnis, Ottawa, 1 November 2018.

22 Constance Backhouse, *Two Firsts: Bertha Wilson and Claire L'Heureux-Dubé at the Supreme Court of Canada* (Toronto: Second Story Press, 2019). Oxner was the first female provincial court judge in the Atlantic provinces: R.E. Kimball, *The Bench: The History of Nova Scotia's Provincial Courts* (Halifax: Province of Nova Scotia, 1989) at 208–9. Halifax-born Oxner had practised with the City of Halifax with Connie Glube. Interview with Sandra Oxner, Toronto, 21 June 2019.

23 Frances Kent Potts, the second female, was appointed to the Provincial Court in 1988. Kimball, *The Bench,* at 208–9. The Task Force on Gender Equality in the Legal Profession, *Touchstones for Change: Equality, Diversity and Accountability* (Ottawa: Canadian Bar Association, 1993) notes at 51 and 186 that by 1993 Nova Scotia's Provincial Court still had thirty-nine male judges out of forty-five. The 13 percent ratio was similar to national figures.

24 Interview with Sandra Oxner.

25 Roscoe was elevated to the Supreme Court in 1989 and to its appellate division in 1992. Stewart was elevated to the Supreme Court in 1992: Charles E. Haliburton, *A Biographical History of the Judges of Nova Scotia, 1754–2004* (Kentville, NS: Gaspereau Press for the Judges of Nova Scotia, 2004) at 129, 305. Kimball, *The Bench,* at 201, lists Family Court judges from 1941.

26 Backhouse, *Two Firsts*; Constance Backhouse, *Claire L'Heureux-Dubé: A Life* (Vancouver: UBC Press, 2017); Erika Rackley, *Women, Judging and the Judiciary* (Abingdon, UK: Routledge, 2012); Sally J. Kenney, *Gender and Justice: Why Women in the Judiciary Really Matter* (Abingdon, UK: Routledge, 2012).

27 Task Force on Gender Equality in the Legal Profession, *Touchstones,* at 192–93.

28 Interview with Judge Sparks, Halifax, 17 August 2018.

29 Task Force on Gender Equality in the Legal Profession, *Touchstones,* at 192–93.

30 Catharine MacKinnon described the double jeopardy of Black women: "You're defined as sexually available. They don't even think of it as a violation. The definition is deep into the white supremacy mindset." Quoted in Linda Hirshman, *Reckoning: The Epic Battle against Sexual Abuse and Harassment* (Boston: Houghton Mifflin Harcourt, 2019) at 53. The combination has been referred to as "misogynoir": Eternity Martis, "Black Women, It's Time Society Fights for Our Lives Too," *Maclean's* (4 June 2020).

31 Interview with Judge Sparks.

32 Black female lawyers and students objected to the absence of racialized members initially on the task force. The task force's *Touchstones* notes at page 4 that "one Woman of Colour said: 'White women lawyers are concerned about how to break through the glass ceiling. We are concerned about how to get through

the front door.'" In 1992, Sparks accepted a belated invitation to join. Sharon McIvor of the Native Women's Association of Canada was also added. Interview with Melina Buckley, Vancouver, 4 May 2020.

33 Nasha Nijhawan and Ben Johnson, "Profile: Judge Corrine Sparks" (2021) Advocates' J 11.

34 Interview with Melina Buckley.

35 "There are very few women from minority groups on the bench. Their responses ... were not encouraging. We look forward to the day when minority women will be sitting at all levels of the Canadian judiciary, bringing their unique insights and understanding of law and life to the judicial process": Task Force on Gender Equality in the Legal Profession, *Touchstones,* at 194.

36 Backhouse, *Two Firsts,* at 225.

37 Interview with Robert S. Wright, Halifax, 14 February 2020.

38 The Delos Davis Law Guild of Ontario was succeeded by the Canadian Association of Black Lawyers (CABL) in 1996.

39 See the National Bar Organization's website.

40 Interview with Judge Sparks. There were objections to the NBA conference costs, something that Judge Hugh Fraser in Ontario also faced when he requested to attend. Equivalent travel funding for others seemed to receive less criticism. There was little recognition of racialized judges' need to meet together. Some colleagues doubted that there was even any need for racialized judges' associations, given that society had "come so far." Interview with Hugh Fraser, Ottawa, 18 September 2019.

41 Women's speech patterns can be subtler than men's, with hyperpolite forms and queries. Communication research suggests that women are socialized to be nonassertive, polite, and proper in language. Their hesitancy contrasts with the tendency of men to communicate more assertively, using self-confident, direct speech patterns. Deborah Tannen, *You Just Don't Understand: Women and Men in Conversation* (New York: Ballantine, 1990).

42 Trial transcript, Nova Scotia Youth Court, 2 December 1994, in *Rodney Darren Small [R.D.S.] v. Her Majesty the Queen* (N.S.) (Criminal) (By Leave), Supreme Court of Canada, Library and Archives Canada (LAC), RG 125, vol. 5231, file 25063A, at 89–93.

43 Her written supplementary reasons were more direct: the officer "appeared nervous when he commenced giving evidence" and "became ruffled" under cross-examination. Yet she still avoided definitive conclusions, noting "*in my view* [Officer Stienburg] became tense," and "this *may have been due* to the racial configuration in the court." She never used the word "racism" and refrained from mentioning that Blacks might feel anxiety, suspicion, and fear in a "white" courtroom. Judge Corrine E. Sparks, "Supplementary Reasons for Judgment," emphasis added.

44 Barry Dorey, "Lawyer Claims Newspaper 'Racist'" *Halifax Chronicle-Herald* (22 December 1994).

45 Barry Dorey, "Decision Reserved in Attempt to Have Teen's Acquittal Stand" *Halifax Chronicle-Herald* (14 October 1995); Marla Cranston, "Judge's Police Remarks Echo Reality, Court Told" *Halifax Daily News* (14 October 1995) 6.

46 Kellee Terrell, "Goodbye to One of the Most Complex Black Women on TV" *New York Times* (14 May 2020), online: <https://www.nytimes.com/2020/05/14/opinion/viola-davis-how-to-get-away-with-murder.html>.

47 Born in Liverpool, Nova Scotia, Williams graduated from University of Toronto law in 1994 and articled with the African Canadian Legal Clinic in Toronto. She obtained a master's in law from New York University in 2001. After working for Jean Augustine, minister of state for multiculturalism and the status of women, in 2004 she became director of the IB&M program at Dalhousie's school of law, where she is now a professor. Interview with Michelle Williams, Halifax, 5 June 2018.

48 Born in East Preston, Bernard was the first African Nova Scotian tenure-track professor at Dalhousie. Interview with Senator Wanda Thomas Bernard, Ottawa, 28 August 2019.

49 Interview with Arleen Huggins, Toronto, 13 May 2019.

50 Hamilton-born Maryka Omatsu graduated from Osgoode Hall law in 1975 and was appointed to the Ontario provincial court in 1992.

51 Interview with Philip Graham, Toronto, 20 December 2019.

52 Interview with Dr. Barrington Walker, Kingston, 25 August 2019.

53 Dartmouth-born Jean Whalen graduated from Dalhousie law, articled at the City of Halifax, opened a solo practice, and then became the first African Nova Scotian woman hired as prosecutor. Interview with Judge Jean Whalen, Halifax, 14 July 2019.

54 Evangeline Cain-Grant founded the Parent-Student Association to lobby for change after the Cole Harbour racism eruption in 1989. She graduated from Dalhousie law and was called to the Nova Scotia bar in 1994. Interview with Evangeline Cain-Grant, Toronto, 20 December 2019.

55 Interview with Delvina Bernard.

56 Toronto-born Morgan graduated from McGill law, practised with the African Canadian Legal Clinic and Falconer LLP, and worked as an antiracism educator at the City of Toronto. Interview with Anthony Morgan, Toronto, 6 September 2019.

57 *Ibid.*

58 R. Blake Brown and Susan S. Jones, "A Collective Biography of the Supreme Court Judiciary of Nova Scotia, 1900–2000" in Philip Girard, Jim Phillips, and

Barry Cahill, eds., *The Supreme Court of Nova Scotia, 1754–2004* (Toronto: University of Toronto Press, 2004) 204 at 212–14.

59 Chelsea Sauvé, "Canada 150: Constance Glube, 1931–2016" *Ottawa Jewish Bulletin* (27 February 2017); Wayne Larsen, "Chief Justice Constance Glube Recalled as 'Feminist Hero'" *Toronto Star* (28 February 2016), online: <https://www.thestar.com/news/insight/2016/02/28/chief-justice-constance-glube-recalled-as-feminist-hero.html>.

60 Interview with Sandra Oxner, describing her conversation with Glube.

61 Jennifer Brown, "Glube Was 'Feminist Hero' in Legal Profession," *Canadian Lawyer* (16 February 2016), online: <https://www.canadianlawyermag.com/news/general/glube-was-feminist-hero-in-legal-profession/273621#:~:text=The%20NSBS%20called%20Glube%20%E2%80%9Ca,justice%20of%20a%20Canadian%20court>.

62 Interview with Richard Devlin, Halifax, 8 March 2018.

63 Dorothy Sterling, ed., *We Are Your Sisters: Black Women in the Nineteenth Century* (New York: W.W. Norton, 1984); Paula Giddings, *When and Where I Enter: The Impact of Black Women on Race and Sex in America* (New York: William Morrow, 1984), ch. 27. Giddings quotes Toni Morrison at 307: "The faces of those white women hovering behind that black girl at the Little Rock school in 1957 do not soon leave the retina of the mind."

64 Born in Wales, El Jones grew up in Winnipeg and graduated in film studies at University of Manitoba. She moved to Halifax in 2002, was named Halifax Municipal Poet, and holds a Chair in Women's Studies at Mount Saint Vincent University. Interview with El Jones.

65 Giddings, *When and Where I Enter,* adding, at 348–49, "The Black woman was able to accomplish so much ... because she had an unshakable conviction: The progress of neither *race nor womanhood* could proceed without her. And she understood the relationship between the two."

66 Interview with El Jones.

67 Interview with Anthony Morgan.

CHAPTER 9: APPEAL TO
THE SUPREME COURT OF CANADA

1 Interview with Rodney Small, Halifax, 9 June 2018.

2 Interview with Denise Kelsie Small, Halifax, 21 August 2018.

3 Rocky Jones had divorced his wife, Joan Jones, in 1993 to marry Sharon, a forty-seven-year-old white banker. Interview with Sharon Jones, Halifax, 17 July 2019; Burnley "Rocky" Jones and James W. St.G. Walker, *Burnley "Rocky" Jones: Revolutionary* (Halifax: Roseway, 2016) at 192–94. Joan Jones, who had been so

involved in the case, had been invited and described her ex-husband as one of her "best friends" but could not afford to attend. Interview with Joan Jones, Halifax, 15 August 2018.

4 Jones and Walker, *Burnley "Rocky" Jones,* at 203; interview with Lynn Jones, Halifax, 4 June 2018.

5 Carolann Wright-Parks and Yvonne Atwell represented the Afro-Canadian Caucus. Wright-Parks explained that she, Atwell, Sherry Bernard, Carol Aylward, Joan Jones, Crystal Mulder, and Tracy Mulder helped to solicit travel funds, including from the National Action Committee on the Status of Women. Interview with Carolann Wright-Parks, Toronto, 23 August 2018; interview with Sherry Bernard, Halifax, 17 July 2019; Carol Aylward, "Take the Long Way Home: *R.D.S. v. R.* – The Journey" (1998) 47 UNBLJ 286 at 293–94.

6 Interview with Lynn Jones.

7 Interview with Denise Kelsie Small.

8 Correspondence with Jewel Amoah, intervener counsel, 4 December 2019. She recalled Melanie Ash as the Black law clerk.

9 Interview with Yola Grant, Toronto, 22 March 2018.

10 Jones and Walker, *Burnley "Rocky" Jones,* at 201–2; interview with Lynn Jones; interview with Vince Kazmierski, Ottawa, 31 July 2018.

11 Interview with Lynn Jones.

12 Jones and Walker, *Burnley "Rocky" Jones,* at 202.

13 Interview with Robert E. Lutes, Halifax, 4 June 2018.

14 Jones and Walker, *Burnley "Rocky" Jones,* 202–3.

15 Interview with Denise Kelsie Small.

16 Jones and Walker, *Burnley "Rocky" Jones,* at 202; interview with Dianne Pothier, Halifax, 20 February 2009.

17 Interview with Yola Grant.

18 Jones, Burey, Grant, Allen, Jewel Amoah (for the African Canadian Clinic), and Douglas Johnson (articling student with Lutes).

19 Aylward, "Take the Long Way Home."

20 Appellant's Factum, in *Rodney Darren Small* [*R.D.S.*] *v. Her Majesty the Queen* (N.S.) (Criminal) (By Leave), Supreme Court of Canada, Library and Archives Canada (LAC), RG 125, vol. 5231, file 25063 [hereafter Appellant's Factum] at 13–14, 26–29, 31; interview with Richard Devlin, Halifax, 9 March 2018.

21 Court Challenges offered government funding for language and equality-rights cases, and Dalhousie law school added funds. Law professors involved included Richard Devlin, Carol Aylward, Dianne Pothier, Wayne MacKay, Archibald Kaiser, and Rollie Thompson, along with law students Vince Kazmierski, Lianne Lagroix, and Bill Watts. Devlin published an article on judicial bias before the hearing: "We Can't Go on Together with Suspicious Minds: Judicial Bias and Racialized Perspective in *R. v. R.D.S.*" (1995) 18 Dal LJ 408.

22 *Nova Scotia (Minister of Community Services) v. S.M.S. et al.* (1992), 110 N.S.R. (2d) 91. Niedermayer graduated Dalhousie law in 1967, practised in Port Hawkesbury and Windsor, Nova Scotia, and with Nova Scotia Legal Aid. He was appointed to Dartmouth Family Court in 1979. R.E. Kimball, *The Bench: The History of Nova Scotia's Provincial Courts* (Halifax: Province of Nova Scotia, 1989) at 177.

23 *R. v. Parks* (1993), 84 C.C.C. (3d) 353, permitting lawyers to question jurors about race bias. Doherty, a former prosecutor, was appointed to the Ontario High Court in 1988 and the Court of Appeal in 1990. The Supreme Court of Canada would later distinguish *Parks* because Doherty referred to expert evidence "documenting the prevalence of anti-black racism in the Metropolitan Toronto area." *R. v. R.D.S.,* [1997] 3 S.C.R. 484 [hereafter SCC 1997] at 536.

24 Appeal Transcript of Oral Argument, *R.D.S. v. The Queen,* Supreme Court of Canada, 10 March 1997, Library and Archives Canada, RG 125, vol. 5231, file 25063A [hereafter Transcript] at 2–5, 14.

25 Interview with Lynn Jones; Jones and Walker, *Burnley "Rocky" Jones,* at 203.

26 Interview with Carolann Wright-Parks.

27 Section 15(1): "Every individual is equal before and under the law and has the right to the equal protection and equal benefit of the law without discrimination and, in particular, without discrimination based on race, national or ethnic origin, colour, religion, sex, age or mental or physical disability."

28 Interview with Dianne Pothier; Pothier, curriculum vitae. Pothier's parents had moved for economic reasons to Halifax from a small Acadian settlement in southwest Nova Scotia. They chose not to speak French to their children because they did not want them to be discriminated against in an English-speaking society. Pothier was determined to learn French and became bilingual as an adult. Private information provided to the author.

29 Dianne Pothier, "Miles to Go: Some Personal Reflections on the Social Construction of Disability" (1992) 14 Dal LJ 526.

30 Transcript at 20–26; Appellant's Factum at 37.

31 Lamer's father, Antonio Lamer, was French Canadian. His mother's ethnicity was part Irish, part French. Her first language was English. "Antonio Lamer," Osgoode Society, oral history, transcript (19 January 1994) at 7–16, 43–48, 57.

32 Transcript at 10–12. Dictionaries describe "honky" as a derogatory term Blacks use to describe whites.

33 Video recording, Supreme Court of Canada Archives; interview with Yola Grant.

34 Transcript at 20–21.

35 *Ibid.* at 21–25.

36 Ruth Goba, Executive Director of the Black Legal Action Centre, pointed out, "You can't call the judges judging your case racist, even though everything on

the ground tells you that there is bias in every structure of the justice system ... prisons, education, child welfare, the health care system. When it comes to the legal field, everybody is very *objective*." Interview with Ruth Goba, Toronto, 18 February 2020.

37 Transcript at 23–24. For further analysis of the race implications of all the questions put by the Supreme Court judges that day, see Constance Backhouse, "Turning the Tables on *R.D.S.*: Racially Revealing Questions Asked by White Judges" (2021) 44:1 Dal LJ 181.

38 Transcript at 25.

39 Interview with Yola Grant.

40 Interview with Lynn Jones.

41 Interview with Sharon Jones.

42 Interview with Chantal Tie (cochair, LEAF legal committee), Ottawa, 30 July 2018.

43 Interview with Michelle Williams, Halifax, 5 June 2018.

44 Bertha Wilson, foreword to LEAF, *Equality and the Charter* (Toronto: Emond Montgomery, 1996) at xi.

45 LEAF was founded in 1985 to advocate a "more woman-centred view of the world" in Canadian law. LEAF, *Equality*, at xi; Sherene Razack, *Canadian Feminism and the Law* (Toronto: Second Story Press, 1992) at 12. The NOIVMWC coalition was founded in 1986 to advance the interests of racialized and immigrant women. It included Hispanic, Chinese, and Filipino women's committees. Roxana Ng, "Managing Female Immigration: The Institutional Sexism and Racism" (1992) 12:3 Can Woman Studies 20; Brenda O'Neill, Elisabeth Gidengil, and Lisa Young, "The Political Integration of Immigrant and Visible Minority Women" (2012) 6:2–3 Can Political Science Rev 185 at 187; Aylward, "Take the Long Way Home," at 291.

46 Interview with Carissima Mathen, Ottawa, 23 April 2018; interview with Jennifer Scott, Toronto, 23 August 2018.

47 Factum of Interveners, LEAF and NOIVMWC, file 25063, at 5.

48 Interview with Yola Grant.

49 *Ibid.*

50 Transcript at 24, 32.

51 Interview with Yola Grant.

52 *Ibid.*

53 LEAF was conscious of its reputation for "whiteness" and committed to diversifying. Interview with Carissima Mathen; interview with Jennifer Scott; Lise Gotell, "Towards a Democratic Practice of Feminist Litigation? LEAF's Changing Approach to *Charter* Equality" in Rahda Jhappan, ed., *Women's Legal Strategies in Canada* (Toronto: University of Toronto Press, 2002) 135.

54 Interview with Carol Allen, Meaford, 31 May 2018.

55 Interview with Yola Grant.

56 Transcript at 40.

57 Interview with Carissima Mathen.

58 Interview with Yola Grant. Grant also argued judicial notice, the rule that judges may rely without further proof on "facts which are so notorious as not to be the subject of dispute among reasonable persons." Because the Halifax trial occurred four years after the Marshall Inquiry, she claimed that assessing interactions between police and Black male youths required recognition of "notorious social facts" about racism: transcript at 31–34; Factum of Interveners, LEAF and NOIVMWC, file 25063, at 5–6, 10–12. Appellants Jones and Pothier had chosen not to focus on judicial notice for two reasons: it had not been raised at trial, and out of concern that if the argument failed, it could be taken as a wider precedent denying the existence of racism. Walker and Jones, *Burnley "Rocky" Jones,* at 201; James W. St.G. Walker, "A Black Day in Court: 'Race' and Judging in *R. v. R.D.S.*" in Barrington Walker, ed., *The African Canadian Legal Odyssey: Historical Essays* (Toronto: University of Toronto Press, 2012) 437 at 454–58. The Supreme Court declined to consider judicial notice because it was not raised by the appellants (at 535). An African Canadian judge of the Ontario Court of Justice, Micheline Rawlins, explained the complexities: "What are you allowed to take judicial notice of? You've got to say the sun rises in the east. You can take that on judicial notice. Can you take judicial notice of driving while Black? What of something that may not be common knowledge among one group because they are exempt due to the colour of their skin? When the judge taking judicial notice has specialized knowledge due to the colour of their skin, does that fit the rule?" Interview with Judge Micheline Rawlins, Windsor, 7 October 2019.

59 Siobhan Alexander, Jewel Amoah, Jacqueline Lawrence, Margaret Parsons, Michelle Williams, and Christopher Wilson worked with Burey. The test-case clinic was established after the 1992 Rodney King verdict and a series of Toronto police shootings of Black citizens.

60 An organization founded in 1987 to provide "advocacy and leadership on socio-economic, cultural and political matters" affecting African Nova Scotians. Interview with Carolann Wright-Parks; Aylward, "Take the Long Way Home," at 291–92.

61 Founded in 1973 as an outgrowth of the Canadian Negro Women's Association. "Congress of Black Women of Canada (CBWC)/Congrès des femmes noires du Canada," Rise Up! A Digital Archives of Feminist Activism, online: <https://riseupfeministarchive.ca/activism/organizations/congress-of-black-women-of-canada-cbwc/>.

62 "April Burey, March 1960–December 12, 1999" online: <https://www.oocities.org/capitolhill/2381/Lawschoolscase/uoftlaw-burey1.html>.

63 Interview with Dr. Sharon Burey, Tecumseh, Ontario, 1 April 2022; interview with Peter Showler, Ottawa, 13 July 2019; interview with Michelle Williams; correspondence from Jewel Amoah, 4 December 2019.

64 Correspondence from Jewel Amoah.

65 Transcript at 44–47.

66 *Ibid.* at 44–48.

67 *Ibid.* at 49.

68 Stephen Bindman, "Racism a Historical Truth, Top Court Told" *Southam Newspapers* (11 March 1997) A3.

69 Interview with Yola Grant; interview with Carissima Mathen.

70 Conversation between Rocky Jones and Shawna Paris-Hoyte, recalled in interview with Paris-Hoyte, Halifax, 14 August 2019; interview with Lynn Jones.

71 Interview with Michelle Williams.

72 Interview with Carol Allen.

73 Interview with Robert Lutes.

74 *Ibid.*

75 Transcript at 50. Lutes later explained that he was told Stienburg had a great reputation within the police force, considered by many to be one of the most tolerant persons there. Interview with Robert Lutes.

76 SCC 1997 at 542–53.

77 Transcript at 50.

78 *Ibid.* at 50, 59–62, 74; Respondent's Factum, file 25063, at 29–30.

79 Respondent's Factum at 8, 27, 34.

80 Jones and Walker, *Burnley "Rocky" Jones,* at 204.

81 Interview with Carol Allen. Yola Grant explained, "It was clear he wasn't an enemy, and he didn't pull any fast ones." Interview with Yola Grant.

82 Transcript at 87–90.

83 CCNC, letter to Canadian Judicial Council, 28 October 1997.

84 "Antonio Lamer: Judge Referred to Chinese As 'Tremendous Gamblers'" *Toronto Star* (4 November 1997).

85 CCNC letter.

86 Dale Anne Freed, "Top Judge Accused of 'Stereotyping'" *Toronto Star* (4 November 1997) A25 [printed version]. The digital version, retrieved with Factiva, Inc., omits Freed's byline and contains additional paragraphs noting that Lamer was one of three dissenting judges, that the Roma Advocacy Centre had a problem with his statements, and that the National Action Committee on the Status of Women wanted him to step down.

87 Nicholas Van Rijn, "Chief Justice Denies Attack on Chinese" *Toronto Star* (5 November 1997) A8.

88 *Ibid.*

89 "A central trend in the development of discrimination law, in every jurisdiction, has been the movement from a requirement of intention to ground a complaint to the recognition as actionable of indirect or adverse effect discrimination": Denise G. Réaume, "Harm and Fault in Discrimination Law: The Transition from Intentional to Adverse Effect Discrimination" (2001) 2 Theoretical Inquiries in L 349.

90 Van Rijn, "Chief Justice Denies."

91 *Ibid.*

92 *Ibid.*

93 Don Sellar, "How the Chief Justice's Side of the Story Got Mangled" *Toronto Star* (8 November 1997) E2. The staff reporter represented the *Star's* "Bureau of Accuracy."

94 *Ibid.* The phrase "journalistic mugging" appears overblown. The wording in both digital and printed versions stated: "Lamer said he was using hypothetical comments when he stated in court that over the years many of his clients were Chinese and were 'very much into gambling.' Later on in the hearing, according to excerpts from a transcript of the appeal, Lamer also took shots at another group: 'What if I take judicial notice of the fact that 95 per cent of gypsies are pickpockets?'" The reporter's phrase "took shots" was the only journalistic assessment, tempered with the qualifying phrase "hypothetical comments."

95 "What We Do," Canadian Judicial Committee, online: <https://cjc-ccm. ca/en/what-we-do>.

96 If he considered a complaint serious enough to merit further consideration, McEachern could refer it to a panel of five committee members who could decide whether a public inquiry was needed. He decided this complaint on his own without public inquiry. McEachern had presided in 1990 over a complaint that Nova Scotia attorney general Tom McInnis lodged against the Nova Scotia appeal judges in the Donald Marshall case. McEachern exonerated the judges, attacking each of the Marshall report criticisms. His dissenting opinion was at odds with the other four committee members, who issued a reprimand. McEachern's dissent was critiqued by Dalhousie law professor Wayne MacKay in "Dispensing Justice in Canada: Exaggerating the Values of Judicial Independence" (1991) 40 UNBLJ 273 at 278–79: "Notwithstanding McEachern CJ's legalistic arguments to the contrary, Marshall should not have been singled out for blame when the criminal justice system, which failed him at every stage, escaped negative comment ... The dissenting approach of Chief Justice McEachern mistakes legalism for justice."

97 Toronto lawyer Eleanor Cronk conducted the review. Correspondence from Jeannie Thomas, Executive Director of the Council, to Dr. Alan Li, CCNC President (22 January 1998), CJC Archives, file 97–120.

98 *Ibid.*; Canadian Judicial Committee, News Release (23 January 1998).

99 Correspondence from Jeannie Thomas, Executive Director of the Council, to Dr. Alan Li, CCNC President (22 January 1998), CJC Archives, file 97–120.

100 In an earlier oral history interview, Lamer referred to another discriminatory stereotype in hypothetical remarks about judges' bail reasons. He said: "If you give [the judge] the magic words 'it is in the public interest' he won't say 'I hate n*****s,' he will say, 'because they are guilty you know...if they are charged with rape, it is because they did it.'" The context of these odd remarks was the need to require judges to cite factors beyond the customary recitation of the "public interest." But the stereotypical reference and use of the full N-word was in the same vein as his comments in the *RDS* hearing. "Antonio Lamer," Osgoode Society, oral history, transcript (10 January 1995), 651–57.

CHAPTER 10: THE SUPREME COURT
OF CANADA'S "GANG OF FIVE"

1 *R. v. S. (R.D.),* [1997] 3 S.C.R. 484 [hereafter SCC 1997]. Although Justice Cory's majority decision is signed only by Iacobucci, five others agreed with his legal test for bias: Lamer, La Forest, Sopinka, Gonthier, and Major. One must read the decisions of Major (signed by Sopinka and Lamer) and Gonthier (signed by La Forest) to confirm. Based on judges' seniority, the dissenting judgment, signed by the chief justice, went first. Next was the decision of La Forest, who simply signed onto portions of decisions that followed. Next was L'Heureux-Dubé's judgment, whose concurrence was at odds with Cory's majority decision, which came last due to his and Iacobucci's status as the newest members.

2 Interview with Anthony Morgan, Toronto, 6 September 2019.

3 Major and Cory's two decisions were signed by Lamer, Sopinka, and Iacobucci: five judges.

4 Oral history interview with Justice Peter Cory (1997–2001), Library and Archives Canada (LAC), R927-70-9-E, acc. 2009-0009 [hereafter LAC, oral history, Cory] at 521; Gil Rémillard, Gerald L. Gall, and Kirk Makin, "Supreme Court of Canada," *Canadian Encyclopedia* (7 February 2006), online: <https://www.thecanadianencyclopedia.ca/en/article/supreme-court-of-canada>.

5 LAC, oral history, Cory at 521.

6 *Ibid.* at 72: "Well, I certainly tried to see if we could reach a consensus and I didn't mind trotting around the various offices to talk to people to see."

7 *Ibid.* at 3.

8 *Ibid.* at 200. The discussion was about the value of juries and the situation in California, where all-white juries assessed cases of Black accused or vice versa.

9 *Ibid.* at 10–24, 47–64, 127, 229, 332.

10 SCC 1997. Cory's decision was signed by Iacobucci. Gonthier and La Forest wrote separately but agreed with Cory's legal test (at 501). Major, Lamer,

and Sopinka wrote separately, agreeing on the test but dissenting on its application (at 500). McLachlin and L'Heureux-Dubé wrote separately on the legal test (at 501). All nine agreed that Sparks's supplementary reasons could not be considered (at 485, 523). They agreed that trial judges' credibility findings would be lacking jurisdiction if tainted by bias (at 526–27).

11 He stated that the "threshold for a finding of real or perceived bias is high," and that the person considering bias must be reasonable and knowledgeable of all relevant circumstances. He added that "the reasonable person should also be taken to be aware of the social reality that forms the background to a particular case, such as societal awareness and acknowledgment of the prevalence of racism or gender bias in a particular community": *ibid.* at 528, 531–32.

12 *Ibid.* at 524.

13 *Ibid.* at 524–25.

14 *Ibid.* at 524, 533.

15 *Ibid.* at 532–34.

16 *Ibid.* at 537–39 (emphasis in original).

17 Oral history interview with Justice Frank Iacobucci (2005–6), LAC, R927-74-6-E, vol. 6719, acc. 2008-0033 [hereafter LAC, oral history Iacobucci]. Iacobucci described himself politically as in the "centre" of the spectrum (17 November 2005) at 39. A first-generation Canadian, Iacobucci was born in Vancouver of Italian parents. His father was a labourer, his mother a part-time domestic. Iacobucci described Vancouver as primarily Anglo-Saxon but his neighbourhood as racially mixed working-class with Scots, Jews, Italians, Hungarians, English, Chinese, and Japanese families, although he had no recollections of Black or Indigenous neighbours. He became president of his high school class, joined a fraternity, obtained a bachelor of commerce from UBC, and ranked second in his graduating UBC law class in 1961. He attended Cambridge on scholarship, practised corporate law on Wall Street in New York City, taught law at the University of Toronto, served as its law dean and vice-president, worked as deputy minister of justice in Ottawa, became chief justice of the Federal Court, and joined the Supreme Court in 1991. He had been a long-time friend of Sopinka's before he arrived at the Supreme Court. He indicated that he had also known Sopinka and Cory professionally; that he, Major, Sopinka, and Cory played sports together; and that his son, Edward, had served as law clerk to Sopinka. "The jocks, the athletic types would get together ... but it wasn't meant as a clique": *ibid* at 149.

18 SCC 1997 at 493–500; Major, Lamer, and Sopinka.

19 *Ibid.* at 500–1; Gonthier and La Forest, joining L'Heureux-Dubé and McLachlin.

20 Citing the Marshall report, Cory noted that "racial tension" existed "at least to some degree between police officers and visible minorities" but that there was "*no* evidence before Judge Sparks that would suggest that antiblack bias

influenced *this particular police officer's reactions*" (emphasis in original): *ibid.* at 543–47.

21 *Ibid.*

22 Appeal Transcript of Oral Argument, *R.D.S. v. the Queen*, Supreme Court of Canada, 10 March 1997, LAC, RG 125, vol. 5231, file 25063A [hereafter Transcript] at 5.

23 Robin DiAngelo, *White Fragility: Why It's So Hard for White People to Talk about Racism* (Boston, MA: Beacon, 2018) at 119–20, 128; Ijeoma Oluo, *So You Want to Talk about Race?* (New York: Seal Press, 2019) at 33. In another problematic pattern, antiracism claims are met with claims of antiwhite racism: Ibram X. Kendi, *How to Be an Antiracist* (New York: One World, 2019) at 130–31.

24 SCC 1997 at 493.

25 *Ibid.* at 495–96, 498 (emphasis in original).

26 *Ibid.* at 498–99. Richard F. Devlin and Dianne Pothier, "Redressing the Imbalances: Rethinking the Judicial Role after *R. v. R.D.S.*" (1999) 31 Ottawa L Rev 1 at 15, describe this as "a false symmetry: victims of sexual assault, prostitutes and children have been historically disempowered and socially constructed as irrational. The [legal reforms] were designed not so much to individualize these types of complainants but to shift the balance so as to *challenge* conventional assumptions about people who fall into these *groups.*"

27 Oral history interview with Justice John Major (2006–7), LAC, R927-75-8-E, acc. 2008-0032 [hereafter LAC, oral history, Major] at 199.

28 *Ibid.* at 362.

29 *Ibid.* at 2–68.

30 Interview with Jack Major, Calgary, 11 November 2020.

31 LAC, oral history, Major at 2–68. Three women had entered the law class in 1954, but only one graduated. Major added, "I just never thought of the two sexes as being unequal. The only complaint I had about women judges was that I thought, in order to balance the numbers, they were appointing some of them too young ... When they began appointing women, the pool was very small; some of the appointments I thought were pretty modest."

32 *Ibid.* at 66–154.

33 *Ibid.* The medical files involved acting for the Canadian Medical Protection Association. The Alberta government cases involved separation of powers and constitutional issues. The tax department files involved Major as counsel to the 1977 McDonald Commission.

34 *Ibid.* at 170–78, 187–88; interview with Brian Mulroney, Montreal, 22 August 2013.

35 Lamer remarked on Major's lack of litigation experience and the unkind rumours that he had only been appointed because he was a "long-standing

Conservative out west": "Antonio Lamer," Osgoode Society, oral history, transcript (10 January 1995) [hereafter Osgoode Society Lamer transcript] at 682–87.

36   SCC 1997 at 493, 495.

37   Constance Backhouse, *Colour-Coded: A Legal History of Racism in Canada, 1900–1950* (Toronto: University of Toronto Press, 1999), ch. 7. When Canadian Pacific Railway fired thirty-six Black male porters during a racially charged union-organizing campaign in 1920, the industrial dispute inquiry failed to mention race: Robin W. Winks, *The Blacks in Canada: A History,* 2nd ed. (Montreal/Kingston: McGill-Queen's University Press, 1997) at 424; Daniel G. Hill, *Negroes in Toronto: A Sociological Study of a Minority Group* (PhD diss., University of Toronto, 1960) [unpublished] at 113–14.

38   Transcript at 62. John Sopinka, Sidney N. Lederman, and Alan W. Bryant, *The Law of Evidence in Canada* (Toronto: Butterworths, 1992) is described as "the leading text on the law of evidence" in Beverley McLachlin's *Truth Be Told: My Journey through Life and the Law* (New York: Simon and Schuster, 2019) at 210, 259. Born into an immigrant Ukrainian family in rural Saskatchewan, Sopinka grew up in the working-class North End of Hamilton, a "pretty tough neighbour-hood," as he described it, with Italians, Poles, and Czechs. He was a symphony-calibre violinist and played professional football during law school, graduating from University of Toronto law in 1958, in the top five of thirty-three students. Sopinka became friends with Jack Major in law school, and their practices occasionally intersected. Sopinka developed a reputation as a top litigator at two large Toronto corporate law firms. He was appointed directly to the Supreme Court of Canada by Prime Minister Brian Mulroney in 1988. He was proud of being one of its first ethnic-minority judges: "John Sopinka," Advocates' Society Project, oral history, 1996; LAC, oral history, Major, at 184, 197–98.

39   Transcript at 10 (emphasis on video, Supreme Court of Canada archives).

40   Montreal-born Lamer was the son of lawyer Antonio Lamer and a mother who worked as a legal secretary. His father left a successful litigation practice to work with the City of Montreal Police Department, where, for two decades, he prosecuted key cases and advised the police on the legality of warrants and arrests. Lamer credited his father with his own sensitivity toward police witnesses, mentioning in his oral history that police officers had often visited their home and that even as defence counsel, his father "never, never badgered police officers" (Osgoode Society Lamer transcript at 34 and 50). Lamer graduated in law from University of Montreal, was called to the Quebec Bar in 1957, and practised in Montreal with Philip Cutler and Jacques Bellemare. He founded the Defence Attorneys' Association of Quebec and taught criminal law at the University of Montreal. His defence practice provided him with insight into "how prosecutors and police really operated," including many "tricks of the trade." Louise Arbour, one of his law

students, described him as "far ahead of his time in terms of his outlook on abuse of power by the state." Lamer claimed that when the Liberal Lesage government supplanted the Union Nationale in 1960, one-third of the Quebec provincial police was fired as corrupt. He also estimated that about 50 percent of the detectives "were smacking people around" (*ibid.* at 154, 497–98). He chaired the Law Reform Commission of Canada when its researchers documented abusive police practices. He was appointed to the Quebec Superior Court in 1969 and the Quebec Court of Appeal in 1978. Prime Minister Pierre Elliott Trudeau appointed him to the Supreme Court in 1980, and Prime Minister Brian Mulroney elevated him to the post of chief justice in 1990. Characterized as a "great raconteur" and a "street-fighter" who viewed the world through the lens of his accused clients, Lamer experienced declining health in his last decade on the court. Increasing "imperial" tendencies exacerbated an impatient temperament and diminished his reputation in his final years as chief justice: McLachlin, *Truth Be Told,* at 210, 258–49; LAC Oral History Major at 193–94; interview with Louise Arbour, Lac Carré Laurentians, 24 July 2014; interview with Ed Ratushny, Ottawa, 15 August 2009; Constance Backhouse, *Claire L'Heureux-Dubé: A Life* (Vancouver: UBC Press, 2017) at 337–40, 347–55, 363–72; Philip Slayton, *Mighty Judgment: How the Supreme Court of Canada Runs Your Life* (Toronto: Penguin, 2012) at 85.

41 Transcript at 59–61.

42 *R. v. Hamilton* (2004), 72 O.R. (3d) 1 (ONCA).

43 Transcript at 72, 76 (Justice L'Heureux-Dubé).

44 Interview with Michael Johnston, Ottawa, 19 July 2018.

45 David Tanovich, "The Charter of Whiteness: Twenty-Five Years of Maintaining Racial Injustice in the Canadian Criminal Justice System" (2008) 40 SCLR 655 at 685.

46 Devlin and Pothier, "Redressing the Imbalance," at 15–16, 24, 31, also describe it as a "formal equality approach" that presumes "if no one talks about race, racial equality has been achieved, with the converse being that introducing race as a factor is introducing racial inequality."

47 Transcript at 8.

48 Sherene Razack, "*R.D.S. v. Her Majesty the Queen:* A Case about Home" (1998) 9:3 Constitutional Forum 59.

49 John Sopinka, "Must a Judge Be a Monk?" (address to the Canadian Bar Association, Toronto, 3 March 1989); A. Wayne MacKay, "Judicial Free Speech and Accountability: Must Judges Be Seen but Not Heard?" 3 NJCL 159.

50 SCC 1997 at 496–98, 500.

51 Montreal-born Gonthier came from a family steeped in law and politics. His grandfather was federal minister of justice; his father was Canada's auditor general. With a French Canadian father and Irish mother, Gonthier became fluently bilingual. He took first-class honours at McGill law, was called to the Quebec bar,

and practised in Montreal. He was appointed to the Quebec Superior Court in 1974, the Quebec Court of Appeal in 1988, and the Supreme Court of Canada in 1989. One colleague described him as a "studious Renaissance man," and the press noted that he maintained "a Sphinx-like silence at judgment-writing time": LAC, oral history, Major, at 200–1; *Globe and Mail* (20 August 1998) A4; interview with Charles Gonthier, Ottawa, 14 September 2008; Backhouse, *Claire L'Heureux-Dubé*, at 387; "The Honourable Charles Doherty Gonthier," Supreme Court of Canada, online: <https://www.scc-csc.ca/judges-juges/bio-eng.aspx?id=charles-doherty-gonthier>.

52 La Forest was born in Grand Falls, New Brunswick. Both parents were francophones with roots in Quebec, but he became fluently bilingual. He graduated from University of New Brunswick law, was called to the New Brunswick bar in 1949, and obtained graduate degrees from Oxford and Yale. Described as an "erudite scholar," he taught law at the Universities of New Brunswick, Alberta, and Ottawa and served as assistant deputy attorney general of Canada. He was appointed to the New Brunswick Court of Appeal in 1981 and to the Supreme Court in 1997: interview with Gérard La Forest, Ottawa, 30 June 2014; McLachlin, *Truth Be Told,* at 258; "The Honourable Gérard Vincent La Forest," Supreme Court of Canada, online: <https://www.scc-csc.ca/judges-juges/bio-eng.aspx?id=gerard-vincent-la-forest>.

53 Writing for himself and La Forest, Gonthier stated: "I am in agreement with and adopt the joint reasons of L'Heureux-Dubé and McLachlin JJ. in their treatment of social context and the manner in which it may appropriately enter the decision-making process as well as their assessment of the trial judge's reasons and comments in the present case": SCC 1997 at 501. Their endorsement also meant three of the four francophone judges supported Judge Sparks.

54 Writing for himself and La Forest, Gonthier stated: "I agree with Cory J. and L'Heureux-Dubé and McLachlin JJ. as to the disposition of the appeal and with their exposition of the law on bias and impartiality and the relevance of context": *ibid.*

CHAPTER 11: THE CONCURRING OPINION IN DEFENCE OF JUDGE SPARKS

1 *R. v. S. (R.D.)*, [1997] 3 S.C.R. 484 [hereafter SCC 1997] at 502.

2 The decision was signed jointly by both, indicating each had contributed to the writing.

3 Bertha Wilson, appointed the first in 1982, retired six years prior to *RDS*: Constance Backhouse, *Two Firsts: Bertha Wilson and Claire L'Heureux-Dubé at the Supreme Court of Canada* (Toronto: Second Story Press, 2019); Constance Backhouse, *Claire L'Heureux-Dubé: A Life* (Vancouver: UBC Press, 2017); Beverley

McLachlin, *Truth Be Told: My Journey through Life and the Law* (New York: Simon and Schuster, 2019).

4 Backhouse, *L'Heureux-Dubé,* chs. 2–9; McLachlin, *Truth Be Told,* chs. 1–12.

5 Backhouse, *L'Heureux-Dubé,* at 148, chs. 11–16; McLachlin, *Truth Be Told,* chs. 13–16.

6 L'Heureux-Dubé was appointed to Quebec Superior Court in 1973, the Quebec Court of Appeal in 1979, and the Supreme Court of Canada in 1987. McLachlin was appointed to the Vancouver County Court and the British Columbia Supreme Court in 1981 and to the British Columbia Court of Appeal in 1985; she became chief justice of the Supreme Court of British Columbia in 1988. In 1989, she was appointed to the Supreme Court of Canada. "The Honourable Claire L'Heureux-Dubé," Supreme Court of Canada, online: <https://www.scc-csc.ca/judges-juges/bio-eng.aspx?id=claire-lheureux-dube>; "The Right Honourable Beverley McLachlin," Supreme Court of Canada, online: <https://www.scc-csc.ca/judges-juges/bio-eng.aspx?id=beverley-mclachlin>.

7 Backhouse, *L'Heureux-Dubé,* chs. 17–27; Backhouse, *Two Firsts,* chs. 9, 13, 15.

8 Philip Slayton, *Mighty Judgment: How the Supreme Court of Canada Runs Your Life* (Toronto: Penguin, 2011) at 150.

9 Backhouse, *Two Firsts,* at 177.

10 *R. v. Ewanchuk,* [1999] 1 S.C.R. 330.

11 Backhouse, *L'Heureux-Dubé,* chs. 1, 36. The Canadian Judicial Council could make a recommendation to Parliament but had no power to remove judges itself.

12 *Ibid.* at 676; Beverley McLachlin, "Crime and Women: Feminine Equality and the Criminal Law" (speech to the Elizabeth Fry Society, Calgary, 17 April 1991).

13 Candace C. White, *Gender Difference in the Supreme Court of Canada* (master's thesis, University of Calgary, 1998) [unpublished] at 55.

14 *Symes v. Canada,* [1993] 4 S.C.R. 695; *R. v. Thibaudeau,* [1995] 2 S.C.R. 627; *R. v. Seaboyer,* [1991] 2 S.C.R. 577; Backhouse, *L'Heureux-Dubé,* chs. 29, 32.

15 Janice Zima, "No Racial Bias in Judge's Comments, S.C.C. Rules" *Lawyers Weekly* (17 October 1997). Interview with Claire L'Heureux-Dubé, Ottawa, 30 June 2014.

16 Backhouse, *L'Heureux-Dubé,* chs. 3–6. McLachlin described Pincher Creek's population as mixed British and Eastern European immigrants, Mennonites, Hutterites, one Chinese café owner, and a few Indigenous people from the Piikani Reserve, but recalled that "everyone who mattered, it seemed, was white": McLachlin, *Truth Be Told,* at 48–49, chs. 1–6.

17 SCC 1997 at 501–4.

18 *Ibid.* at 506.

19 Jennifer Nedelsky, "Embodied Diversity and the Challenges to Law" (1997) 42 McGill LJ 91 at 106–7 (emphasis added). Martha Minow, in "'Stripped Down Like a Runner' or Enriched by Experience: Bias and Impartiality of Judges and Jurors" (1992) 33:4 Wm and Mary L Rev 1201, describes the "open mind" principle at 1207–9, 1214, 1217 as a "willingness to be surprised, rather than always to be confirmed." We hope for "the open mind from those who judge," she writes, "not the mind as a sieve without prior reference points and commitments."

20 Canadian Judicial Council, *Commentaries on Judicial Conduct* (Cowansville, QC: Éditions Yvon Blais, 1991) at 12, as quoted by L'Heureux-Dubé and McLachlin, SCC 1997 at 504.

21 SCC 1997 at 504, 506, 513.

22 *Ibid.* at 506–7, 509.

23 *Ibid.* at 508–9.

24 *Ibid.* at 513.

25 Shalin Sugunasiri, "Contextualism: The Supreme Court's New Standard of Analysis and Accountability" (1999) 22 Dal LJ 126, traces the broader theoretical dimensions of the concept, its foundations in philosophy, sociology, political science, linguistics, science, and education, how it came into being in legal analysis, and how it expanded during the 1990s to encompass decision making well beyond the Charter.

26 Appeal Transcript of Oral Argument, *R.D.S. v. the Queen,* Supreme Court of Canada, 10 March 1997, Library and Archives Canada (LAC), RG 125, vol. 5231, file 25063A [hereafter Transcript] at 72, 76.

27 Bruce P. Archibald, "The Lessons of the Sphinx: Avoiding Apprehensions of Judicial Bias in a Multi-racial, Multi-cultural Society" (1998) 10 CR (5th) 54.

28 Marilyn MacCrimmon, "Generalizing about Racism" (1998) 10 CJWL 184 at 194. Richard Devlin and Dianne Pothier, "Redressing the Imbalances: Rethinking the Judicial Role after *R. v. R.D.S.*" (1999) 31 Ottawa Law Rev 1, query at 14, "Would a white officer have arrested an elderly white woman astride a bicycle who interrupted an arrest in an affluent white neighbourhood?" Audrey Kobayashi, "Do Minority Women Judges Make a Difference?" (1998) 10 CJWL 199 at 204, urges judges to speak frankly about their thought processes, labelling as "problematic" the "assumption that judges should give opinions without holding opinions."

29 Interview with Sylvia Parris-Drummond, Halifax, 8 March 2018; interview with Sherry Bernard, Halifax, 17 July 2019; interview with Carolann Wright-Parks, Toronto, 23 August 2018; interview with Joan Jones, Halifax, 4 June 2018.

30 Transcript at 72, 76.

31 The Commission, *Royal Commission on the Donald Marshall, Jr., Prosecution,* vol. 4, *Discrimination against Blacks in Nova Scotia* (Halifax: The Royal Commission, 1989) at 69–70.

32 SCC 1997 at 511 (emphasis in original).

33 *Ibid.* at 511–13.

34 *Ibid.* at 512 (emphasis in original).

35 Archibald, "Lessons of the Sphinx," at 54.

36 Minow, "Stripped Down Like a Runner," at 1204–7, 1213. Devlin and Pothier, in "Redressing the Imbalances," at 15, use the metaphor of "a judge dropped in from Mars," suggesting that such an entity would be unable to assess testimony without reference points.

37 Catharine A. MacKinnon, *Butterfly Politics: Changing the World for Women* (Cambridge, MA: Harvard University Press, 2017) at 266–71.

38 Carol A. Aylward, "Take the Long Way Home: *R.D.S. v. R.* – The Journey" (1998) 47 UNBLJ 249 at 254; Nedelsky, "Embodied Diversity," at 101.

39 Kobayashi, "Minority Women Judges."

40 Canadian Bar Association Task Force on Canadian Equality, *Touchstones for Change: Equality, Diversity and Accountability* (Ottawa: Canadian Bar Association, 1993) at 4.

41 Caroline Criado Perez, *Invisible Women: Data Bias in a World Designed for Men* (New York: Abrams Books, 2019) at 270.

42 Kobayashi, "Minority Women Judges," at 206.

43 Richard F. Devlin, in "We Can't Go on Together with Suspicious Minds: Judicial Bias and Racialized Perspective in *R. v. R.D.S.*" (1995) 18 Dal LJ 408, notes at 422–23 that one explanation for the absence of earlier complaints is that white judges "have been extremely sensitive to issues of racial inequality, and that, unlike many Canadians, they have risen above racial prejudice." Alternatively, he suggests, racialized minorities have been so marginalized and excluded that they saw little point in raising white bias.

44 Without magistrates' court transcripts, his memoirs are sourced to demonstrate the racist sentiments he brought to court: Colonel George T. Denison, *Recollections of a Magistrate* (Toronto: Musson Book Company, 1920), as cited in Carolyn Strange, *Toronto's Girl Problem: The Perils and Pleasures of the City, 1880–1930* (Toronto: University of Toronto Press, 1995) at 16, 153, 250.

45 William Renwick Riddell, "Administration of Criminal Law in the Far North of Canada" (1929) 20 J Crim L, Criminology and Police Science 294; Canadian Social Hygiene Council, Social Health 1:11 (1925); Strange, *Toronto's Girl Problem*, at 250; Robin W. Winks, *The Blacks in Canada: A History*, 2nd ed. (Montreal/Kingston: McGill-Queen's University Press, 1997) at 298.

46 There was no bias appeal, and a subsequent Judicial Council complaint found his remarks "unfortunate" but not worthy of judicial discipline: Robert Martin, "An Open Legal System" (1985) 23 UWO L Rev 169 at 179. See also discussion of Judge Nichols, ch. 6, this book.

47 The study included sixty-nine cases involving Indigenous offenders and/ or victims: Margo L. Nightingale, "Judicial Attitudes and Differential Treatment: Native Women in Sexual Assault Cases" (1991) 23 Ottawa L Rev 71 at 80–86. In one illustration, Territorial Court judge Michel Bourassa responded to complaints about low sentences for sexual assault offenders by saying that "the majority of rapes in the Northwest Territories occur when the woman is drunk and passed out," adding, "A man comes along, sees a pair of hips and helps himself. That contrasts sharply to the cases I dealt with before (in southern Canada) of the dainty co-ed who gets jumped from behind." See also Laurie Sarkadi, "Native Women Call for Judge to Resign" *Edmonton Journal* (20 December 1989) A1. In 1984, Bourassa sentenced three Inuit men to a week in jail for having sex with a thirteen-year-old mentally ill girl, because he believed the "morality of values of the people here is that when a girl begins to menstruate, she is considered ready to engage in sexual relations." Laurie Sarkadi, "Protests against Judge 'Out of Hand'" *Edmonton Journal* (30 January 1990) A3. Although there were no bias appeals, the Territories Judicial Council reviewed Bourassa's remarks. Its discussion centred on whether Bourassa specifically referred to "natives" since he had not mentioned race, another example of the pattern of erasing race in legal matters. Since Indigenous people made up the majority of the population and of the criminal cases, others described the debate as bizarre. "Judge's Remarks Worthy of Story" *Edmonton Journal* (29 May 1990) A4. The Territories Judicial Council found no misbehaviour, holding that the comments did not "affect his ability as a judge." It stated: "Certainly there is no evidence to indicate that Judge Bourassa has exercised a conscious bias, and ... these comments are not indicative of any actual hidden bias [nor] apprehension of bias": Judicial Council of the Northwest Territories, *In the Matter of An Inquiry Pursuant to Section 13(2) of the Territorial Court Act ... and In the Matter of an Inquiry into the Conduct of Judge R.M. Bourassa* (28 September 1990) at xiv–xv, xv–xxi. Don Thomas, "Women Upset Judge Was Cleared; Northern Judges Needed a 'Message'" *Edmonton Journal* (13 October 1990) A4.

48 Wayne MacKay, "Judicial Free Speech and Accountability" (1994) 3 NJCL 159 at 175, 181.

49 The Commission, *Royal Commission on the Donald Marshall, Jr., Prosecution,* vol. 1, *Findings and Recommendations* (Halifax: Province of Nova Scotia, 1989) at 156–57, and vol. 4, *Discrimination against Blacks in Nova Scotia.*

50 Joan Jones, "Marshall Inquiry Lessons Have Yet to Be Learned" *Halifax Chronicle-Herald* (18 May 1995) B2.

51 The Commission, *Report of the Commission on Systemic Racism in the Ontario Criminal Justice System* (Toronto: Queen's Printer for Ontario, 1995) at i, vi, 20–27, 230, quoted respondents: "At present, although certain individuals are notorious, nothing is done by the system. By tolerating their behaviour it is

condoned, continues and increases ... At both the provincial and general division levels, but particularly the provincial division, the bench is saturated with elitist, racist and sexist individuals."

52 Canadian Bar Association, *Racial Equality in the Canadian Legal Profession* (Ottawa: Canadian Bar Association, 1999) at 24.

53 "Sparks Did Make Mistakes" *Halifax Daily News* (7 May 1995) 20.

54 Interview with Anthony Ross, Toronto, 26 May 2019. Ross noted that one judge who served on the Halifax County Court and later the Supreme Court was so racist that Ross refused to appear before him. Others agreed with this assessment: interview with Donald Oliver, Halifax, 18 July 2019.

55 *Commonwealth of Pennsylvania v. Local Union 542, International Union of Operating Engineers,* 388 F. Supp. 155 (1974). Black plaintiffs were seeking damages for race discrimination, and the white defendants sought to disqualify Higginbotham because he gave a speech criticizing Supreme Court race decisions.

56 *Ibid.* at 163, 165, 177, 180–82. Bromley Armstrong, appointed to the Ontario Labour Relations Board in 1980, faced one of the first challenges to a Black adjudicator in Canada. An antiracist activist who had campaigned for racial equality in immigration, education, employment, and policing, he faced impeachment from his own adjudicator-colleagues. They suggested he recuse himself from a case with a Black complainant because there would be a "perception of bias." Armstrong agreed to do so only if his white colleagues recused themselves from every other case: Bromley L. Armstrong and Sheldon Eric Alister Taylor, *Bromley: Tireless Champion of Just Causes* (Pickering, ON: Vitabu, 2000); Ron Csillag, "Civil-Rights Champion Was a Gentleman and a Scrapper" *Globe and Mail* (5 September 2018) B20.

In 1994, three white Ontario Divisional Court judges removed Frederica Douglas from the tripartite Ontario Police Complaints Board on a successful bias challenge. She had been assigned to hear a complaint from a Black woman strip searched by white police officers. The African Canadian vice-president of the Toronto chapter of the Congress of Black Women had commented publicly to the media about the case. Douglas was removed because she was president of the Mississauga chapter of the same organization: *Dulmage v. Ontario (Police Complaints Commissioner)* (1994), 21 O.R. (3d) 356 (Gen Div). *Touchstones for Change* notes at 192–94 that women judges were being refused assignment to sexual assault cases on the ground that they could not be impartial. Some male judges also badgered their female colleagues with complaints that "feminists were unsuited for the judicial role because of their radical and biased views."

57 Devlin and Pothier, "Redressing the Imbalances," at 21–23. Outsider judges can also hold different contextualized frameworks. Some Black adjudicators might be inclined to believe a workplace racial harassment complaint because they have

personally experienced similar problems. Others might develop an "up-by-the-bootstraps" philosophy, quick to blame Black employees for failing to surmount challenges. It was what Rodney Small initially anticipated when he faced Sparks. White adjudicators might dismiss a complaint because they have no personal experience with race discrimination or because racism complaints make them defensive. Alternately, they might feel so guilty about racism that they lean toward overcompensating a complainant. Martha Minow, in "Stripped Down," considers similar possibilities regarding sexual harassment at 1207–9, 1214, 1217, adding: "These alternatives simply point to the multiple directions that bias can take, but not to its absence."

58 Martha Minow, *Making All the Difference: Inclusion, Exclusion, and American Law* (Ithaca, NY: Cornell University Press, 1990), ch. 1.

59 Devlin and Pothier, "Redressing the Imbalances," at 24, 35–36.

60 Paul Barnsley, "Question of Bias; Nova Scotia Judge's Decision" *Windspeaker Aboriginal Multi-media Society of Alberta* (7 November 1997) 6.

61 Constance Backhouse, "Bias in Canadian Law: A Lopsided Precipice" (1998) 10 CJWL 170 at 174–55.

62 Reg Graycar, "Gender, Race, Bias and Perspective: Or, How Otherness Colours Judgement" (2008) 15 Int J Leg Profession 73 at 82.

63 SCC 1997 at 508.

64 Interview with El Jones, Halifax, 15 October 2019.

65 Kobayashi, "Minority Women Judges," at 200, 202, 206–7, 212.

CHAPTER 12: EPILOGUE

1 Interviews with Rodney D. Small, Halifax, 9 June and 14 August 2018. Alex Mason, "How a Landmark Case Heard 20 Years Ago Today Shaped a Black Teen" *CBC News* (10 March 2017), online: <https://www.cbc.ca/news/canada/nova-scotia/rodney-small-landmark-case-1.4015878>.

2 "I found out on the plane that I won the case. I called home to my Nan, and it was true": interviews with Rodney Small.

3 *Ibid.* On Jones's divorce from Joan and remarriage to Sharon, see ch. 9, note 3.

4 Interviews with Rodney Small.

5 Cassidy Chisholm, "Halifax Man Reflects on Racial Profiling" *CBC News* (5 June 2020), online: <https://www.cbc.ca/news/canada/nova-scotia/halifax-man-reflects-on-racial-profiling-by-police-1.5600309>.

6 Interviews with Rodney Small; Greg Mercer, "Africville 2.0" *Globe and Mail* (28 December 2020) A1, A15.

7 Mason, "How a Landmark Case."

8 Interviews with Rodney Small; Scott Baker, dir., *RDS vs: A Story of Race and Justice* (Toronto: Canadian Race Relations Foundation, 2020), online: <https://crrf-fcrr.box.com/s/6tr1a84ylhw03gpi8c6pi7gr1p4jnhk7>.

9 Interviews with Rodney Small. The portrait, painted by Bruce John Wood, was commissioned by the Dalhousie Black Law Students' Association in 2014.

10 Interview with Donald Stienburg, Halifax, 28 September 2018.

11 Steve MacLeod, "Top Court Backs Judge Sparks" *Halifax Daily News* (27 September 1997) 3; Brian Underhill, "Black Judge's Remarks 'Troubling,' Not Biased" *Halifax Chronicle-Herald* (27 September 1997).

12 MacLeod, "Top Court."

13 Burnley "Rocky" Jones and James W. St.G. Walker, *Burnley "Rocky" Jones: Revolutionary* (Black Point, NS: Roseway, 2016) at 203–5.

14 Jones and Derrick filed a complaint against an officer who strip searched three junior high school girls on suspicion of a ten-dollar theft. The officer did not contact their parents or advise the girls of their right to counsel or to refuse the search. She was later disciplined for the improper search. Halifax police chief Vince MacDonald denied that police would have acted differently if the girls were white: "My view is we stand on our record. We have a very good record as a police department." The officer then sued the two lawyers personally for calling her "racist," although they had never used that word. She obtained the largest sum ever awarded in a Nova Scotia defamation trial; with costs, Jones and Derrick faced a $315,000 payment. Nova Scotia Court of Appeal justice Elizabeth Roscoe reversed the award, citing lawyers' responsibility to speak out against injustice. Constance Glube concurred. Eva Hoare, "Chief Denies Racism Played Role in Search" *Halifax Chronicle-Herald* (7 April 1995) A1; *Campbell v. Jones,* [2001] N.S.J. No. 373 (T.D.); *Campbell v. Jones,* [2002] N.S.J. No. 450 (C.A.); Jones and Walker, *Burnley "Rocky" Jones,* at 205–23.

15 Jones and Walker, *Burnley "Rocky" Jones,* at 231–33, 246–47. Joan Jones speculated in "All Judiciary Members Bring Experiences to Jobs" *Halifax Chronicle-Herald* (2 October 1997) B2, that if "someone from the 'old boys club'" had achieved a similar victory in *RDS*, "prestigious law firms would now be interviewing him to bring him into their fold." David Woods added, "Rocky has been a champion of all kinds of things. He drops his life and jumps on things, with no filters about what is economically good for him or not. He gave an awful lot of his time to so many causes": interview with David Woods, Halifax, 6 June 2018.

16 Jones and Walker, *Burnley "Rocky" Jones,* at 230–33, 247–53.

17 Interview with Michelle Williams, Halifax, 5 June 2018.

18 Jones and Walker, *Burnley "Rocky" Jones,* at 253–54.

19 Interview with El Jones, Halifax, 15 October 2019.

20 Jones and Walker, *Burnley "Rocky" Jones,* at 254–68.

21 Interview with Dianne Pothier, Halifax, 20 February 2009; Dianne Pothier, curriculum vita; Pothier and Devlin, "Redressing the Imbalances: Rethinking the Judicial Role after *R. v. R.D.S.*" (1999) 31 Ottawa L Rev 1; Canadian Bar Association, "CBA President's Award," online: <https://www.cba.org/Sections/ Governance-and-Equality/Awards/CBA-President-s-Award>; Kim Brooks, "Dianne Louise Pothier, Lives Lived" *Globe and Mail* (1 May 2017) S10; obituary, Dianne Louise Pothier (1954–2017), J.A. Snow Funeral Home.

22 Canadian Bar Association, New Release, "OBA Randall Echlin Mentorship Award: Honoured Award Recipient Yola Grant" (24 February 2021), online: <https://www.cbapd.org/details_en.aspx?id=on_on21lab03i>.

23 Interview with Alabama lawyer Jim Blacksher, Beach Meadows, 13 August 2019.

24 April Burey, "No Dichotomies: Reflections on Equality for African Canadians in *R. v. R.D.S.*" (1998) 21:1 Dal LJ 199 at 211, 217–18. She lodged a race discrimination complaint against the University of Toronto, where she taught law part-time for fifteen years: April Burey, "An Open Letter to Ron Daniels Faculty of Law, University of Toronto, from a Colleague, April Burey" (24 August 1997), online: <http://geocitiessites.com/CapitolHill/2381/Lawschoolscase/uoftlaw-burey. html>. The Canadian Association of Black Lawyers, the Jamaican Canadian Association, the Arts and Science Students' Union, and the African Canadian Legal Clinic supported her complaint: "Systemic Racism at the University of Toronto Page," online: <https://www.oocities.org/capitolhill/2381/Lawschoolscase/uof t-systemicracism.html>.

25 Obituary, "April Burey, March 1960–December 12, 1999" online: <https:// www.oocities.org/capitolhill/2381/Lawschoolscase/uoftlaw-burey1.html>.

26 Regarding her response to debilitating multiple sclerosis, the column continued: "To keep up her spirits, she occasionally wheeled herself grandly into Toronto's King Edward Hotel, dressed in Afro-Jamaican finery, for a power lunch at Café Victoria ... Equally comfortable with a Black Power salute or with sushi and a bottle of Perrier, she took the joys of living wherever she could find them." The "Lives Lived" column was co-authored by Lois Lehmann and Justice Ian Binnie, contacts from her Department of Justice litigation, who described themselves as "friends of April Burey." Binnie had been appointed to the Supreme Court of Canada in 1998, a year after the *RDS* case. *Globe and Mail* (26 January 2000) A22.

27 Interview with Richard (Rick) B. Miller, Halifax, 17 August 2018; Nova Scotia Barristers' Society, list of current members (available on the organization website); "Richard B. Miller," Canadian Law List, online: <http://www.canadian-lawlist.com/listingdetail/contact/richard-b-miller-576669/>.

28 Information available online from the Nova Scotia Public Prosecution Services website.

29 Interview with Rick Miller.

30 Interview with Robert E. Lutes, Halifax, 4 June 2018; interview with Mark Knox, Halifax, 16 July 2019; *Youth Criminal Justice Act,* S.C. 2002, c.1, proclaimed 2003; Lee Tustin and Robert E. Lutes, QC, *A Guide to the Young Offenders Act* (Markham, ON: Butterworths, 2002). The revisions covered diversion, flexibility in sentencing, rehabilitation, and victims' rights.

31 Wendy King, "Names in the News," *Lawyers Weekly* (30 January 1998). The Nova Scotia Association of Women and the Law bestowed the awards.

32 Interview with Judge Sparks, Halifax, 8 December 2021.

33 Interview with Judge Sandra Oxner, Toronto, 21 June 2019.

34 Devlin, "We Can't Go on Together with Suspicious Minds: Judicial Bias and Racialized Perspective in *R. v. R.D.S.*" (1995) 18 Dal LJ 408. Her words to Devlin at the function were "You cut my throat." Interview with Richard Devlin, Halifax, 9 March 2018.

35 *The Courts of Nova Scotia* (Halifax: Queen's Printer, 2006).

36 Allison Lawlor, "Obituary, Constance Glube" *Globe and Mail* (15 February 2016), online: <https://www.theglobeandmail.com/news/national/constance-glube -nova-scotias-first-female-supreme-court-judge-dies-aged-84/article28759964/>.

37 Interview with Chief Justice Glube, Halifax, 28 October 2014.

38 Ontario Retirement Dinner for Claire L'Heureux-Dubé, Toronto, 6 May 2002, DVD, copy in possession of the author.

39 "Tribute for Constance Glube," 2016, written upon her death by the dean of Dalhousie's law school, Kim Brooks; copy in possession of the author. Michelle Williams, director of the IB&M program at Dalhousie, also heard "that this might be one case that gave her pause": interview with Michelle Williams.

40 "Edward John Flinn, Doctor of Laws," Saint Mary's University, Patrick Power Library, University Archives, online: <https://www.smu.ca/academics/ archives/edward-john-flinn.html>; obituary, "Edward John Flinn, 1935–2002," BillionGraves, online: <https://billiongraves.com/grave/Edward-John-Flinn/907 0422?referrer=myheritage>.

41 "Pugsley, Ronald Newton" *Globe and Mail* (9 May 2000), online: <https:// www.legacy.com/ca/obituaries/theglobeandmail/name/justice-pugsley-obituary ?pid=189712473>.

42 "The Honourable Justice Gerald Borden Freeman Retires," Society Record [NS Barristers' Society] 24:4 (August 2006) 10.

43 Interview with Gerald Freeman, Beach Meadows, 13 August 2019.

44 "Obit. Gerald B. (Hon. Justice) Freeman" *Halifax Chronicle-Herald* (6 June 2020).

45 Oral history interview with Justice Peter Cory (1997–2001), Library and Archives Canada, R927-70-9-E, acc. 2009-0009, at 520–21.

46 Elizabeth Raymer, "Former Supreme Court Justice Peter Cory Dead at 94," *Canadian Lawyer* (13 April 2020), online: <https://www.canadianlawyermag.com/news/general/former-supreme-court-justice-peter-cory-dead-at-94/328557>.

47 Interview with Jack Major, Calgary, 11 November 2020.

48 *Ibid.*

49 Constance Backhouse, *Claire L'Heureux-Dubé: A Life* (Vancouver: UBC Press, 2017); Constance Backhouse, *Two Firsts: Bertha Wilson and Claire L'Heureux-Dubé at the Supreme Court of Canada* (Toronto: Second Story Press, 2019), ch. 18.

50 On continuing animus, see Backhouse, *Claire L'Heureux-Dubé*, chs. 26–28.

51 Interview with Claire L'Heureux-Dubé, Ottawa, 30 June 2014.

52 Beverley McLachlin, *Truth Be Told: My Journey through Life and Law* (New York: Simon and Schuster, 2019).

53 Chief Justice Beverley McLachlin, "Address to Canada's Judicial Advisory Committees" Video, mandatory training for all members, viewed by the author as a member of the federal judicial advisory committee on the appointment of superior court judges in Ontario east and north, appointed by Minister of Justice David Lametti for a term in 2019–21.

54 Interview with Judge Sparks, Halifax, 8 December 2021.

55 Interview with Judge Sandra Oxner, Toronto, 21 June 2019.

56 Interview with (then chief judge) Pamela S. Williams, Dartmouth, 15 October 2019.

57 Charles Saunders, "Justice for Judge Corrine Sparks" *Halifax Daily News* (5 October 1997) 18.

58 Harry Flemming, "A Judge Isn't a Social Critic" *Halifax Daily News* (1 October 1997) 13.

59 Eight judges were appointed to the Nova Scotia Supreme Court (Family Division). Three were assigned to Sydney, five to Halifax: Charles E. Haliburton, *A Biographical History of the Judges of Nova Scotia, 1754–2004* (Kentville, NS: Gaspereau Press for the Judges of Nova Scotia, 2004) at 30–31.

60 Interview with El Jones, Halifax, 15 October 2019.

61 Interview with Douglas Ruck, Halifax, 16 July 2019.

62 Open letter from Dr. Esmeralda Thornhill to Justice Minister Anne McLellan, signed by many organizations and individuals, 27 March 1999; Esmeralda M.A. Thornhill "Re-thinking and Re-framing *RDS:* A Black Woman's Perspective" in Michele A. Johnson and Funké Aladejebi, eds., *Unsettling the Great White North: Black Canadian History* (Toronto: University of Toronto Press, 2022) 538.

63 Interview with Gerald Freeman.

64 Interview with Robert S. Wright, Halifax, 14 February 2020.

65 Correspondence from law professor Philip Girard, 30 September 2018.

66 Interview with Sandra Oxner.

67 Thornhill, "Re-thinking and Re-framing *RDS*," at 562–63, 570.

68 Charles Saunders, "Judge's Fate Already Sealed" *Halifax Daily News* (11 April 1999) 21.

69 "An Uncertain Future for a Black Role Model" *Toronto Star* (5 April 1999) 1.

70 Stephen Smith, "Youngsters Add Voices" *National Post* (16 June 1999) A10.

71 Judge Sparks led seminars on social-context training for the New Judges' Program, the Canadian Association of Provincial Court Judges, the National Judicial Institute, the Commonwealth Judicial Education Centre, and the International Association of Women Judges: "The Hon. Judge Corrine Sparks," *African Nova Scotian Affairs,* Government of Nova Scotia (13 March 2021); Nova Scotia Judiciary Communications, "Province's First African Nova Scotian Judge Retiring" (30 December 2021); interview with Judge Sandra Oxner.

72 John D. Comeau, appointed chief judge of the Provincial Family Court in 2000, supported a leave reducing her judicial duties by one-third while completing the degree. Other judges also received support for LLM study; interview with Judge Sparks, Halifax, 14 July 2019.

73 (LLM thesis, Dalhousie University, 2001). Sparks noted at 107 that Japanese Canadians, also forcibly relocated, sought apology and reparation from politicians, after concluding no litigation redress was possible because of "racial bias within the judiciary." The thesis notes in passing that relocation compensation for Africville residents was reduced by payments to furniture stores such as Glubes, to cover residents' outstanding bills (*ibid.* at 68–69). For another course, Sparks wrote about George Webber Roache Davis, the second Nova Scotian-born Black to graduate from Dalhousie law in 1952.

74 Evelyn C. White, "Judge Corrine Sparks," *Pamphlet for the 30th Anniversary Celebrating African Nova Scotian Judges* (Halifax: Delmore "Buddy" Daye Learning Institute, 2018); Nova Scotia Judiciary Communications, "Province's First African Nova Scotian Judge Retiring" (30 December 2021).

75 Interview with Judge Sparks, Halifax, 8 December 2021.

76 *Ibid.*

77 *CABL News* (November 1997) 6.

78 "Sharon Melson Fletcher, "Corinne [sic] Sparks Biography," *Contemporary Black Biography: Profiles from the International Black Community,* vol. 53 (Farmington Hills, MI: Thomson Gale, 2006) at 151.

79 The award was developed with the support of the IB&M Initiative, which continues to administer it: Dalhousie Law School, *Hearsay Magazine* (2007); interview with Michelle Williams.

80 Canadian Bar Association, "Touchstone Award," online: <https://www.cba.org/Who-We-Are/About-us/Awards-and-Recognition/Search-Awards/Equality-Awards/Touchstone-Award>.

81 "The Hon. Judge Corrine Sparks" *African Nova Scotian Affairs,* Government of Nova Scotia (13 March 2021); Stephanie Hurley, "Judge Corrine Sparks" *Dal News Archives* (2 November 2020), online: <https://www.dal.ca/faculty/law/news-events/news/2020/11/02/judge_corrine_sparks_named_2020_recipient_of_weldon_award_for_unselfish_public_service.html>. Her Weldon Award came one year after Ronald Pugsley's. The irregularities of land grants to Black Loyalists and other Black citizens are discussed in ch. 3.

82 Delmore "Buddy" Daye Learning Institute, the IB&M Initiative, Dalhousie School of Law, and the Dalhousie Black Law Students' Association, "Honouring African Nova Scotian Judges," Video (9 February 2018), Halifax Central Library.

83 Interview with Evelyn C. White, Halifax, 22 May 2018.

84 *Ibid.*

CONCLUSION

1 Esmeralda M.A. Thornhill "Re-thinking and Re-framing *RDS:* A Black Woman's Perspective" in Michele A. Johnson and Funké Aladejebi, eds., *Unsettling the Great White North: Black Canadian History* (Toronto: University of Toronto Press, 2022) 538–81.

2 I am indebted to the insight of Professor Michelle Williams of Dalhousie law school, who described this as the pedagogical method she uses to teach the *RDS* case in her law classes.

3 *Murdoch v. Murdoch,* [1975] 1 S.C.R. 423; Vanessa Gruben, Angela Cameron, and Angela Chaisson, "The Courts Have Turned Women into Slaves for the Men of the World: Irene Murdoch's Quest for Justice" in Eric Tucker, James Muir, Bruce Ziff, eds., *Property on Trial: Canadian Cases in Context* (Toronto: Irwin Law, 2012) 159–92.

4 Interview with Michael MacDonald, Halifax, 16 October 2019.

Illustration Credits

Note: Photos are by author unless attributed below. A reasonable attempt has been made to secure permission to reproduce all material used. If there are errors or omissions they are wholly unintentional and the publisher would be grateful to learn of them.

30 Courtesy of the Jones Family (*The Coast*)

31 *top* Courtesy of the *Chronicle-Herald*
   bottom James St.G. Walker and Burnley "Rocky" Jones, *Burnley "Rocky" Jones Revolutionary: An Autobiography by Burnley "Rocky"* Jones (Halifax: Fernwood Publishing, 2016)

32 Courtesy of the Jones Family (*The Coast*)

36 Dalhousie University Archives, Item PC1, Box 26, Folder 38

37 R.E. Kimball, *The Bench: The History of Nova Scotia's Provincial Courts* (Halifax: Province of Nova Scotia, 1989), photo by Robert F. Calnen

38 Courtesy of Corrine Sparks

40 *N.S. Gazette and Weekly Chronicle* (1 September 1772), Nova Scotia Archives

42 Delmore "Buddy" Daye Learning Institute

45 Afrikan Canadian Heritage and Friendship Centre, Guysborough Academy

47 Black Cultural Centre for Nova Scotia

48 *Toronto Star* (24 January 1987), p. B5, Saint Mary's University Archives, 2016.002.1, Box 14, Series 5, File 2

51 Craig Marshall Smith, *The Journey Continues: An Atlantic Canadian Black Experience* (Halifax: Black Green and Red Educational Products, 2010), p. 106

53 Courtesy of Jean Whalen

54 Stu Ducklow, *Halifax Daily News*

63 *Mail-Star* (7 April 1995), Saint Mary's University Archives

68 Charles E. Haliburton, ed., *A Biographical History of the Judges of Nova Scotia, 1754–2004* (Kentville, NS: Judges of Nova Scotia, 2004)

71 *Chronicle-Herald* (9 December 1994), Saint Mary's University Archives, 2016.002.1, Box 14, Series 5, Subseries 4, File3

72 Charles E. Haliburton, ed., *A Biographical History of the Judges of Nova Scotia, 1754–2004* (Kentville, NS: Judges of Nova Scotia, 2004)

74 *top* Saint Mary's University Archives, 01/18077
    bottom Carrie M. Best, *That Lonesome Road* (Clarion Publishing, 1977)

76 Nova Scotia House of Assembly

79 Courtesy of Corrine Sparks

82 Dalhousie University Archives

87 *top* Charles E. Haliburton, ed., *A Biographical History of the Judges of Nova Scotia, 1754–2004* (Kentville, NS: Judges of Nova Scotia, 2004)
    bottom Executive Office of the Nova Scotia Judiciary

90 *Halifax Daily News* (20 April 1995), p. 5

95 *top Chronicle-Herald* (18 May 1995), Saint Mary's University Archives, 2016.002.1, Box 14, Series 5, Subseries 4, File 3

99 Charles E. Haliburton, ed., *A Biographical History of the Judges of Nova Scotia, 1754–2004* (Kentville, NS: Judges of Nova Scotia, 2004)

100 Charles E. Haliburton, ed., *A Biographical History of the Judges of Nova Scotia, 1754–2004* (Kentville, NS: Judges of Nova Scotia, 2004)

104 Charles E. Haliburton, ed., *A Biographical History of the Judges of Nova Scotia, 1754–2004* (Kentville, NS: Judges of Nova Scotia, 2004)

109 George Elliott Clarke, ed., *Fire on the Water: An Anthology of Black Nova Scotian Writing,* vol. 2 (Porter's Lake, NS: Pottersfield, 1991–92), photo by Alex Murchison

114 *top* Dalhousie University Archives
    bottom UNB Archives & Special Collections

115 *top* University of Calgary Digital Collections, CU1140946
    bottom Courtesy of Corrine Sparks

119 Courtesy of Michelle Y. Williams

120 CBC Licensing

126 Courtesy of Yola Grant, photo by William Knox

130 Courtesy of Richard Devlin

131 Courtesy of Claire L'Heureux-Dubé

132 Courtesy of Yola Grant, photo by William Knox

134 Courtesy of Sharon Burey

142 Photo by Paul Couvrette

143 © Supreme Court of Canada, photo by Larry Munn

147 © Supreme Court of Canada, photo by Philippe Landreville

151 *left* © Supreme Court of Canada, photo by Larry Munn
    right Photo by Paul Couvrette

155   Courtesy of Claire L'Heureux-Dubé

159   *left* Courtesy of Claire L'Heureux-Dubé
     right © Supreme Court of Canada, photo by Roy Grogan

165   *Law Times* (10–16 November 1997), p. 20

167   *Chronicle-Herald* (2 October 1997), p. B2, Saint Mary's University Archives,
     Lynn Jones African-Canadian and Diaspora Heritage Collection

170   Courtesy of Françoise Baylis

172   James St.G. Walker and Burnley "Rocky" Jones, *Burnley "Rocky" Jones
     Revolutionary: An Autobiography by Burnley "Rocky"* Jones (Halifax: Fernwood
     Publishing, 2016)

176   Chris Wattie/Reuters/Alamy

182   Courtesy of Corrine Sparks

184   Courtesy of Corrine Sparks

186   Courtesy of Adjacent Possibilities

Index

Note: Page numbers with (f) refer to illustrations.

Lamer, Antonio (father), 239*n*31, 247*n*40
land titles, 41, 43, 184
Laskin, Bora, 88, 226*n*39
Laval University Law School, 155
law schools: Black student dropouts, 35, 203*n*47, 204*n*49; first law school in English Canada, 113; gender discrimination, 84–85, 155–56; insiders and outsiders, 204*n*49; race discrimination, 257*n*24; US graduate schools, 85, 133, 224*n*18. *See also* Dalhousie University Law School; Dalhousie University Law School, Indigenous Blacks & Mi'kmaq Initiative (IB&M)
Lawrence, Calvin, 56–57
Lawrence, Ray, 12, 112, 200*n*11
lawyers, Black female: about, 113–21, 114(f), 115(f); discriminatory hiring, 218*n*60; early history, 203*n*47, 204*nn*48–49; gendered criticism, 118–21; insiders and outsiders, 108, 115, 204*n*49; list of practising lawyers in NS (2018), 221*n*31; Task Force on Gender Equality (CBA), 206*n*66, 234*n*32. *See also* Burey, April (*RDS* intervener counsel); Dalhousie University Law School; Dalhousie University Law School, Indigenous Blacks & Mi'kmaq Initiative (IB&M)
lawyers, Black female, firsts: lawyer in Canada (1954) (Henry), 113, 115(f), 233*n*19; lawyer in ON (1960) (Smith), 113; lawyer to graduate from Dalhousie Law (1976) (Healey), 113, 114(f), 233*n*13; lawyer to open solo law practice (Cain-Grant), 120, 236*n*54; lawyer to practise in NS

(1980) (Sparks), 113, 114(f); prosecutor in NS (1989) (Whalen), 52, 53(f), 81, 236*n*53
lawyers, Black male: discrimination, 37, 205*n*60, 218*n*60; early history, 203*n*47, 204*nn*48–49; insiders and outsiders, 108; list of practising lawyers in NS (2018), 221*n*31; senators, 213*n*3. *See also* Dalhousie University Law School; Dalhousie University Law School, Indigenous Blacks & Mi'kmaq Initiative (IB&M)
lawyers, female: about, 113–18; awards, 175–76; demographics, 113, 148, 233*n*12; with disabilities, 128, 133–34, 173; discrimination against, 85; gendered criticism, 118–21; hiring by Halifax City, 35, 85, 113, 204*n*53, 225*n*24; motherhood, 85
lawyers, female, firsts: all-female firm in Dartmouth (1981) (Sparks and Foote), 36, 115, 115(f), 204*n*55; white female lawyer in Canada (1897) (Martin), 113; white female lawyer in NS (1918) (Fish), 113, 114(f), 175
lawyers and judges, female. *See* judges, female; lawyers, Black female; lawyers, female
Le Jeune, Oliver, 207*n*4
LEAF (Women's Legal Education and Action Fund) (*RDS* intervener), 130–33, 132(f), 173–74, 240*n*45, 240*n*53, 241*n*58
legal clinics. *See* African Canadian Legal Clinic (*RDS* intervener); Dalhousie University Law School
legal community: about, 187–92; on anti-Black racism, 94–96, 191;

282 | *Index*

access to trial recording (1995),
70–72, 71(f), 107, 197*n*7, 199*n*2,
199*n*8; police complaint of
Sparks's "bias," 70–73, 71(f);
SCC's decisions, 135, 165(f),
167(f), 180; Sparks's decision
at trial, 118–19; Sparks's nonelevation to Unified Court, 180–
83, 259*n*59
prostitution, 52, 146–47, 157, 213*n*2,
246*n*26
Provincial Court, Nova Scotia. *See*
Nova Scotia Family Court; Nova
Scotia Provincial Court; Nova
Scotia Youth Court
Pugsley, Ronald Newton, 99–103,
100(f), 177, 229*n*11, 260*n*81. *See
also* Nova Scotia Court of Appeal,
RDS (October 1995)

Quebec: first Black judge and female
judge (1999) (Westmoreland-
Traoré), 93, 185; first female judge
on SCC (1987) (L'Heureux-Dubé),
155(f); Jewish lawyers, 155

race: intersectionality, 121–23, 167–
68, 232*n*1, 234*n*32; socially constructed myth, 4. *See also* race,
terminology; race and racism
race, terminology: about, 4, 66;
African Canadian, 104; African
Nova Scotian, 197*n*3, 200*n*21;
Black, 104, 197*n*3, 200*n*21;
capitalization of Black and Negro,
197*n*3; Caucasian, 101, 229*n*16;
coloured, 197*n*3, 200*n*21; honky,
239*n*32; legal language as insufficient, 187; Negro, 197*n*3, 200*n*21,
223*n*51; nonwhite, 4, 14, 66, 70,

78–79, 104; N-word, 54–55, 57,
205*n*60, 244*n*100; racialized
people, 4; racism, 66; scare quotes
for "race," 4; settled people vs
white settler colonists, 213*n*67;
terminology of choice, 197*n*3,
200*n*21; whites as norm, 14, 102
race and racism: about, 4, 66, 187–
92; antiwhite racism, 246*n*23;
Blackness as threat, 232*n*4; covert
racism, 94; critical race theory,
162–63; denials of racism, 61–64,
63(f); gendered racism, 121–23,
232*n*1; importance of *RDS*, 187–
92; intent, 138, 243*n*89; normal-
ization of racism, 163; political
correctness, 152; race as fiction
vs racism as reality, 4; reflections
on, 187–92; stereotypes of Black
people, 46, 56, 58–59, 92, 107,
127, 163–64, 231*n*42; as term, 4,
66, 187; white erasures, 29, 46, 55,
61–64, 252*n*47; white fragility,
64, 187; white male views, nor-
malization, 77, 102, 163; white
racism, 5; white supremacists, 44,
55, 57, 234*n*30. *See also* African
Nova Scotians, discrimination
and racism; race, terminology
race and racism in the legal system:
about, 187–92; court cases, 127–
28, 228*n*1, 239*nn*22–23; court
recognition vs silencing, 158–62;
criminality as individual vs community problem, 214*n*10; double
standard for white male judges,
127–28, 147, 163–68; expert evidence, 149–50, 158–61; expert
perspectives, 57–60, 158–59; formal equality approach and silences,

248*n*46; individual vs systemic, 151, 164, 168, 188–89; judicial council complaints, 198*n*13, 220*n*24; *RDS* as challenge to silences, 94–96; *RDS* concurring opinion on racism as context, 158–60, 166–68, 249*nn*53–54; *RDS*'s importance, 187–92; reasonable apprehension of bias, 191; responses to naming racism, 61–64, 63(f), 246*n*23. *See also* judicial bias; judicial bias, reasonable apprehension of bias; policing; *RDS*

Rawlins, Micheline, 93–94, 200*n*13, 227*n*64, 241*n*58

RDS: about, 3–4, 187–92; Black female identity, 113–18; cases cited, 127–28, 239*nn*22–23; chronology, 193–96; first judicial race bias case (SCC), 3, 163, 187–88, 252*n*43; personal toll on individuals, 188; racialized masculinity, 111–13; records, 6, 197*n*7, 199*n*8; reflections on, 187–92

RDS trial. *See* Nova Scotia Youth Court, *RDS* trial (December 1994); Small, Rodney Darren; Small, Rodney, facts and criminal charges (October 1993); Small, Rodney, trial (December 1994)

RDS appeal (NSSC). *See* Nova Scotia Supreme Court, *RDS* (April 1995)

RDS appeal (NSCA). *See* Nova Scotia Court of Appeal, *RDS* (October 1995)

RDS appeal (SCC). *See* Supreme Court of Canada, *RDS* (1997)

Read, Horace, 85

REAL Women of Canada, 156–57

Regan, Gerald, 82, 205*n*61

Reid, Adrian Charles: about, 82, 82(f); judicial real "bias," 83–84, 102, 136, 224*n*12; legal career, 55–56, 174–75, 224*n*7; *RDS* prosecution (NSSC), 81–84, 82(f). *See also* Nova Scotia Supreme Court, *RDS* (April 1995)

religion: Black churches, 26, 33–34, 33(f), 43–44, 135; judicial complaints, 198*n*13, 220*n*24. *See also* Jewish community

Renner, Edward, 60

resistance, Black. *See* Black resistance

Riddell, William Renwick, 163–64

Rocky. *See* Jones, Rocky (Burnley Allan)

Rodney, use of his name, 5. *See also* Small, Rodney Darren

Rodney Darren Small [R.D.S.] v. Her Majesty the Queen (N.S.), 198*n*1. See also *RDS*

Roma people, 129, 138, 139–40, 242*n*86, 243*n*94

Roscoe, Elizabeth Ann, 116, 225*n*31, 234*n*25, 256*n*14

Ross, E. Anthony, 53, 75, 108, 164, 203*n*47, 221*n*31, 231*n*45, 254*n*54

Royal Commission on the Donald Marshall, Jr., Prosecution (1989). *See* Marshall Inquiry (1986–89)

Ruck, Calvin W., 221*nn*30–31

Ruck, Douglas G., 35–37, 76, 77(f), 180–81, 203*n*47, 204*n*48, 205*n*57, 221*n*31

Saunders, Charles, 55, 180, 226*n*42, 226*n*45

SCC. *See* Supreme Court of Canada (SCC)

288 | *Index*